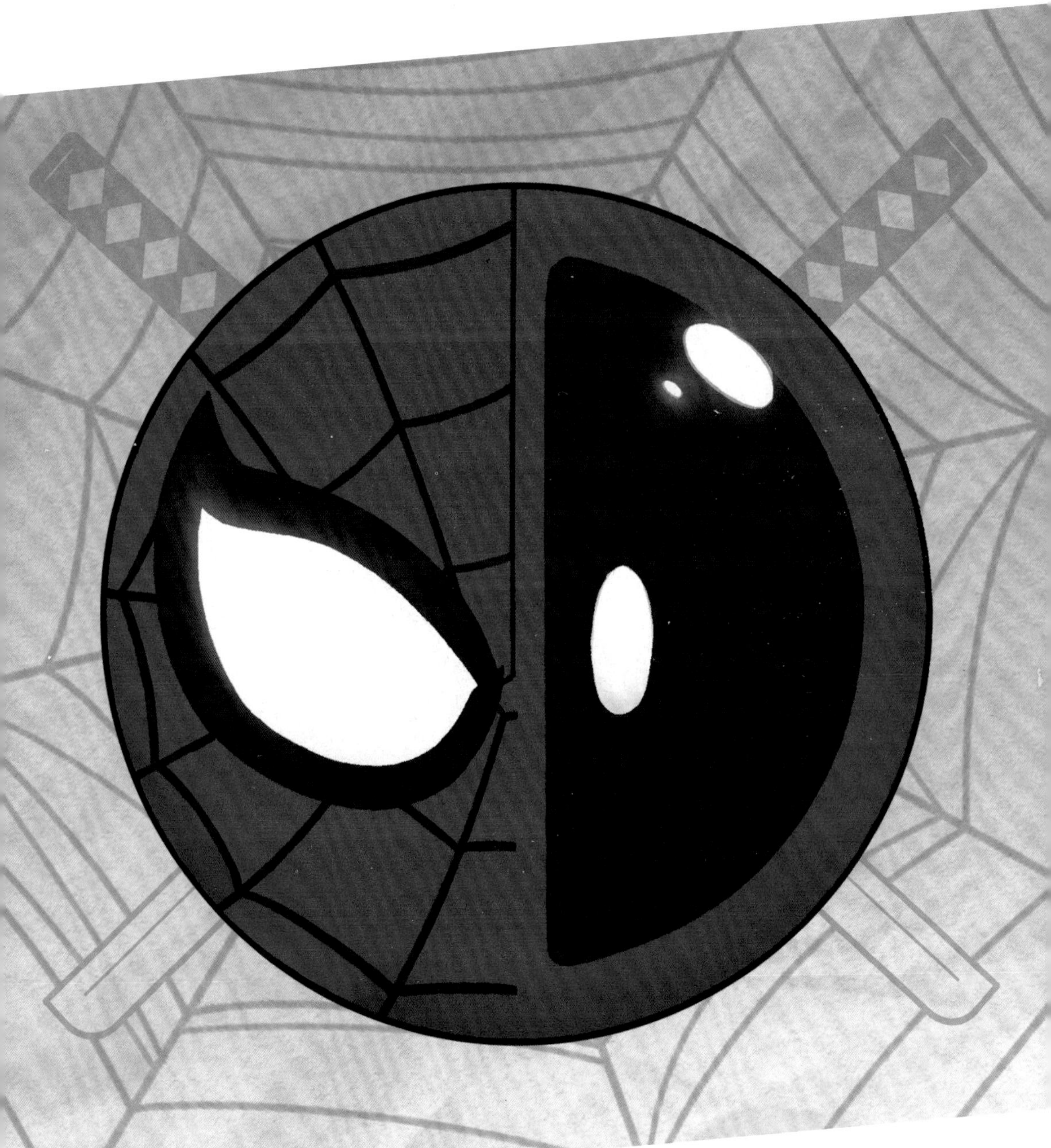

ARMS RACE

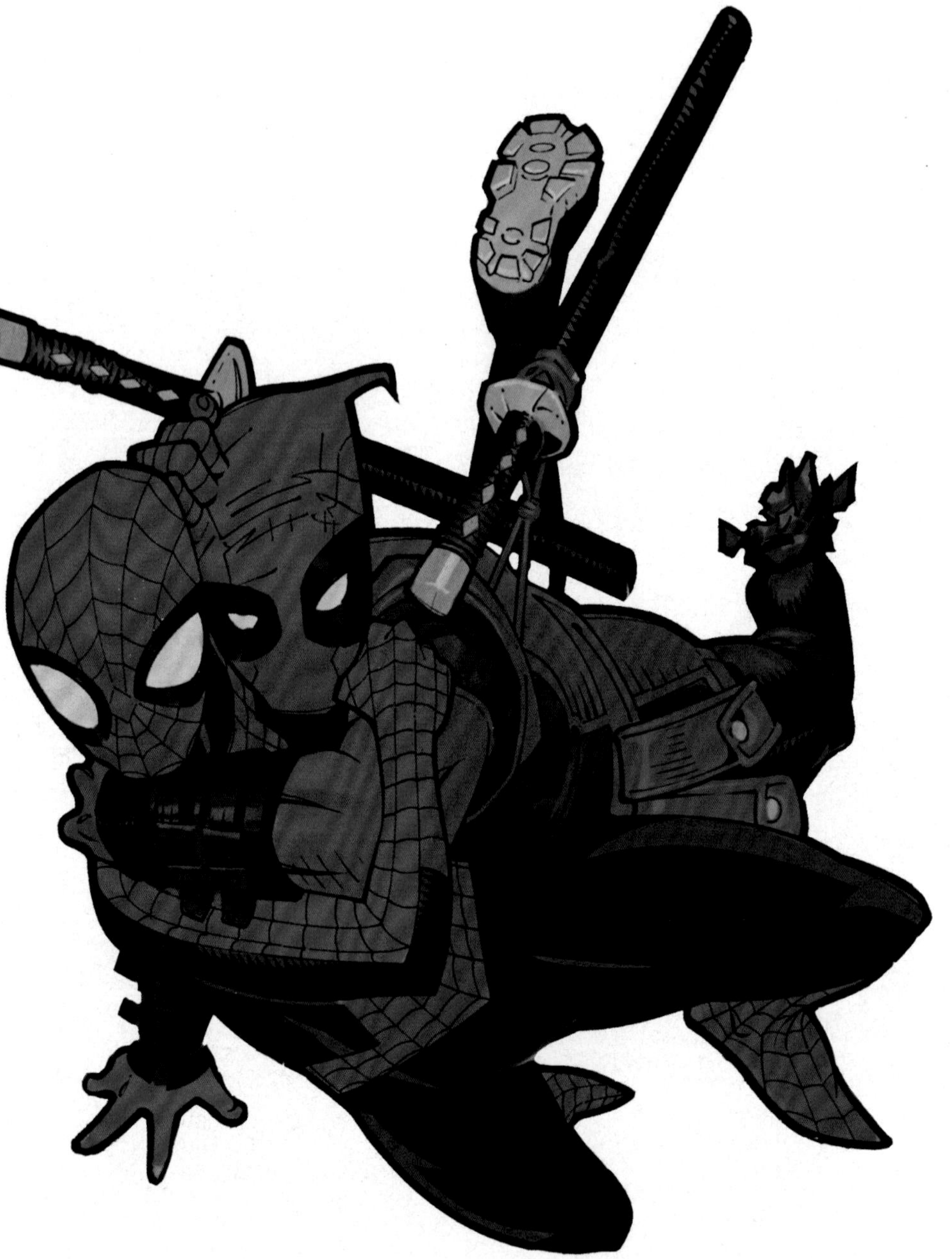

Collection Editor **JENNIFER GRÜNWALD**
Assistant Editor **CAITLIN O'CONNELL**
Associate Managing Editor **KATERI WOODY**
Editor, Special Projects **MARK D. BEAZLEY**

VP Production & Special Projects **JEFF YOUNGQUIST**
SVP Print, Sales & Marketing **DAVID GABRIEL**
Book Designer **ADAM DEL RE**

Editor In Chief **C.B. CEBULSKI**
Chief Creative Officer **JOE QUESADA**
President **DAN BUCKLEY**
Executive Producer **ALAN FINE**

SPIDER-MAN/DEADPOOL VOL. 5: ARMS RACE. Contains material originally published in magazine form as SPIDER-MAN/DEADPOOL #23-28. First printing 2018. ISBN 978-1-302-91047-1. Published by MARVEL WORLDWIDE, INC., a subsidiary of MARVEL ENTERTAINMENT, LLC. OFFICE OF PUBLICATION: 135 West 50th Street, New York, NY 10020. **Printed in Canada.** DAN BUCKLEY, President, Marvel Entertainment; JOHN NEE, Publisher; JOE QUESADA, Chief Creative Officer; TOM BREVOORT, SVP of Publishing; DAVID BOGART, SVP of Business Affairs & Operations, Publishing & Partnership; DAVID GABRIEL, SVP of Sales & Marketing, Publishing; JEFF YOUNGQUIST, VP of Production & Special Projects; DAN CARR, Executive Director of Publishing Technology; ALEX MORALES, Director of Publishing Operations; SUSAN CRESPI, Production Manager; STAN LEE, Chairman Emeritus. For information regarding advertising in Marvel Comics or on Marvel.com, please contact Vit DeBellis, Custom Solutions & Integrated Advertising Manager, at vdebellis@marvel.com. For Marvel subscription inquiries, please call 888-511-5480. **Manufactured between 2/16/2018 and 3/20/2018 by SOLISCO PRINTERS, SCOTT, QC, CANADA.**

10 9 8 7 6 5 4 3 2 1

MARVEL COMICS
BEGRUDGINGLY PRESENTS...

PETER PARKER WAS BITTEN BY AN IRRADIATED SPIDER, GRANTING HIM AMAZING ABILITIES, INCLUDING THE PROPORTIONAL SPEED, STRENGTH AND AGILITY OF A SPIDER, AS WELL AS ADHESIVE FINGERTIPS AND TOES. AFTER LEARNING THAT WITH GREAT POWER, THERE MUST ALSO COME GREAT RESPONSIBILITY, HE BECAME THE WORLD'S GREATEST SUPER HERO! HE'S...

THE WORLD'S GREATEST SUPER HERO!
The AMAZING SPIDER-MAN

AVENGER...ASSASSIN...SUPERSTAR! WADE WILSON WAS CHOSEN FOR A TOP-SECRET GOVERNMENT PROGRAM THAT GAVE HIM A HEALING FACTOR THAT ALLOWS HIM TO HEAL FROM ANY WOUND. DESPITE EARNING A SMALL FORTUNE AS A GUN FOR HIRE, WADE HAS BECOME THE WORLD'S MOST BELOVED HERO, AND IS THE STAR OF THE WORLD'S GREATEST COMICS MAGAZINE (NO MATTER WHAT THAT JERK IN THE WEBS MAY THINK). CALL HIM THE MERC WITH THE MOUTH...CALL HIM THE REGENERATIN' DEGENERATE...CALL HIM...

DEADPOOL

— ARMS RACE —

ROBBIE THOMPSON
Writer

CHRIS BACHALO (#23-25, #27-28), SCOTT HEPBURN (#25-27), MARCUS TO (#27) & MATT HORAK (#28)
Pencilers

TIM TOWNSEND (#23-24, #28), AL VEY (#23-25), RICHARD FRIEND (#23), WAYNE FAUCHER (#24-25, #27-28), VICTOR OLAZABA (#24-25, #27-28), LIVESAY (#24-25, #27-28), SCOTT HEPBURN (#25-27), CHRIS BACHALO (#27), MARCUS TO (#27) & MATT HORAK (#28)
Inkers

CHRIS BACHALO (#23-25), CHRIS O'HALLORAN (#25, #27-28) & IAN HERRING (#26-27)
Colorists

CHRIS BACHALO & TIM TOWNSEND (#23), CHRIS BACHALO, TIM TOWNSEND & BRIAN REBER (#24); DAVE JOHNSON (#25); AND SCOTT HEPBURN & IAN HERRING (#26-28)
Cover Artists

VC's JOE SABINO
Letterer

ALLISON STOCK
Assistant Editor

JORDAN D. WHITE & NICK LOWE
Editors

SPIDER-MAN created by STAN LEE & STEVE DITKO

DEADPOOL created by ROB LIEFELD & FABIAN NICIEZA

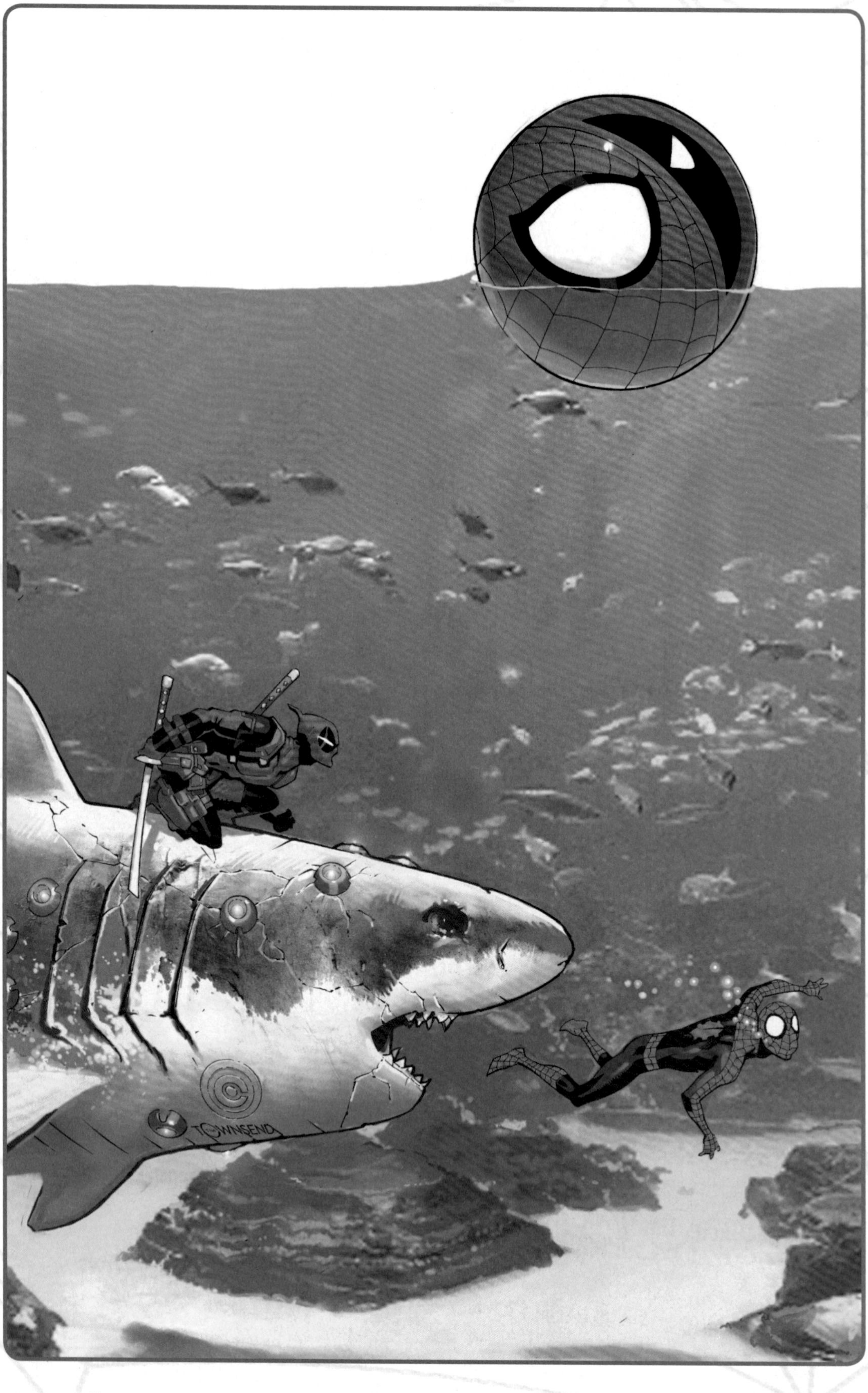
TOWNSEND

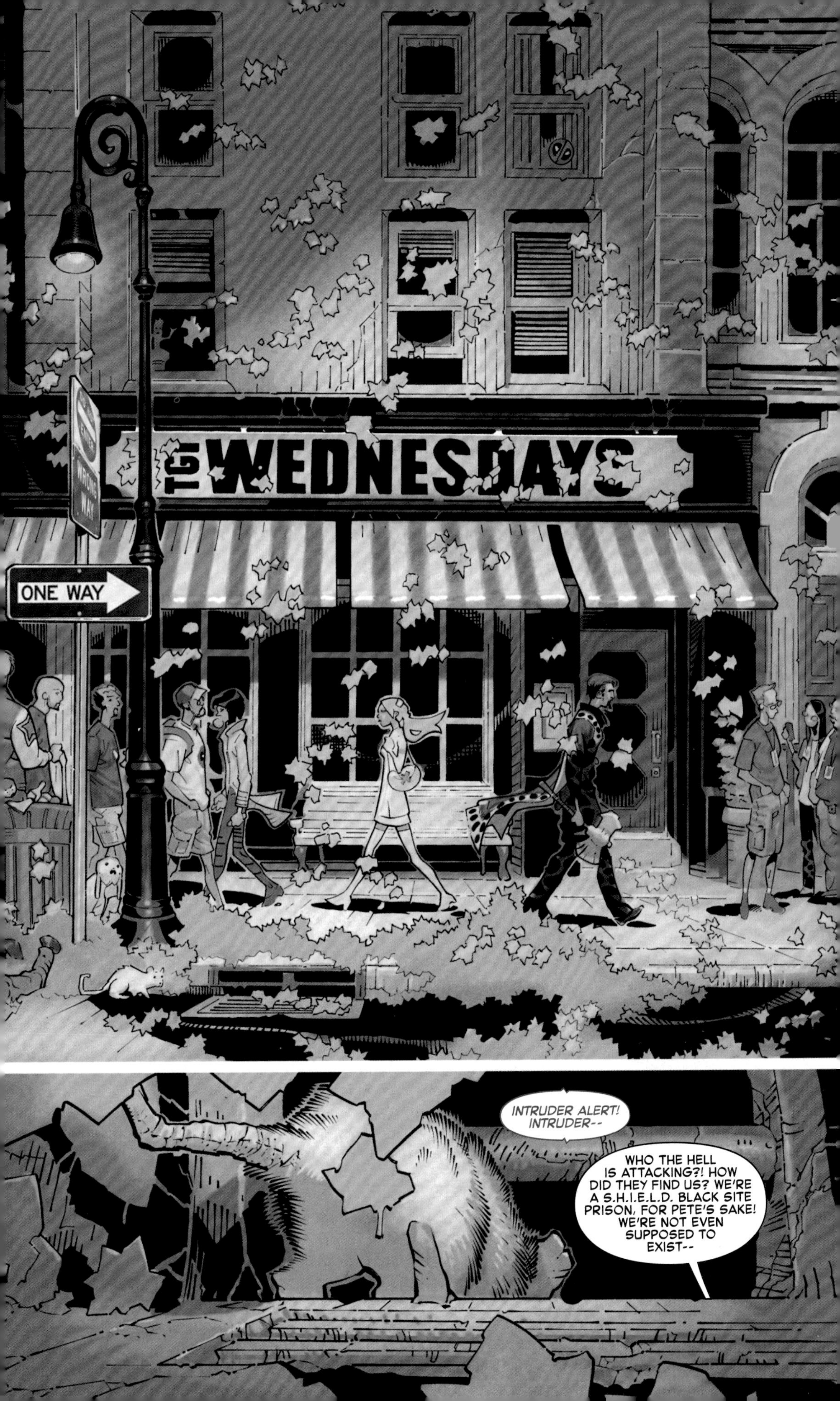
WEDNESDAYS
ONE WAY
WRONG WAY
INTRUDER ALERT! INTRUDER--
WHO THE HELL IS ATTACKING?! HOW DID THEY FIND US? WE'RE A S.H.I.E.L.D. BLACK SITE PRISON, FOR PETE'S SAKE! WE'RE NOT EVEN SUPPOSED TO EXIST--

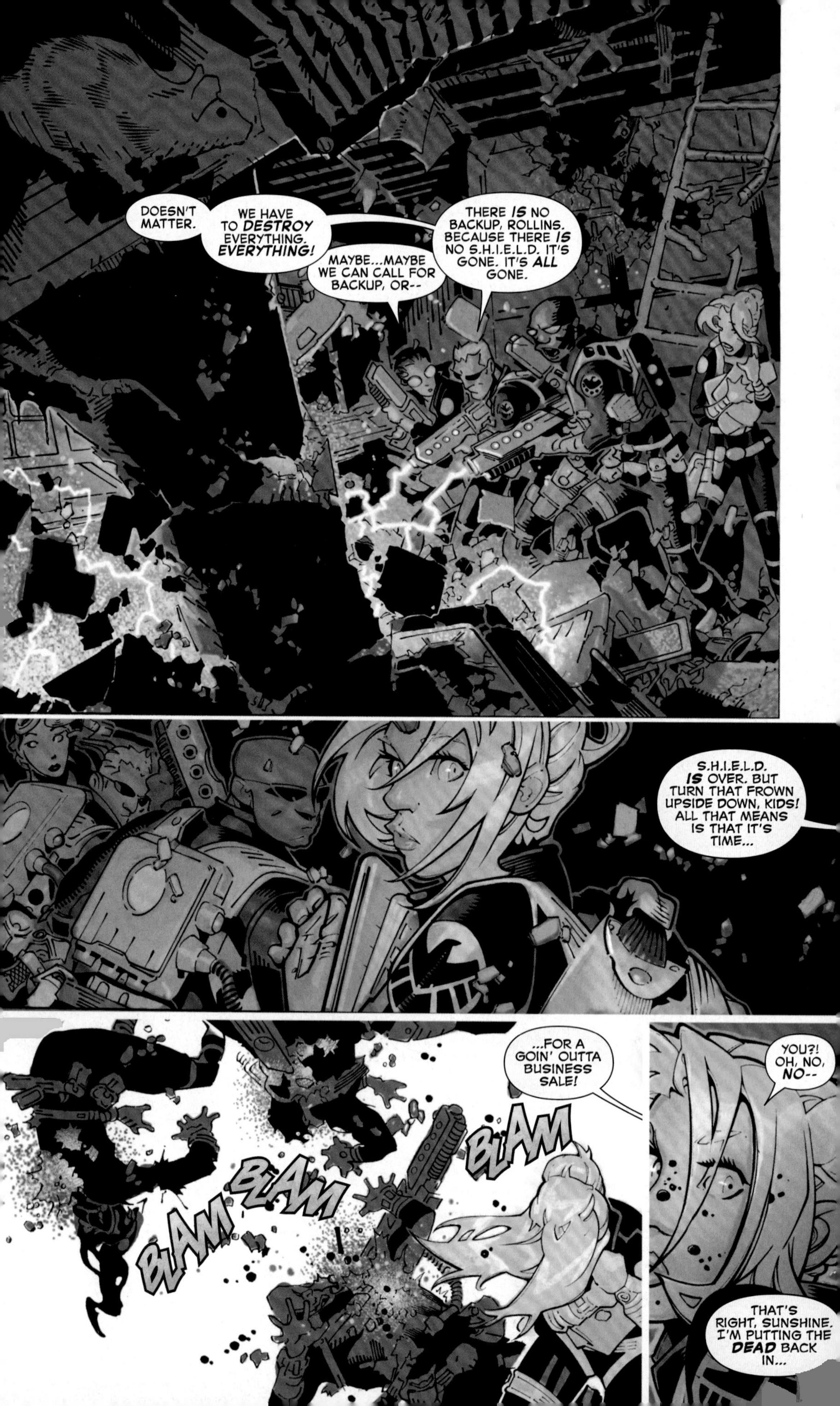

DOESN'T MATTER.
WE HAVE TO DESTROY EVERYTHING. EVERYTHING!
MAYBE...MAYBE WE CAN CALL FOR BACKUP, OR--
THERE IS NO BACKUP, ROLLINS. BECAUSE THERE IS NO S.H.I.E.L.D. IT'S GONE. IT'S ALL GONE.
S.H.I.E.L.D. IS OVER. BUT TURN THAT FROWN UPSIDE DOWN, KIDS! ALL THAT MEANS IS THAT IT'S TIME...
...FOR A GOIN' OUTTA BUSINESS SALE!
BLAM
BLAM
BLAM
YOU?! OH, NO, NO--
THAT'S RIGHT, SUNSHINE. I'M PUTTING THE DEAD BACK IN...

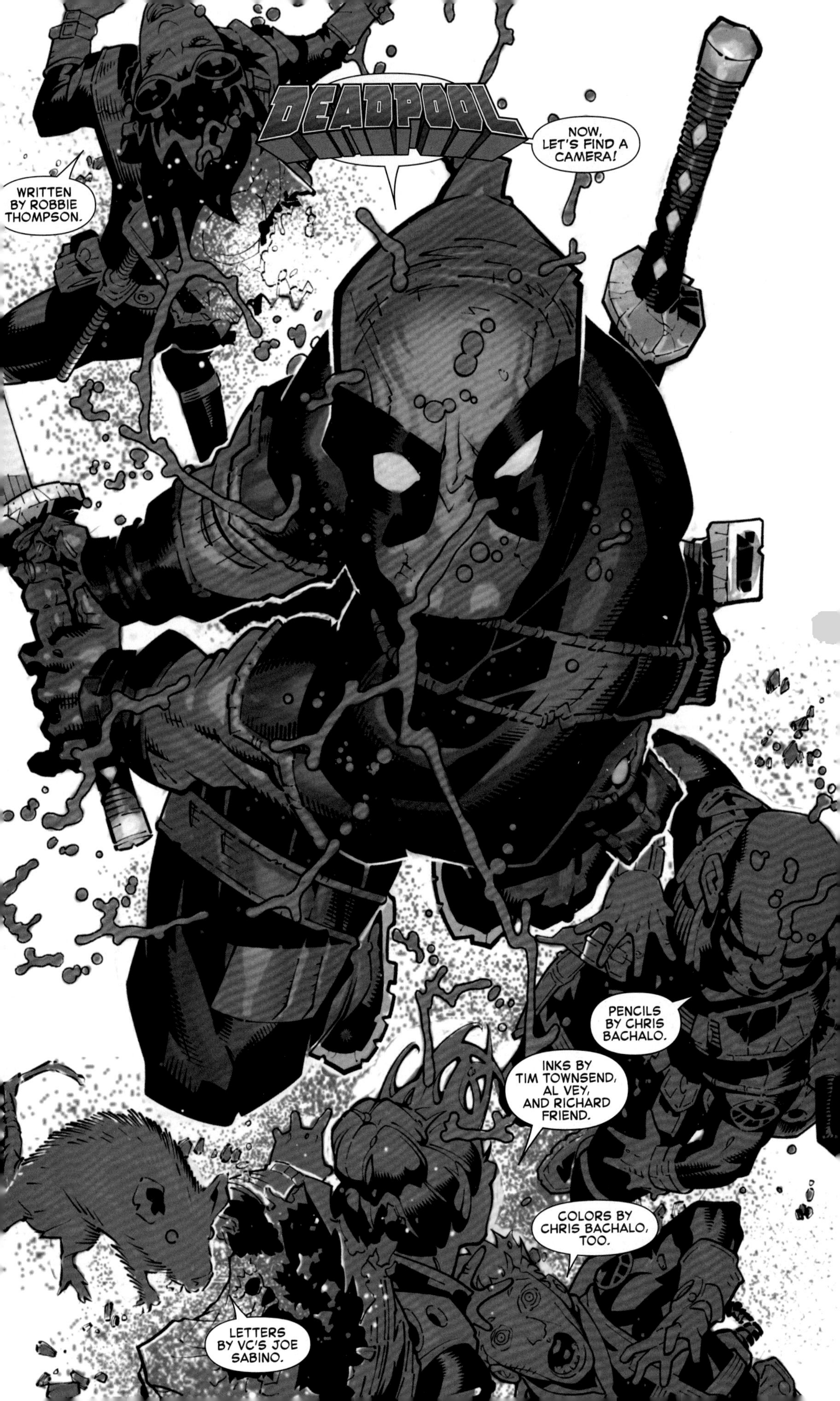
DEADPOOL
NOW, LET'S FIND A CAMERA!
WRITTEN BY ROBBIE THOMPSON.
PENCILS BY CHRIS BACHALO.
INKS BY TIM TOWNSEND, AL VEY, AND RICHARD FRIEND.
COLORS BY CHRIS BACHALO, TOO.
LETTERS BY VC'S JOE SABINO.

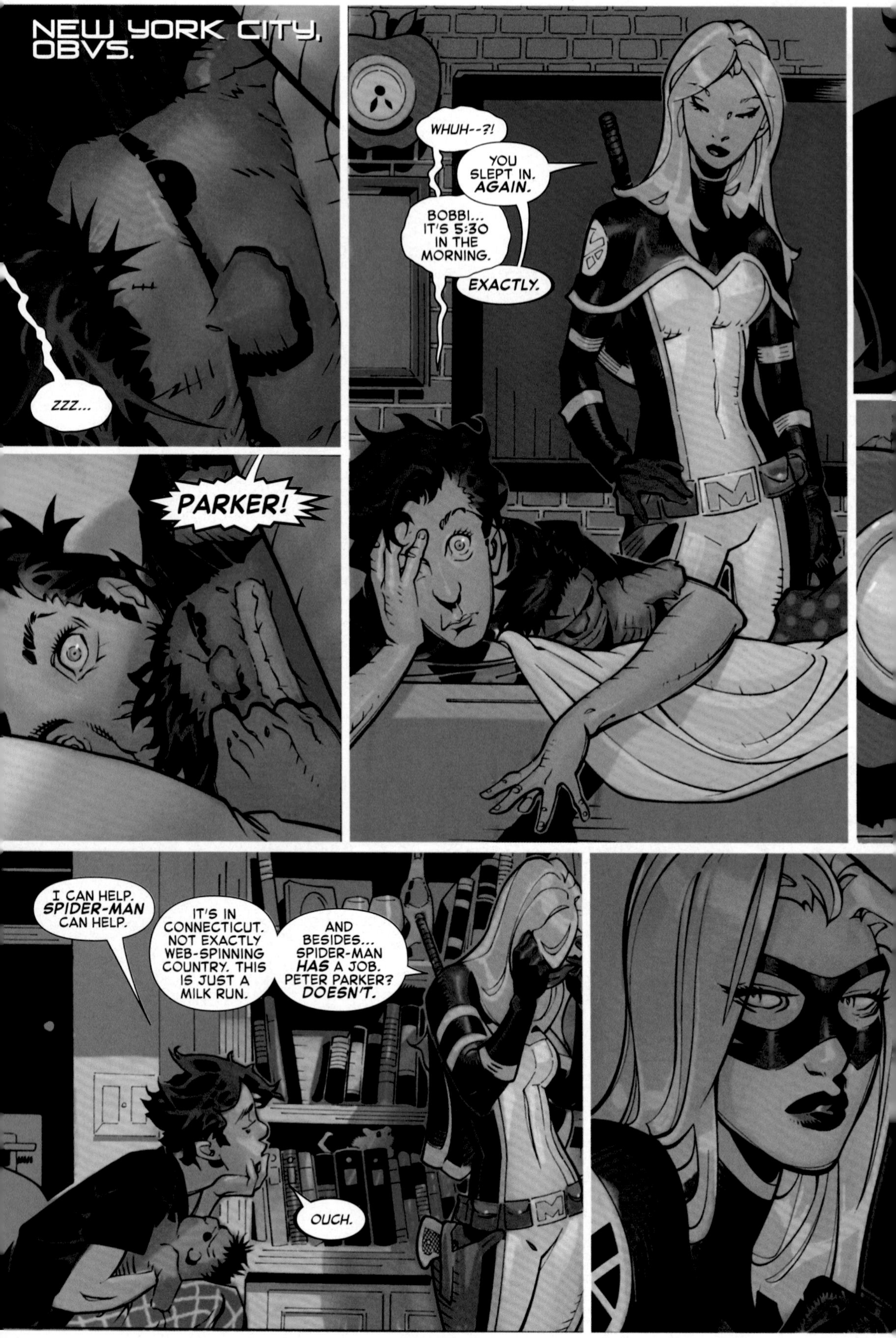

NEW YORK CITY, OBVS.
ZZZ...
PARKER!
WHUH--?!
YOU SLEPT IN. AGAIN.
BOBBI... IT'S 5:30 IN THE MORNING.
EXACTLY.
I CAN HELP. SPIDER-MAN CAN HELP.
IT'S IN CONNECTICUT. NOT EXACTLY WEB-SPINNING COUNTRY. THIS IS JUST A MILK RUN.
AND BESIDES... SPIDER-MAN HAS A JOB. PETER PARKER? DOESN'T.
OUCH.

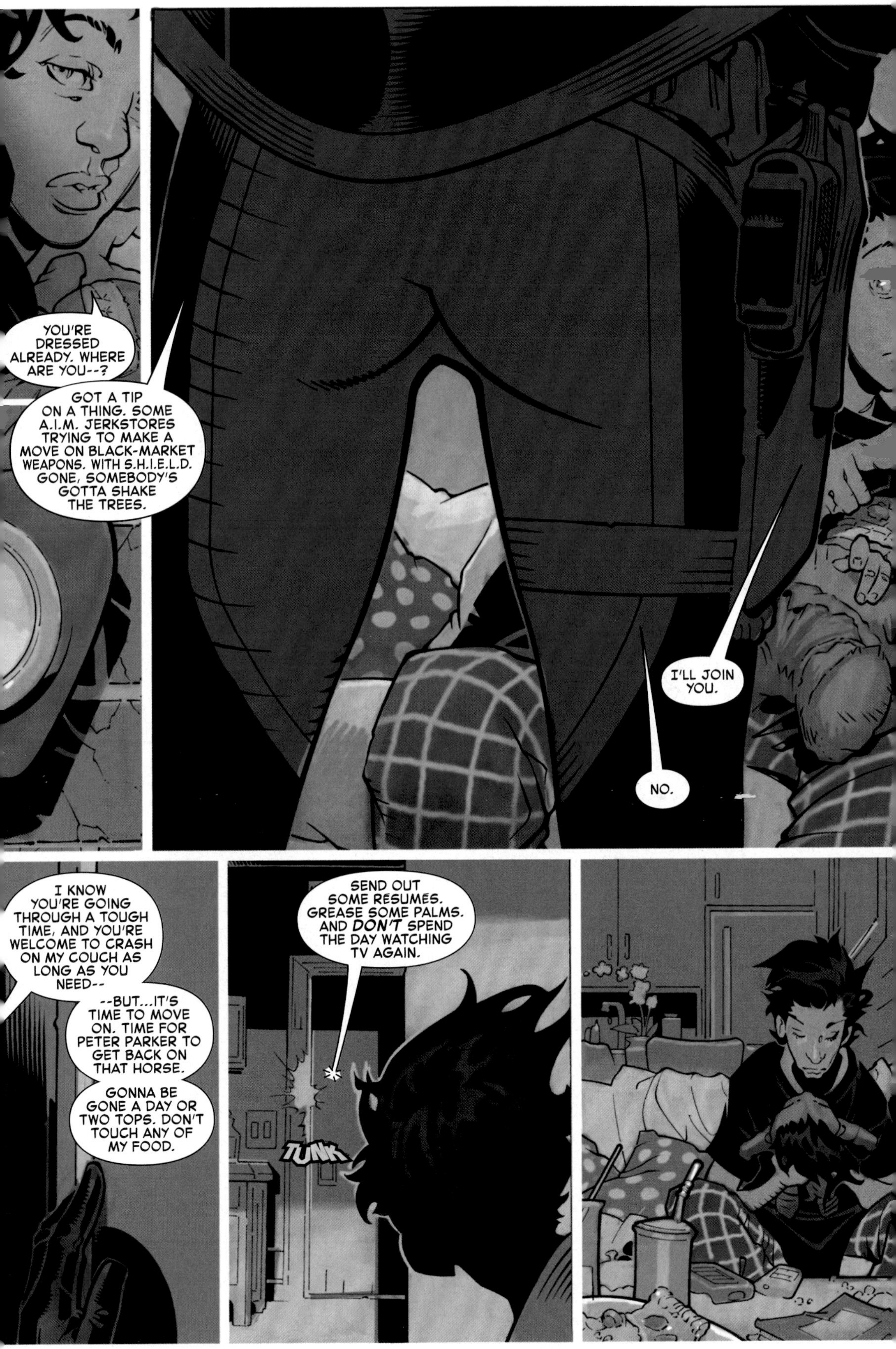
YOU'RE DRESSED ALREADY. WHERE ARE YOU--?
GOT A TIP ON A THING. SOME A.I.M. JERKSTORES TRYING TO MAKE A MOVE ON BLACK-MARKET WEAPONS. WITH S.H.I.E.L.D. GONE, SOMEBODY'S GOTTA SHAKE THE TREES.
I'LL JOIN YOU.
NO.
I KNOW YOU'RE GOING THROUGH A TOUGH TIME, AND YOU'RE WELCOME TO CRASH ON MY COUCH AS LONG AS YOU NEED--
--BUT...IT'S TIME TO MOVE ON. TIME FOR PETER PARKER TO GET BACK ON THAT HORSE.
GONNA BE GONE A DAY OR TWO TOPS. DON'T TOUCH ANY OF MY FOOD.
SEND OUT SOME RESUMES. GREASE SOME PALMS. AND DON'T SPEND THE DAY WATCHING TV AGAIN.
TUNK

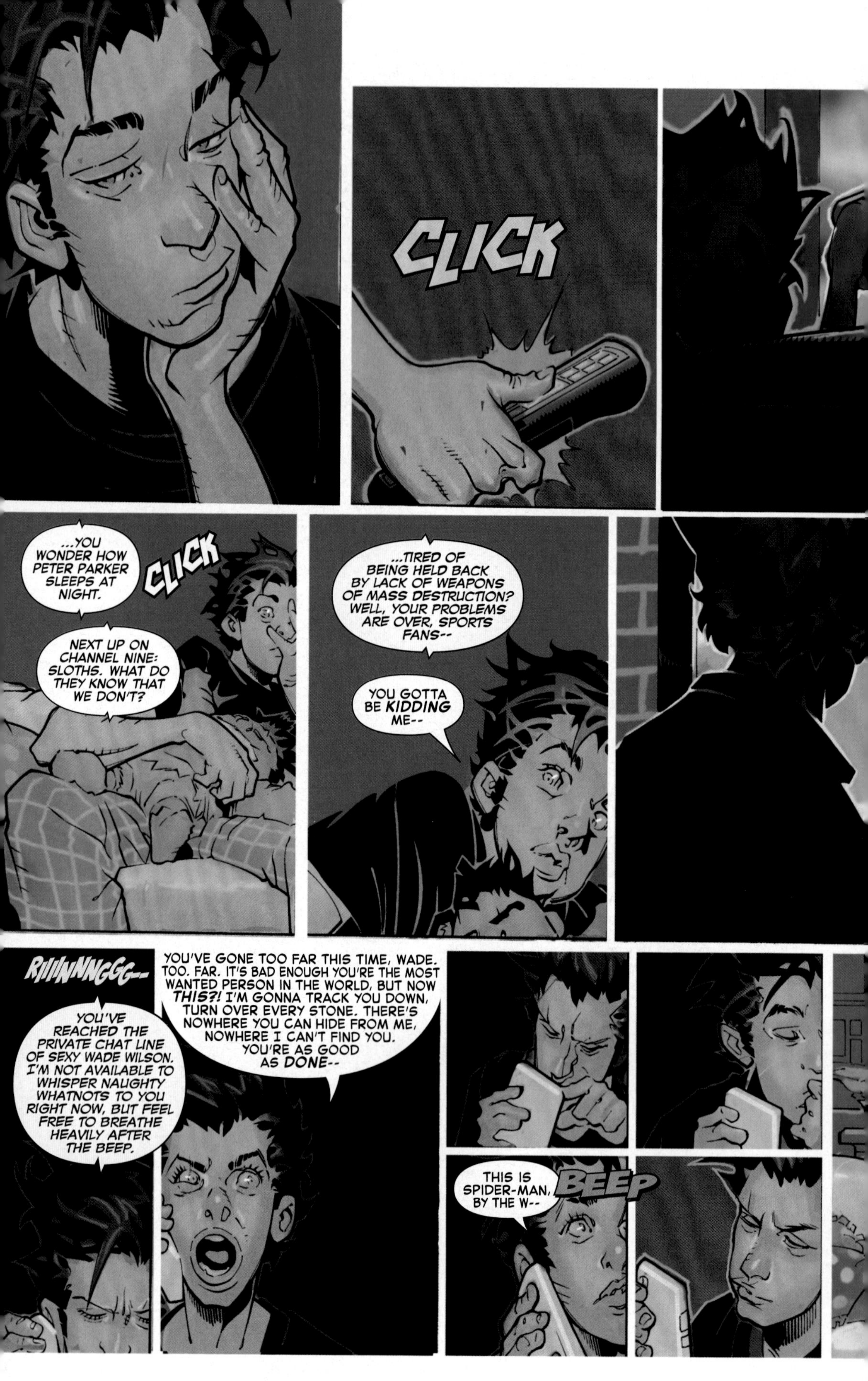
CLICK
...YOU WONDER HOW PETER PARKER SLEEPS AT NIGHT.
CLICK
NEXT UP ON CHANNEL NINE: SLOTHS. WHAT DO THEY KNOW THAT WE DON'T?
...TIRED OF BEING HELD BACK BY LACK OF WEAPONS OF MASS DESTRUCTION? WELL, YOUR PROBLEMS ARE OVER, SPORTS FANS--
YOU GOTTA BE KIDDING ME--
RIIIINNNGGG--
YOU'VE REACHED THE PRIVATE CHAT LINE OF SEXY WADE WILSON. I'M NOT AVAILABLE TO WHISPER NAUGHTY WHATNOTS TO YOU RIGHT NOW, BUT FEEL FREE TO BREATHE HEAVILY AFTER THE BEEP.
YOU'VE GONE TOO FAR THIS TIME, WADE. TOO. FAR. IT'S BAD ENOUGH YOU'RE THE MOST WANTED PERSON IN THE WORLD, BUT NOW THIS?! I'M GONNA TRACK YOU DOWN, TURN OVER EVERY STONE. THERE'S NOWHERE YOU CAN HIDE FROM ME, NOWHERE I CAN'T FIND YOU. YOU'RE AS GOOD AS DONE--
THIS IS SPIDER-MAN, BY THE W--
BEEP

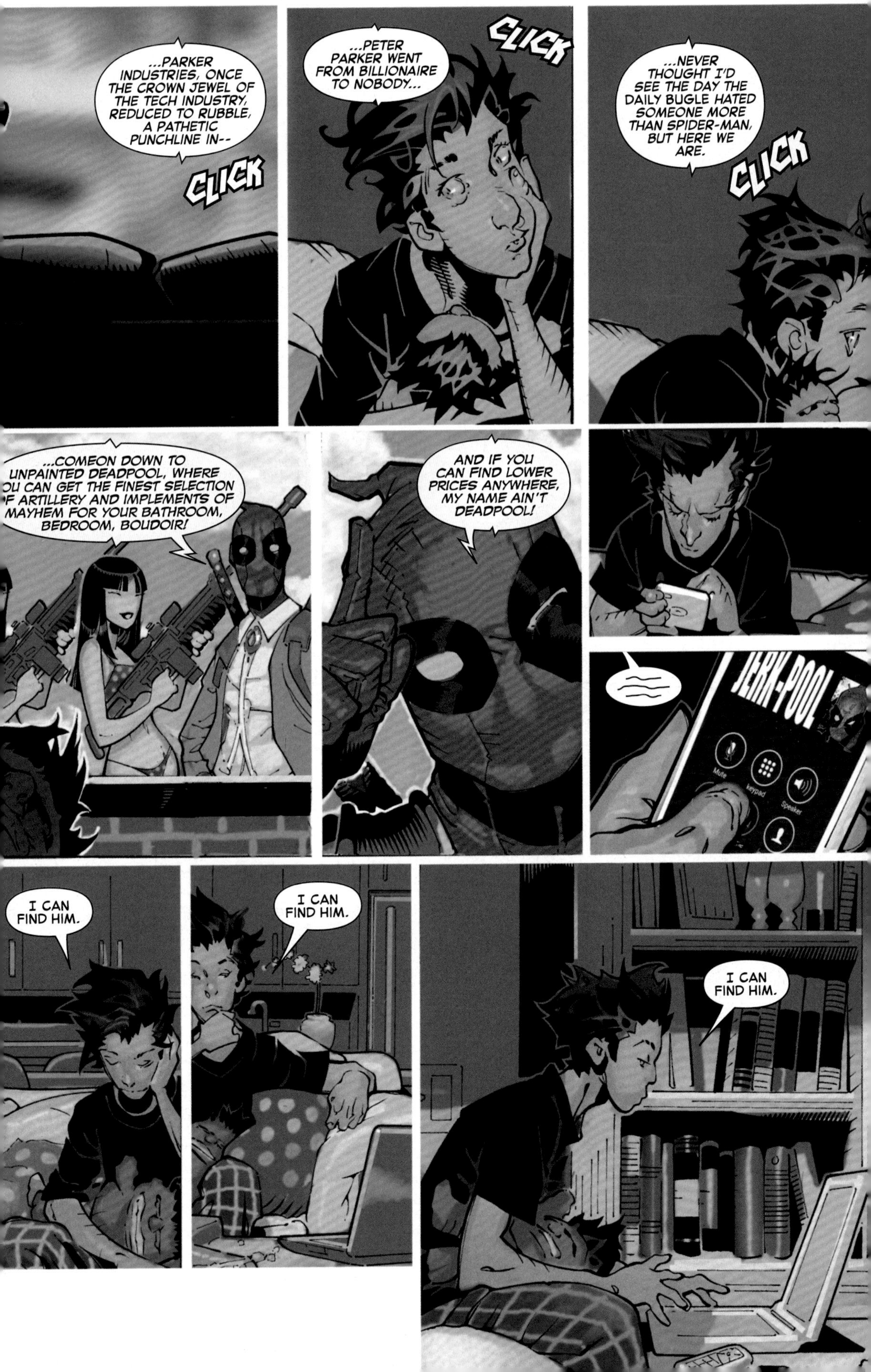
...PARKER INDUSTRIES, ONCE THE CROWN JEWEL OF THE TECH INDUSTRY, REDUCED TO RUBBLE, A PATHETIC PUNCHLINE IN--
CLICK
...PETER PARKER WENT FROM BILLIONAIRE TO NOBODY...
CLICK
...NEVER THOUGHT I'D SEE THE DAY THE DAILY BUGLE HATED SOMEONE MORE THAN SPIDER-MAN, BUT HERE WE ARE.
CLICK
...COMEON DOWN TO UNPAINTED DEADPOOL, WHERE OU CAN GET THE FINEST SELECTION F ARTILLERY AND IMPLEMENTS OF MAYHEM FOR YOUR BATHROOM, BEDROOM, BOUDOIR!
AND IF YOU CAN FIND LOWER PRICES ANYWHERE, MY NAME AIN'T DEADPOOL!
JERK-POOL
Mute
keypad
Speaker
I CAN FIND HIM.
I CAN FIND HIM.
I CAN FIND HIM.

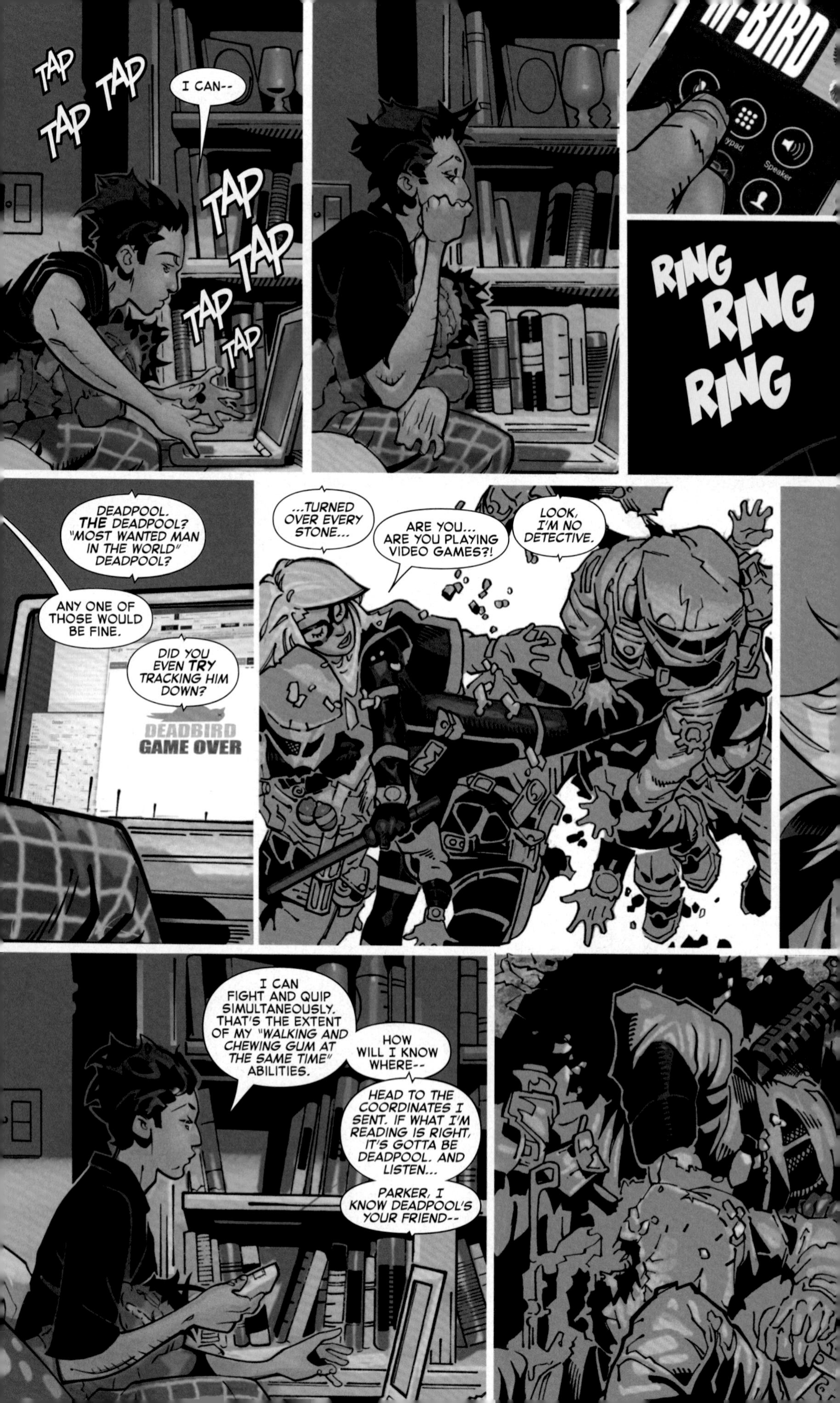

TAP
TAP TAP
I CAN--
TAP
TAP
TAP
TAP
M-BIRD
Speaker
RING
RING
RING
DEADPOOL. THE DEADPOOL? "MOST WANTED MAN IN THE WORLD" DEADPOOL?
ANY ONE OF THOSE WOULD BE FINE.
DID YOU EVEN TRY TRACKING HIM DOWN?
DEADBIRD
GAME OVER
...TURNED OVER EVERY STONE...
ARE YOU... ARE YOU PLAYING VIDEO GAMES?!
LOOK, I'M NO DETECTIVE.
I CAN FIGHT AND QUIP SIMULTANEOUSLY. THAT'S THE EXTENT OF MY "WALKING AND CHEWING GUM AT THE SAME TIME" ABILITIES.
HOW WILL I KNOW WHERE--
HEAD TO THE COORDINATES I SENT. IF WHAT I'M READING IS RIGHT, IT'S GOTTA BE DEADPOOL. AND LISTEN...
PARKER, I KNOW DEADPOOL'S YOUR FRIEND--

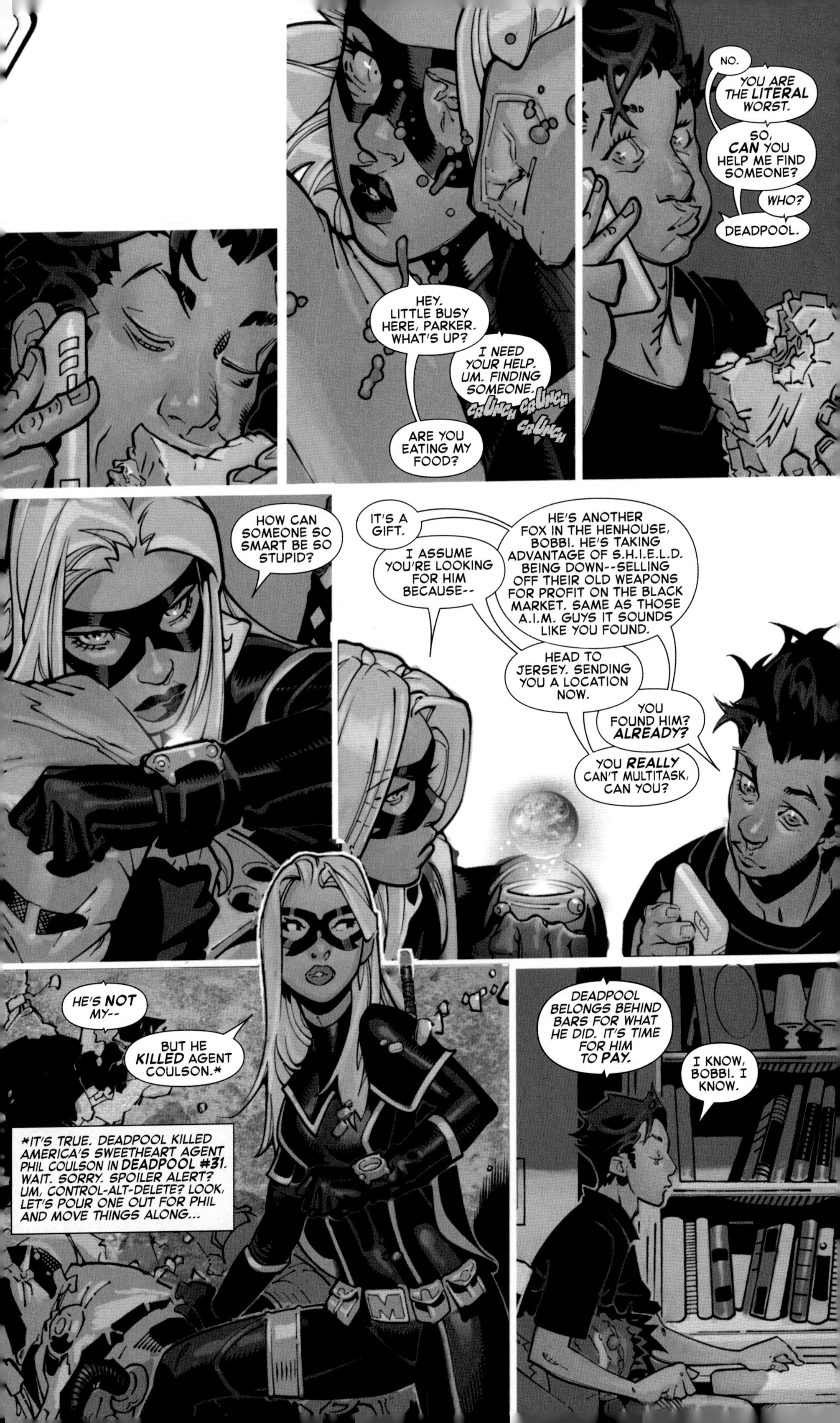
HEY. LITTLE BUSY HERE, PARKER. WHAT'S UP?
I NEED YOUR HELP. UM. FINDING SOMEONE.
CRUNCH CRUNCH CRUNCH
ARE YOU EATING MY FOOD?
NO.
YOU ARE THE LITERAL WORST.
SO, CAN YOU HELP ME FIND SOMEONE?
WHO?
DEADPOOL.
HOW CAN SOMEONE SO SMART BE SO STUPID?
IT'S A GIFT.
I ASSUME YOU'RE LOOKING FOR HIM BECAUSE--
HE'S ANOTHER FOX IN THE HENHOUSE, BOBBI. HE'S TAKING ADVANTAGE OF S.H.I.E.L.D. BEING DOWN--SELLING OFF THEIR OLD WEAPONS FOR PROFIT ON THE BLACK MARKET. SAME AS THOSE A.I.M. GUYS IT SOUNDS LIKE YOU FOUND.
HEAD TO JERSEY. SENDING YOU A LOCATION NOW.
YOU FOUND HIM? ALREADY?
YOU REALLY CAN'T MULTITASK, CAN YOU?
HE'S NOT MY--
BUT HE KILLED AGENT COULSON.*
*IT'S TRUE. DEADPOOL KILLED AMERICA'S SWEETHEART AGENT PHIL COULSON IN DEADPOOL #31. WAIT. SORRY. SPOILER ALERT? UM, CONTROL-ALT-DELETE? LOOK, LET'S POUR ONE OUT FOR PHIL AND MOVE THINGS ALONG...
DEADPOOL BELONGS BEHIND BARS FOR WHAT HE DID. IT'S TIME FOR HIM TO PAY.
I KNOW, BOBBI. I KNOW.

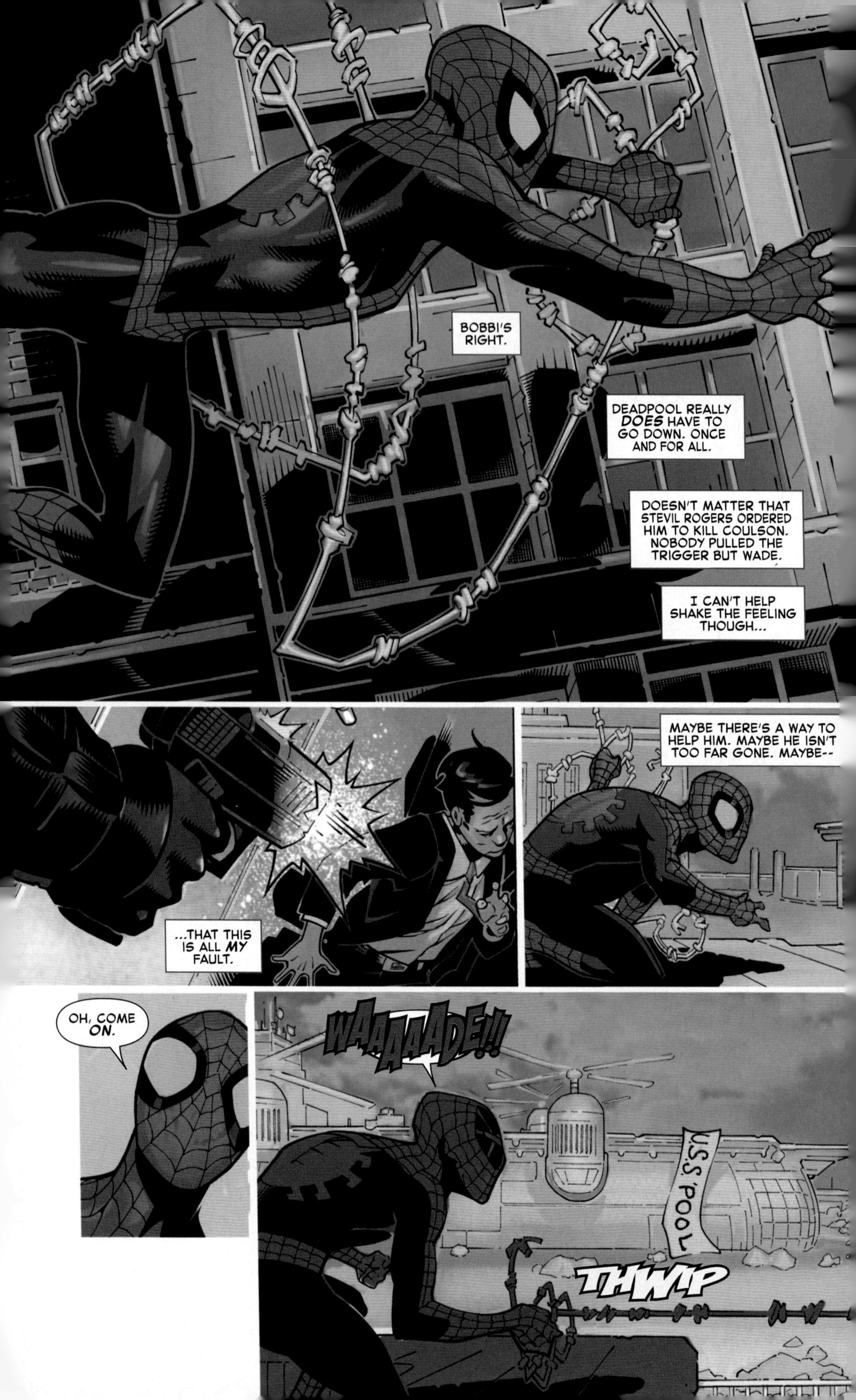

BOBBI'S RIGHT.
DEADPOOL REALLY DOES HAVE TO GO DOWN. ONCE AND FOR ALL.
DOESN'T MATTER THAT STEVIL ROGERS ORDERED HIM TO KILL COULSON. NOBODY PULLED THE TRIGGER BUT WADE.
I CAN'T HELP SHAKE THE FEELING THOUGH...
...THAT THIS IS ALL MY FAULT.
MAYBE THERE'S A WAY TO HELP HIM. MAYBE HE ISN'T TOO FAR GONE. MAYBE--
OH, COME ON.
WAAAAAADE!!!
U.S.S. POOL
THWIP

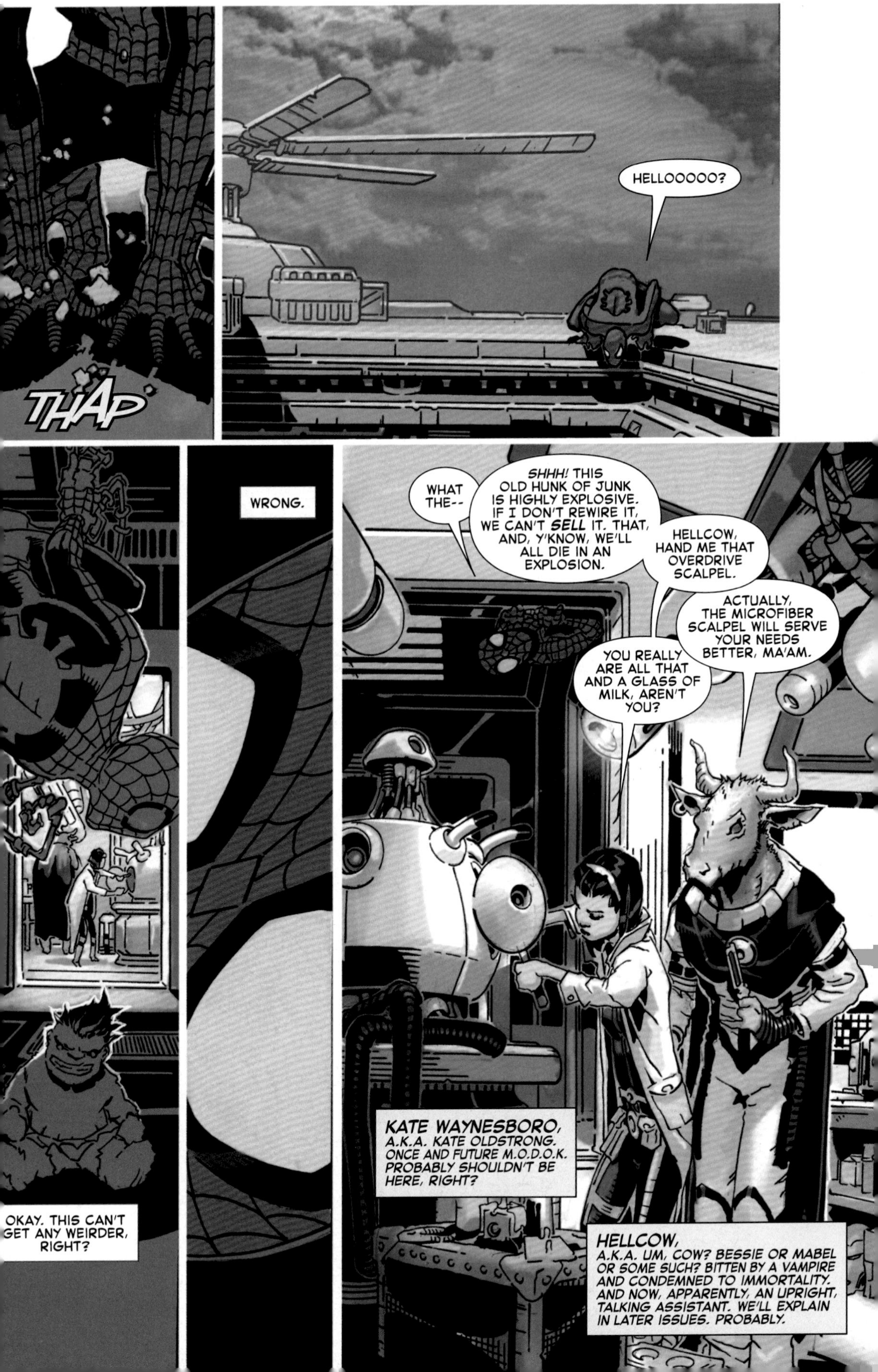

THAP
HELLOOOOO?
WRONG.
OKAY. THIS CAN'T GET ANY WEIRDER, RIGHT?
WHAT THE--
SHHH! THIS OLD HUNK OF JUNK IS HIGHLY EXPLOSIVE. IF I DON'T REWIRE IT, WE CAN'T SELL IT. THAT, AND, Y'KNOW, WE'LL ALL DIE IN AN EXPLOSION.
HELLCOW, HAND ME THAT OVERDRIVE SCALPEL.
ACTUALLY, THE MICROFIBER SCALPEL WILL SERVE YOUR NEEDS BETTER, MA'AM.
YOU REALLY ARE ALL THAT AND A GLASS OF MILK, AREN'T YOU?
KATE WAYNESBORO, A.K.A. KATE OLDSTRONG. ONCE AND FUTURE M.O.D.O.K. PROBABLY SHOULDN'T BE HERE, RIGHT?
HELLCOW, A.K.A. UM, COW? BESSIE OR MABEL OR SOME SUCH? BITTEN BY A VAMPIRE AND CONDEMNED TO IMMORTALITY. AND NOW, APPARENTLY, AN UPRIGHT, TALKING ASSISTANT. WE'LL EXPLAIN IN LATER ISSUES. PROBABLY.

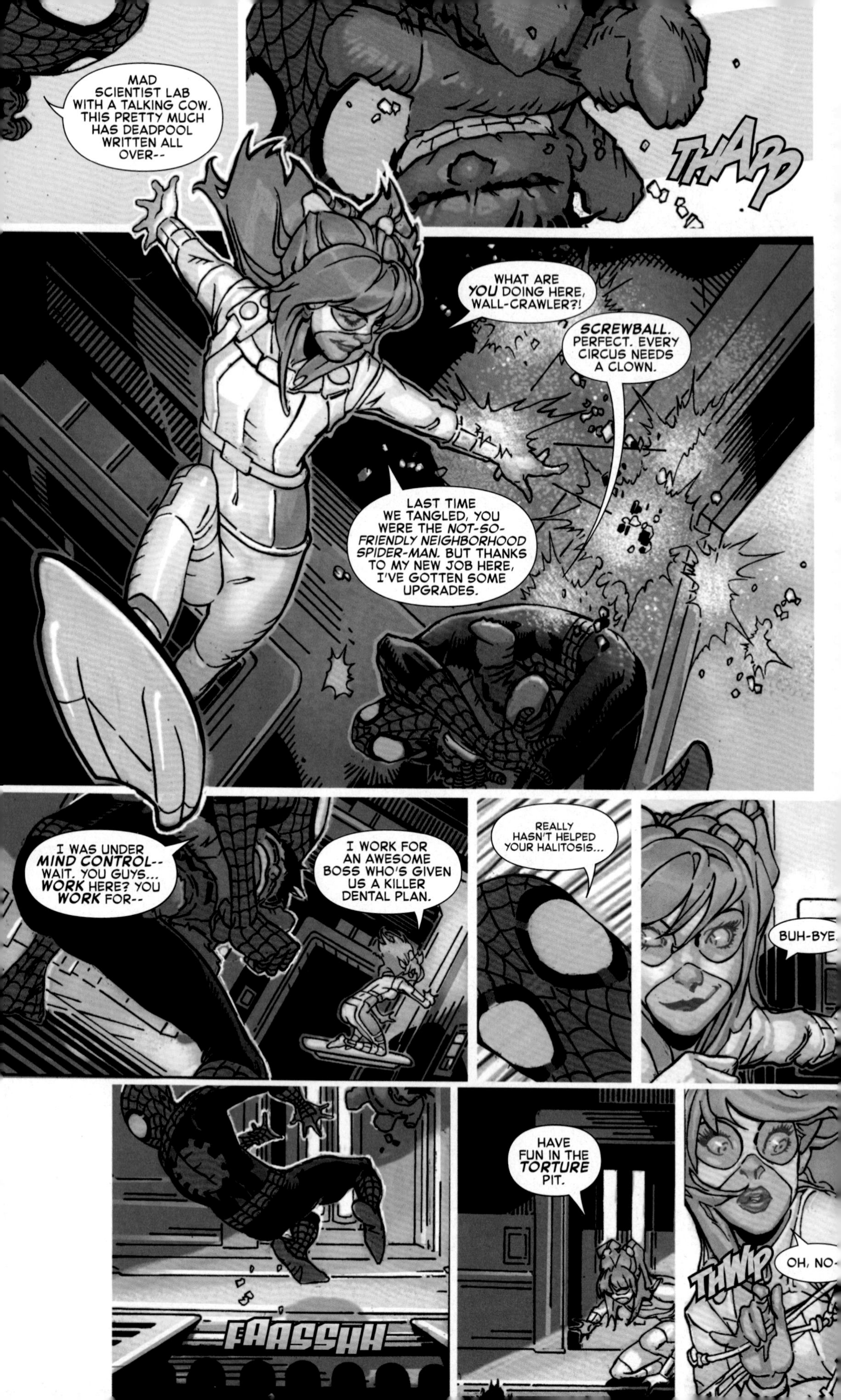
MAD SCIENTIST LAB WITH A TALKING COW. THIS PRETTY MUCH HAS DEADPOOL WRITTEN ALL OVER--
THAPP
WHAT ARE YOU DOING HERE, WALL-CRAWLER?!
SCREWBALL. PERFECT. EVERY CIRCUS NEEDS A CLOWN.
LAST TIME WE TANGLED, YOU WERE THE NOT-SO-FRIENDLY NEIGHBORHOOD SPIDER-MAN. BUT THANKS TO MY NEW JOB HERE, I'VE GOTTEN SOME UPGRADES.
I WAS UNDER MIND CONTROL-- WAIT. YOU GUYS... WORK HERE? YOU WORK FOR--
I WORK FOR AN AWESOME BOSS WHO'S GIVEN US A KILLER DENTAL PLAN.
REALLY HASN'T HELPED YOUR HALITOSIS...
BUH-BYE.
FAASSHH
HAVE FUN IN THE TORTURE PIT.
THWIP
OH, NO-

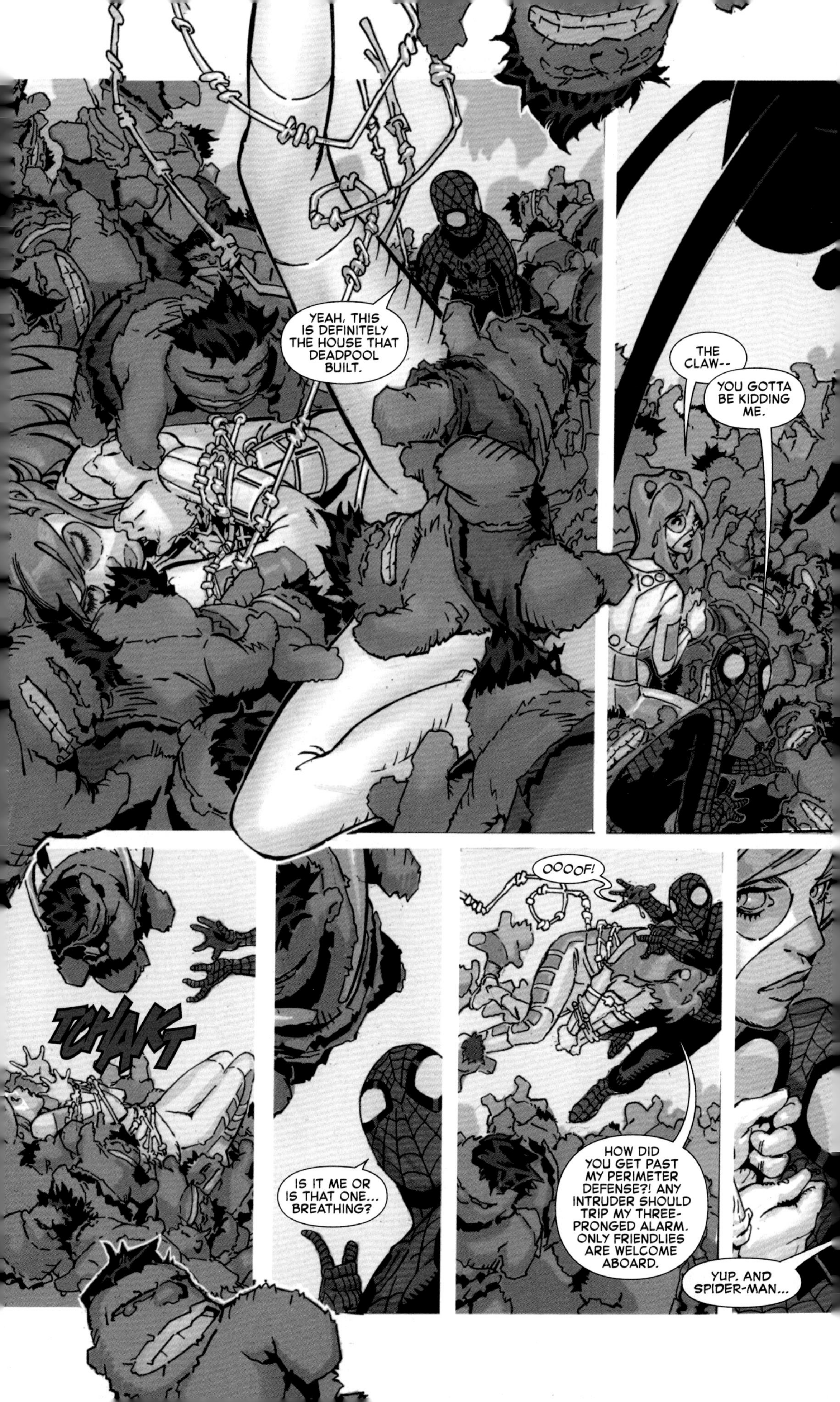
YEAH, THIS IS DEFINITELY THE HOUSE THAT DEADPOOL BUILT.
THE CLAW--
YOU GOTTA BE KIDDING ME.
TCHAKT
IS IT ME OR IS THAT ONE... BREATHING?
OOOOF!
HOW DID YOU GET PAST MY PERIMETER DEFENSE?! ANY INTRUDER SHOULD TRIP MY THREE-PRONGED ALARM. ONLY FRIENDLIES ARE WELCOME ABOARD.
YUP. AND SPIDER-MAN...

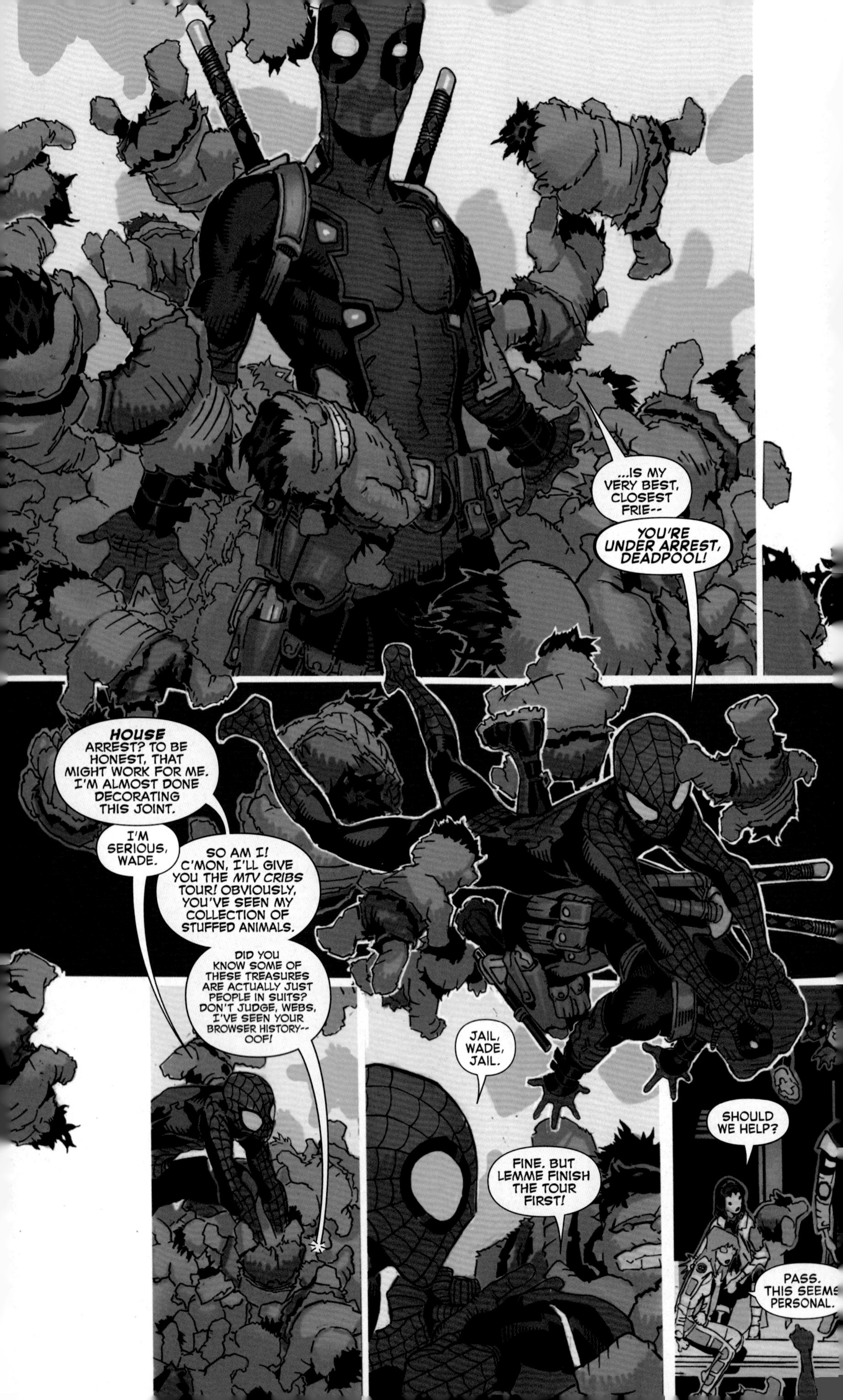

...IS MY VERY BEST, CLOSEST FRIE--
YOU'RE UNDER ARREST, DEADPOOL!
HOUSE ARREST? TO BE HONEST, THAT MIGHT WORK FOR ME. I'M ALMOST DONE DECORATING THIS JOINT.
I'M SERIOUS, WADE.
SO AM I! C'MON, I'LL GIVE YOU THE MTV CRIBS TOUR! OBVIOUSLY, YOU'VE SEEN MY COLLECTION OF STUFFED ANIMALS.
DID YOU KNOW SOME OF THESE TREASURES ARE ACTUALLY JUST PEOPLE IN SUITS? DON'T JUDGE, WEBS, I'VE SEEN YOUR BROWSER HISTORY-- OOF!
JAIL, WADE, JAIL.
FINE. BUT LEMME FINISH THE TOUR FIRST!
SHOULD WE HELP?
PASS. THIS SEEMS PERSONAL.

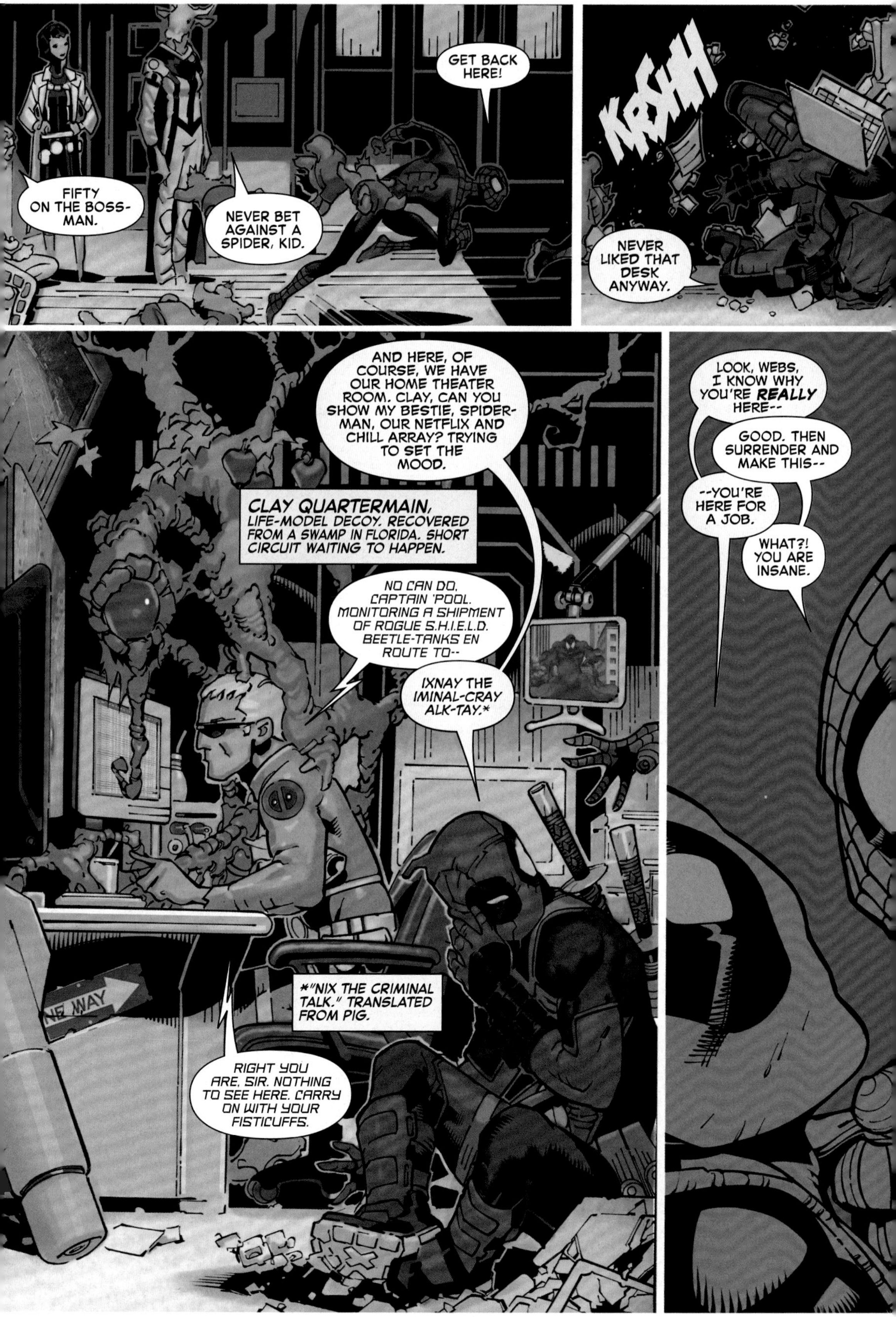
FIFTY ON THE BOSS-MAN.
NEVER BET AGAINST A SPIDER, KID.
GET BACK HERE!
KRSHH
NEVER LIKED THAT DESK ANYWAY.
AND HERE, OF COURSE, WE HAVE OUR HOME THEATER ROOM. CLAY, CAN YOU SHOW MY BESTIE, SPIDER-MAN, OUR NETFLIX AND CHILL ARRAY? TRYING TO SET THE MOOD.
CLAY QUARTERMAIN, LIFE-MODEL DECOY. RECOVERED FROM A SWAMP IN FLORIDA. SHORT CIRCUIT WAITING TO HAPPEN.
NO CAN DO, CAPTAIN 'POOL. MONITORING A SHIPMENT OF ROGUE S.H.I.E.L.D. BEETLE-TANKS EN ROUTE TO--
IXNAY THE IMINAL-CRAY ALK-TAY.*
*"NIX THE CRIMINAL TALK." TRANSLATED FROM PIG.
ONE WAY
RIGHT YOU ARE, SIR. NOTHING TO SEE HERE. CARRY ON WITH YOUR FISTICUFFS.
LOOK, WEBS, I KNOW WHY YOU'RE REALLY HERE--
GOOD. THEN SURRENDER AND MAKE THIS--
--YOU'RE HERE FOR A JOB.
WHAT?! YOU ARE INSANE.

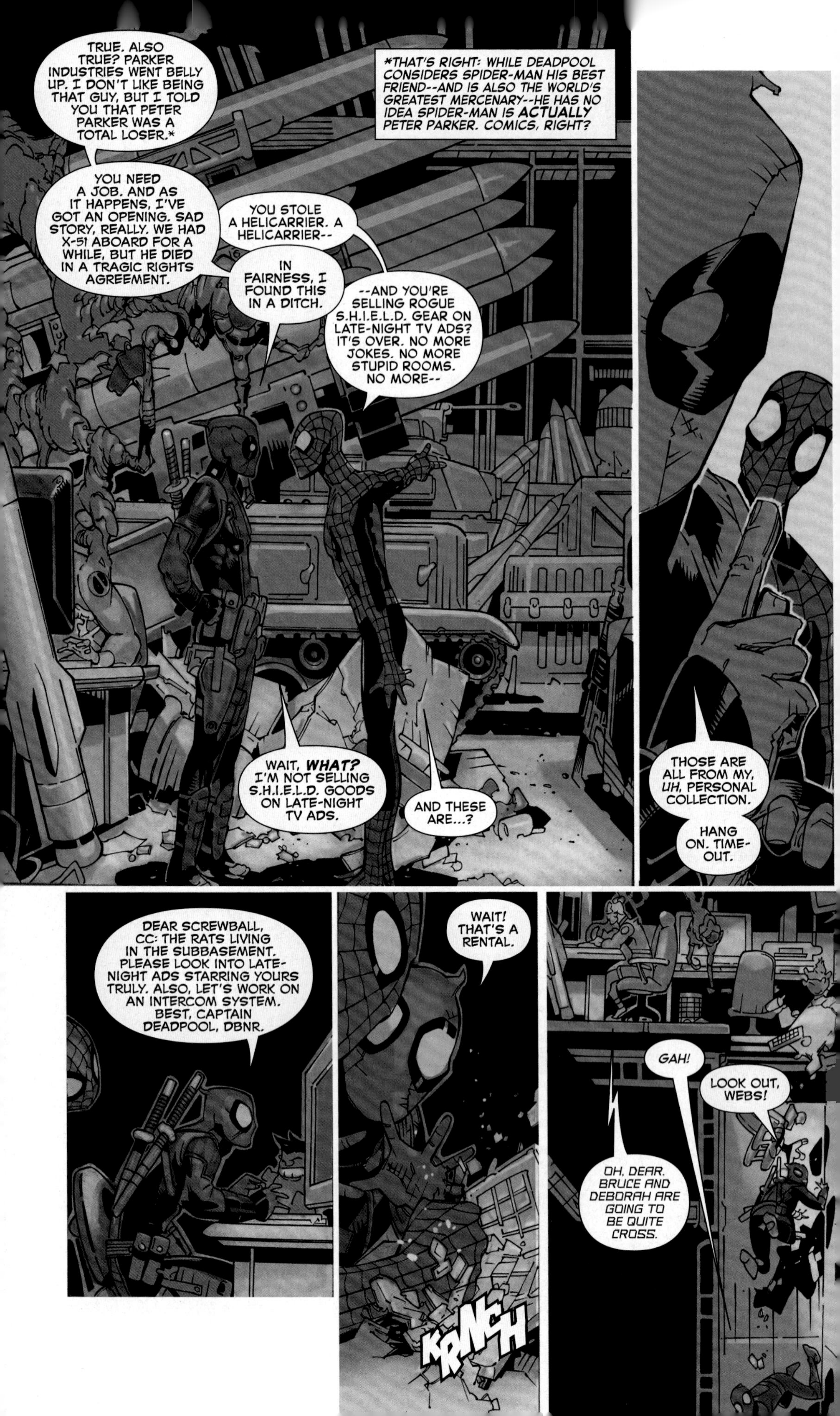
TRUE. ALSO TRUE? PARKER INDUSTRIES WENT BELLY UP. I DON'T LIKE BEING THAT GUY, BUT I TOLD YOU THAT PETER PARKER WAS A TOTAL LOSER.*
*THAT'S RIGHT: WHILE DEADPOOL CONSIDERS SPIDER-MAN HIS BEST FRIEND--AND IS ALSO THE WORLD'S GREATEST MERCENARY--HE HAS NO IDEA SPIDER-MAN IS ACTUALLY PETER PARKER. COMICS, RIGHT?
YOU NEED A JOB. AND AS IT HAPPENS, I'VE GOT AN OPENING. SAD STORY, REALLY. WE HAD X-51 ABOARD FOR A WHILE, BUT HE DIED IN A TRAGIC RIGHTS AGREEMENT.
YOU STOLE A HELICARRIER. A HELICARRIER--
IN FAIRNESS, I FOUND THIS IN A DITCH.
--AND YOU'RE SELLING ROGUE S.H.I.E.L.D. GEAR ON LATE-NIGHT TV ADS? IT'S OVER. NO MORE JOKES. NO MORE STUPID ROOMS. NO MORE--
WAIT, WHAT? I'M NOT SELLING S.H.I.E.L.D. GOODS ON LATE-NIGHT TV ADS.
AND THESE ARE...?
THOSE ARE ALL FROM MY, UH, PERSONAL COLLECTION.
HANG ON. TIME-OUT.
DEAR SCREWBALL, CC: THE RATS LIVING IN THE SUBBASEMENT. PLEASE LOOK INTO LATE-NIGHT ADS STARRING YOURS TRULY. ALSO, LET'S WORK ON AN INTERCOM SYSTEM. BEST, CAPTAIN DEADPOOL, DBNR.
WAIT! THAT'S A RENTAL.
KRNCH
GAH!
LOOK OUT, WEBS!
OH, DEAR. BRUCE AND DEBORAH ARE GOING TO BE QUITE CROSS.

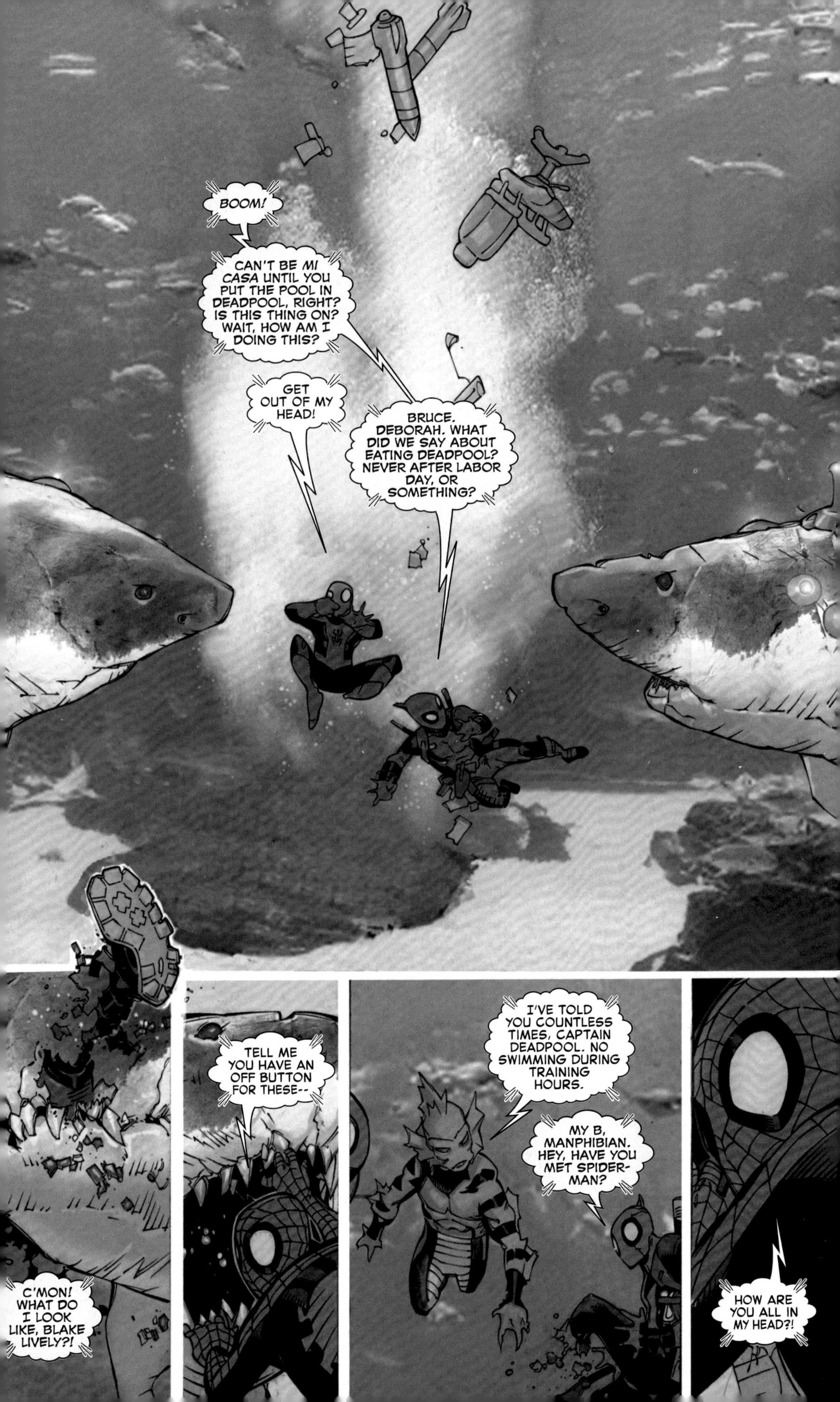
BOOM!
CAN'T BE MI CASA UNTIL YOU PUT THE POOL IN DEADPOOL, RIGHT? IS THIS THING ON? WAIT, HOW AM I DOING THIS?
GET OUT OF MY HEAD!
BRUCE. DEBORAH. WHAT DID WE SAY ABOUT EATING DEADPOOL? NEVER AFTER LABOR DAY, OR SOMETHING?
C'MON! WHAT DO I LOOK LIKE, BLAKE LIVELY?!
TELL ME YOU HAVE AN OFF BUTTON FOR THESE--
I'VE TOLD YOU COUNTLESS TIMES, CAPTAIN DEADPOOL. NO SWIMMING DURING TRAINING HOURS.
MY B, MANPHIBIAN. HEY, HAVE YOU MET SPIDER-MAN?
HOW ARE YOU ALL IN MY HEAD?!

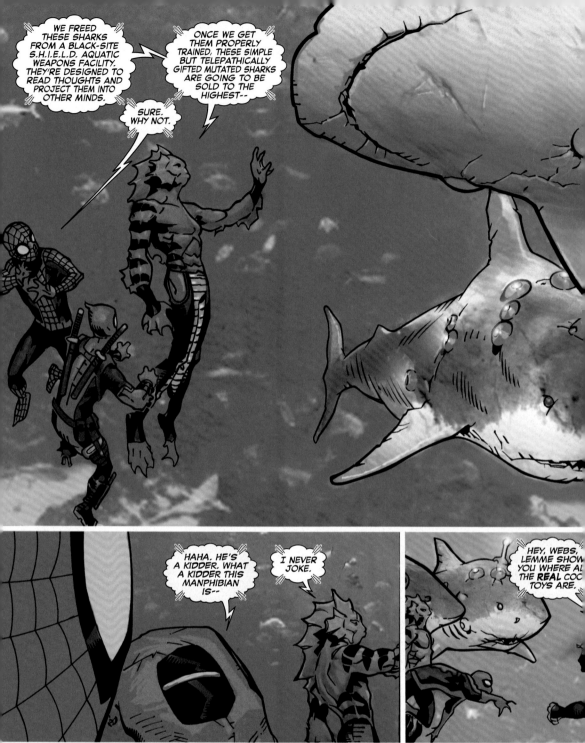

WE FREED THESE SHARKS FROM A BLACK-SITE S.H.I.E.L.D. AQUATIC WEAPONS FACILITY. THEY'RE DESIGNED TO READ THOUGHTS AND PROJECT THEM INTO OTHER MINDS.

ONCE WE GET THEM PROPERLY TRAINED, THESE SIMPLE BUT TELEPATHICALLY GIFTED MUTATED SHARKS ARE GOING TO BE SOLD TO THE HIGHEST--

SURE. WHY NOT.

HAHA, HE'S A KIDDER. WHAT A KIDDER THIS MANPHIBIAN IS--

I NEVER JOKE.

HEY, WEBS, LEMME SHOW YOU WHERE AI THE REAL COC TOYS ARE.

THAT'S ENOUGH FOR TODAY, BRUCE AND DEBORAH.

FREE SWIM FOR THE REST OF THE EVENING.

SOON, WE WILL CONSUME THEM ALL.

YES, MY DEAR BROTHER. BUT FIRST...LET'S DOWNLOAD THE NEW EPISODES OF STRANGER THINGS.

THE NEW SEASON IS OUT ALREADY? I DO SO HOPE ELEVEN IS ALL RIGHT.

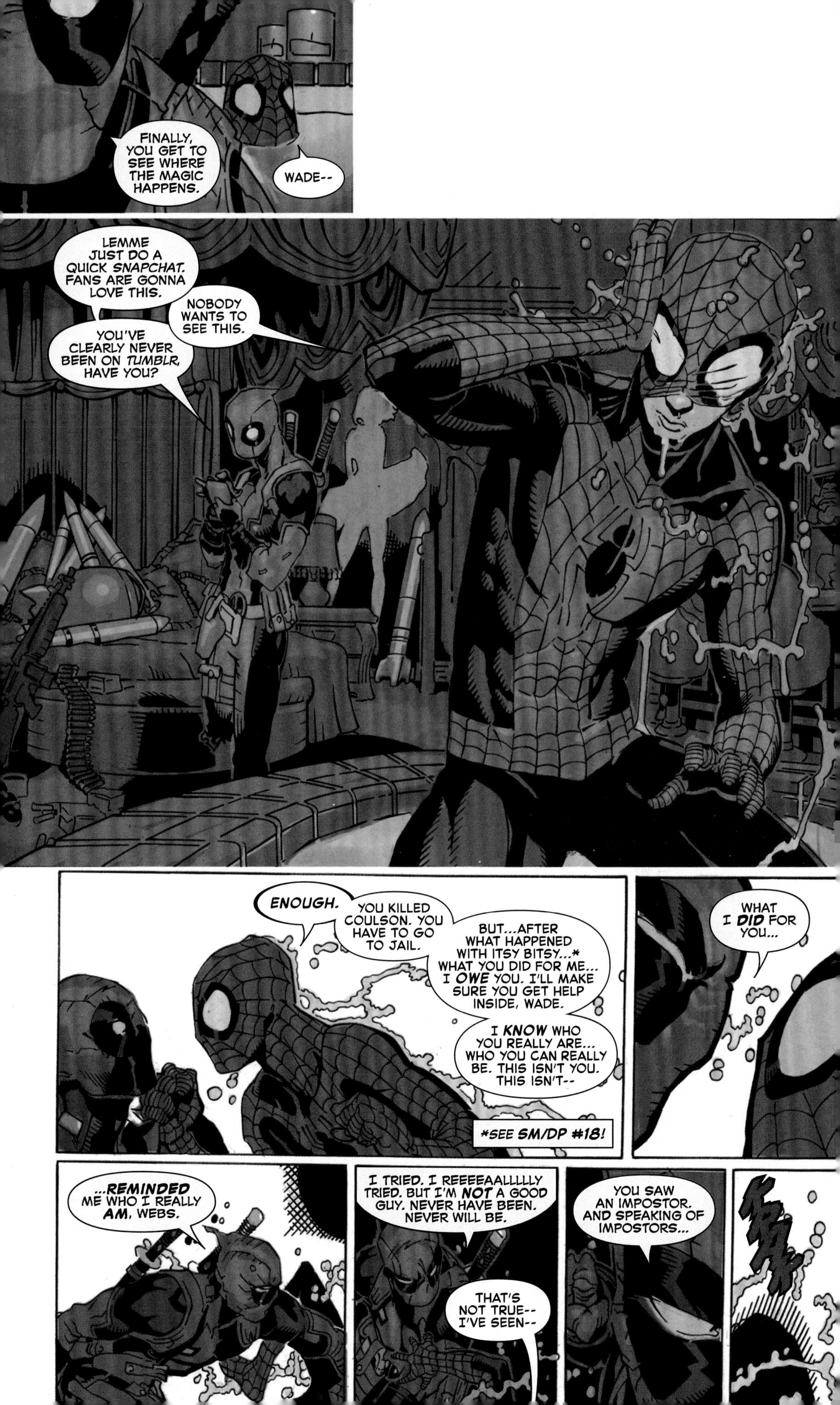
FINALLY, YOU GET TO SEE WHERE THE MAGIC HAPPENS.
WADE--
LEMME JUST DO A QUICK SNAPCHAT. FANS ARE GONNA LOVE THIS.
NOBODY WANTS TO SEE THIS.
YOU'VE CLEARLY NEVER BEEN ON TUMBLR, HAVE YOU?
ENOUGH.
YOU KILLED COULSON. YOU HAVE TO GO TO JAIL.
BUT...AFTER WHAT HAPPENED WITH ITSY BITSY...* WHAT YOU DID FOR ME... I OWE YOU. I'LL MAKE SURE YOU GET HELP INSIDE, WADE.
I KNOW WHO YOU REALLY ARE... WHO YOU CAN REALLY BE. THIS ISN'T YOU. THIS ISN'T--
*SEE SM/DP #18!
WHAT I DID FOR YOU...
...REMINDED ME WHO I REALLY AM, WEBS.
I TRIED. I REEEEAALLLLLY TRIED. BUT I'M NOT A GOOD GUY. NEVER HAVE BEEN. NEVER WILL BE.
THAT'S NOT TRUE-- I'VE SEEN--
YOU SAW AN IMPOSTOR. AND SPEAKING OF IMPOSTORS...

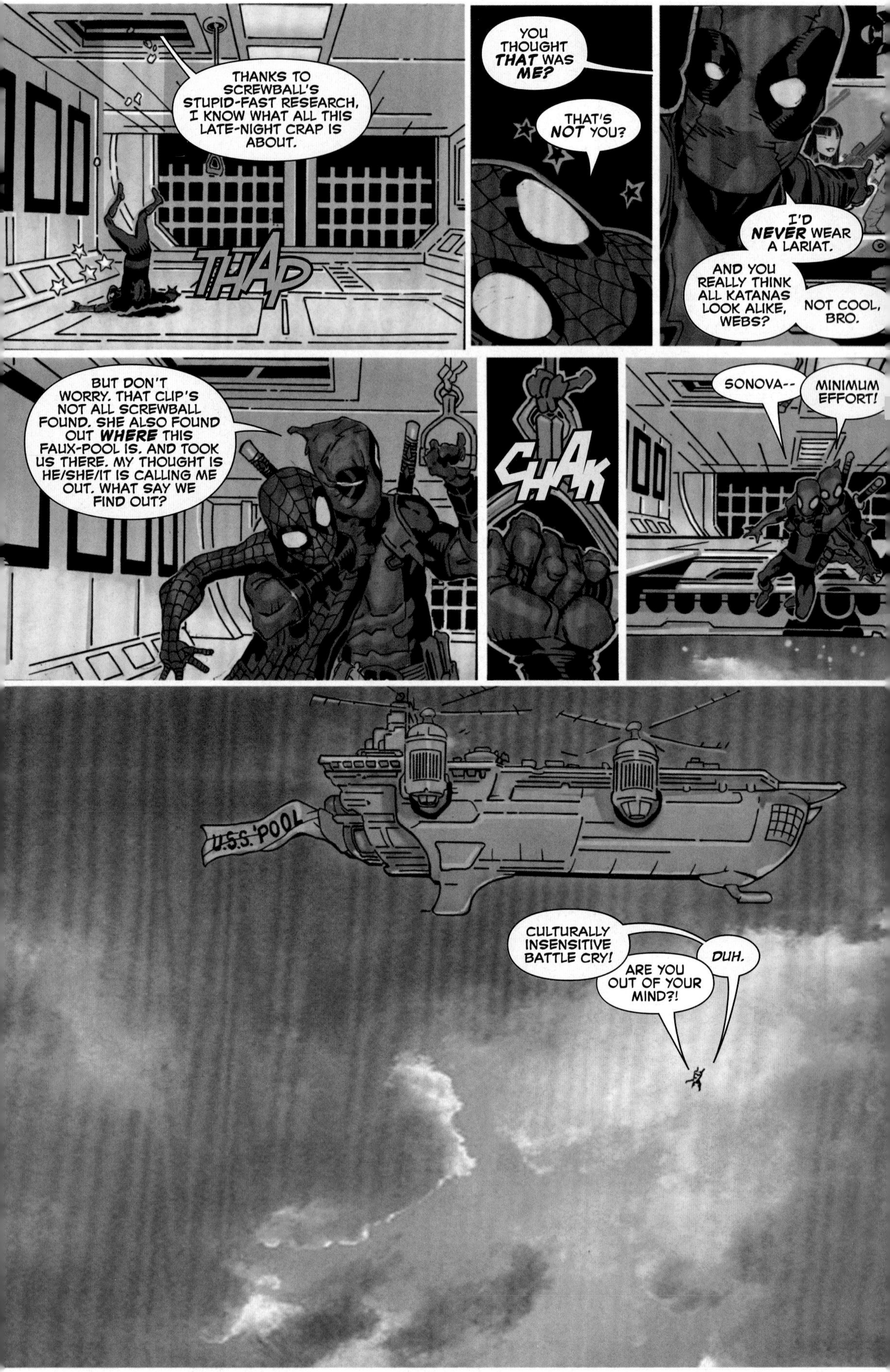

THANKS TO SCREWBALL'S STUPID-FAST RESEARCH, I KNOW WHAT ALL THIS LATE-NIGHT CRAP IS ABOUT.
THAP
YOU THOUGHT THAT WAS ME?
THAT'S NOT YOU?
I'D NEVER WEAR A LARIAT.
AND YOU REALLY THINK ALL KATANAS LOOK ALIKE, WEBS?
NOT COOL, BRO.
BUT DON'T WORRY. THAT CLIP'S NOT ALL SCREWBALL FOUND. SHE ALSO FOUND OUT WHERE THIS FAUX-POOL IS. AND TOOK US THERE. MY THOUGHT IS HE/SHE/IT IS CALLING ME OUT. WHAT SAY WE FIND OUT?
CHAK
SONOVA--
MINIMUM EFFORT!
U.S.S. 'POOL
CULTURALLY INSENSITIVE BATTLE CRY!
DUH.
ARE YOU OUT OF YOUR MIND?!

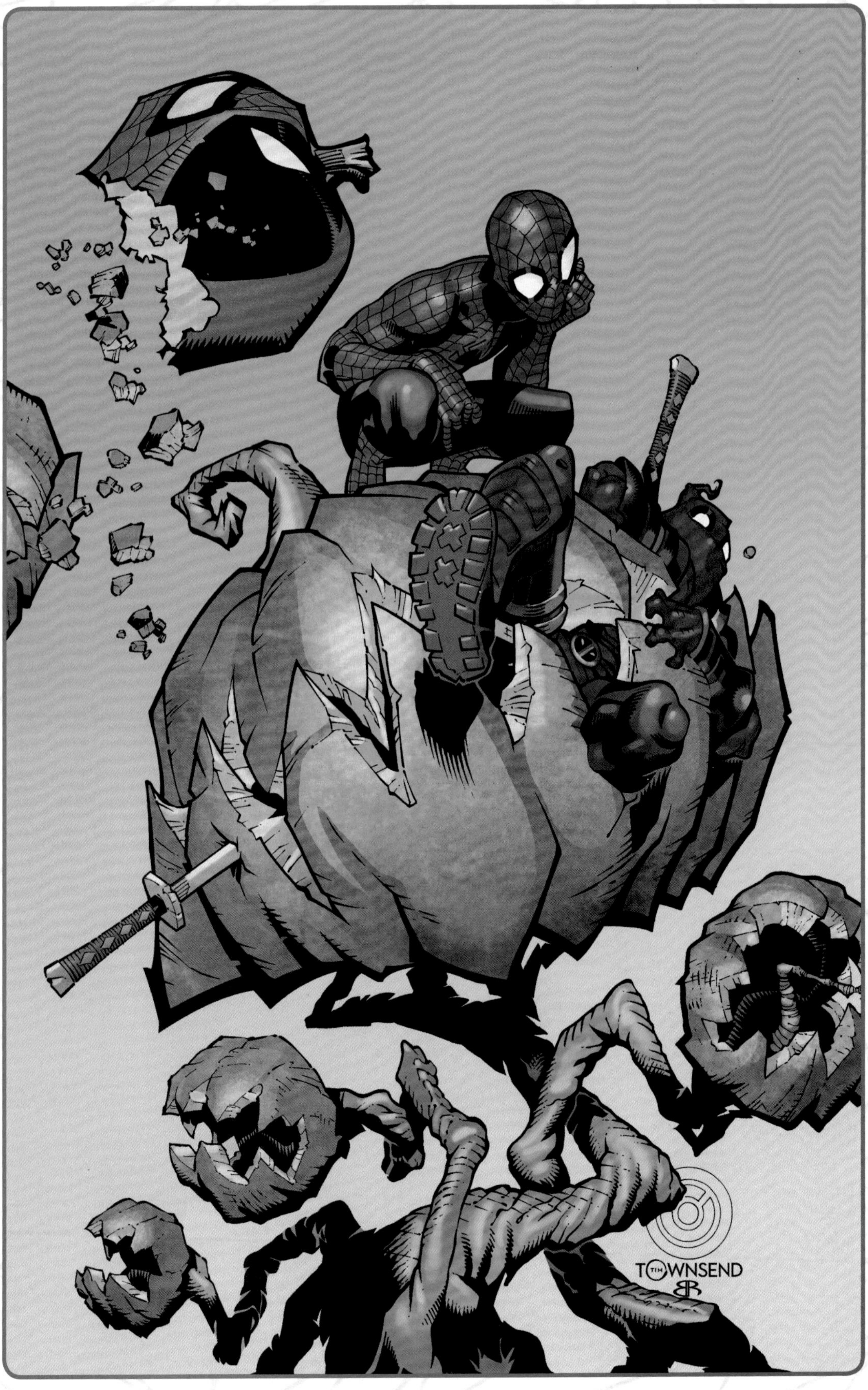
TIM TOWNSEND

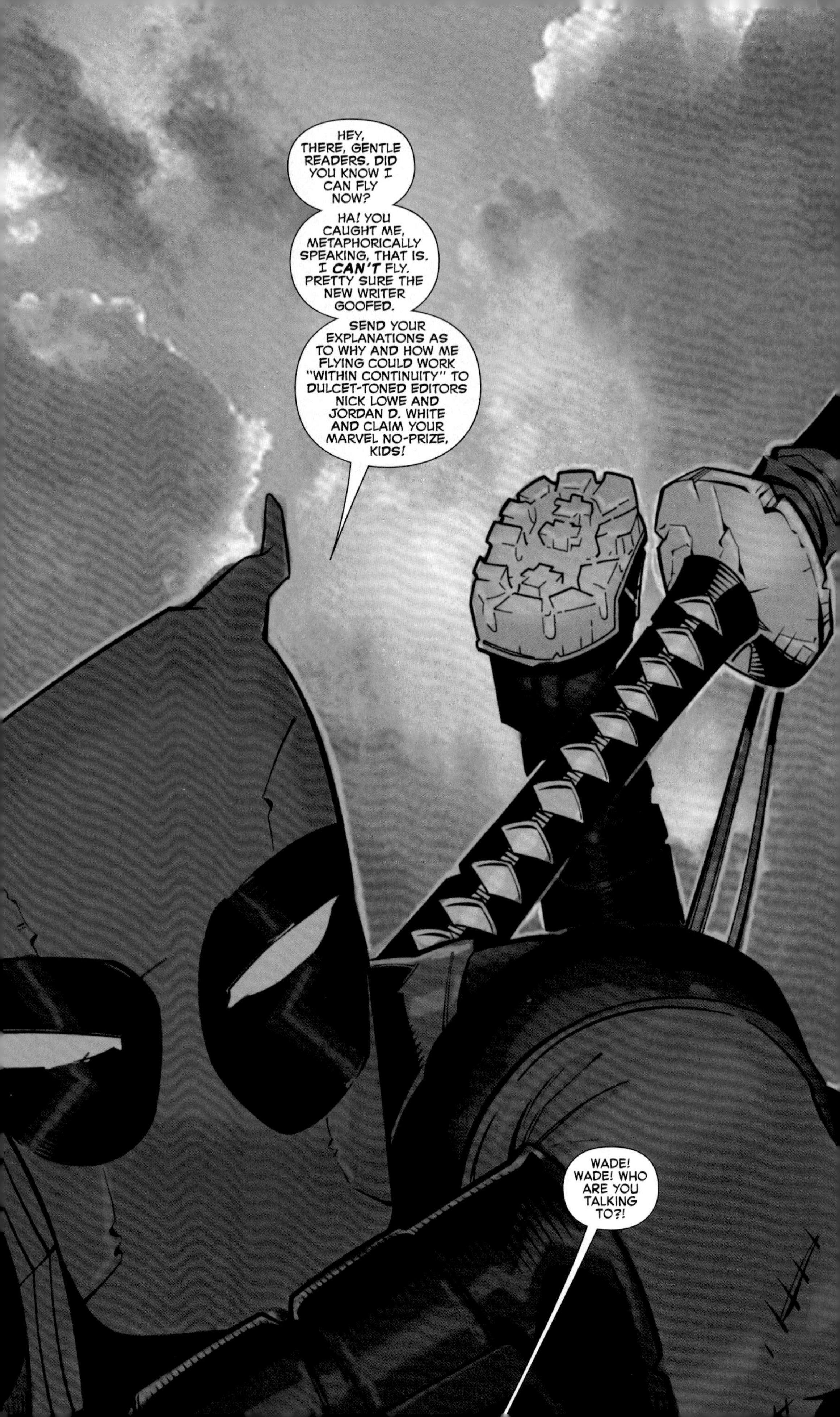
HEY, THERE, GENTLE READERS. DID YOU KNOW I CAN FLY NOW?
HA! YOU CAUGHT ME, METAPHORICALLY SPEAKING, THAT IS. I **CAN'T** FLY. PRETTY SURE THE NEW WRITER GOOFED.
SEND YOUR EXPLANATIONS AS TO WHY AND HOW ME FLYING COULD WORK "WITHIN CONTINUITY" TO DULCET-TONED EDITORS NICK LOWE AND JORDAN D. WHITE AND CLAIM YOUR MARVEL NO-PRIZE, KIDS!
WADE! WADE! WHO ARE YOU TALKING TO?!

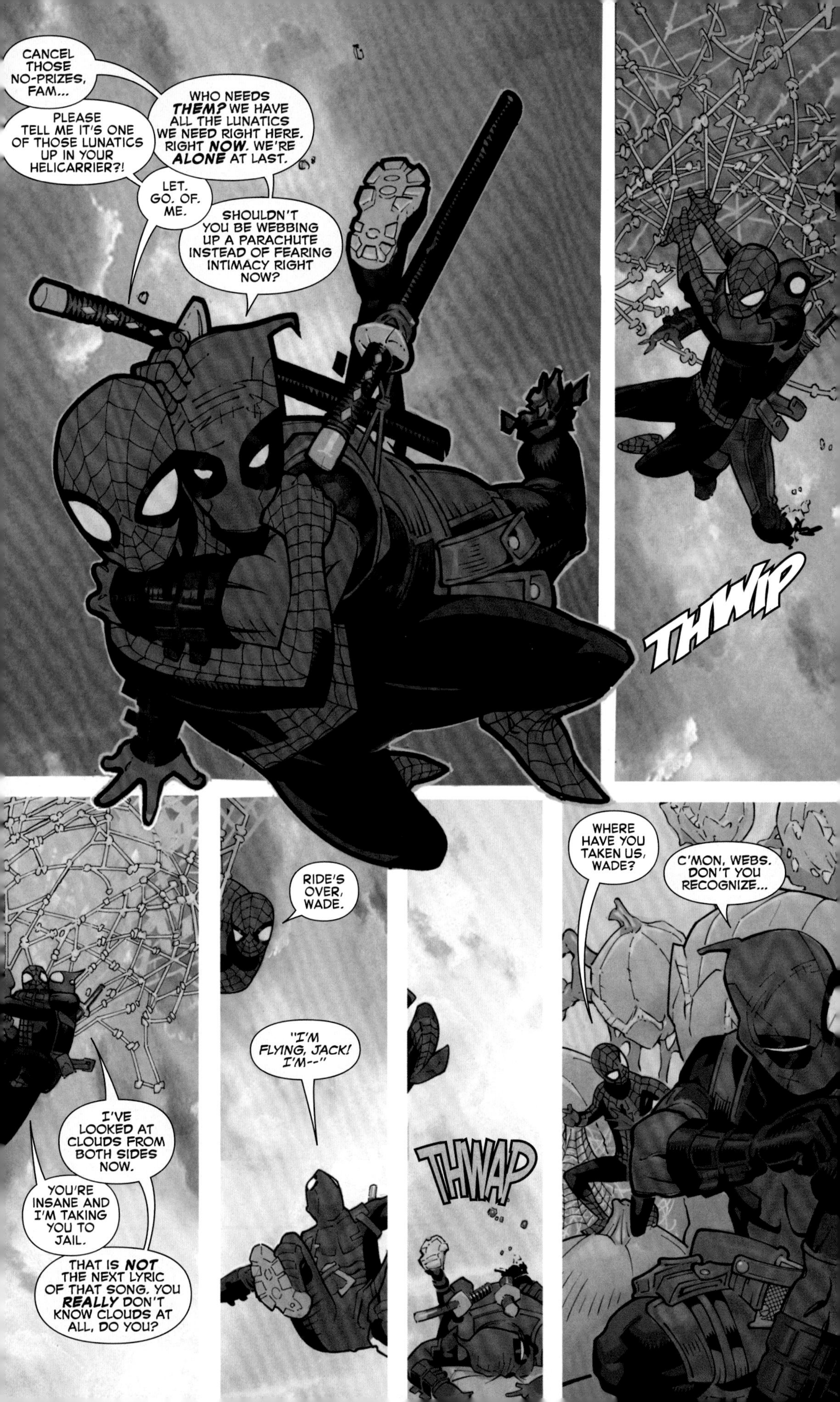
CANCEL THOSE NO-PRIZES, FAM...
WHO NEEDS THEM? WE HAVE ALL THE LUNATICS WE NEED RIGHT HERE. RIGHT NOW. WE'RE ALONE AT LAST.
PLEASE TELL ME IT'S ONE OF THOSE LUNATICS UP IN YOUR HELICARRIER?!
LET. GO. OF. ME.
SHOULDN'T YOU BE WEBBING UP A PARACHUTE INSTEAD OF FEARING INTIMACY RIGHT NOW?
THWIP
I'VE LOOKED AT CLOUDS FROM BOTH SIDES NOW.
YOU'RE INSANE AND I'M TAKING YOU TO JAIL.
THAT IS NOT THE NEXT LYRIC OF THAT SONG. YOU REALLY DON'T KNOW CLOUDS AT ALL, DO YOU?
RIDE'S OVER, WADE.
"I'M FLYING, JACK! I'M--"
THWAP
WHERE HAVE YOU TAKEN US, WADE?
C'MON, WEBS. DON'T YOU RECOGNIZE...

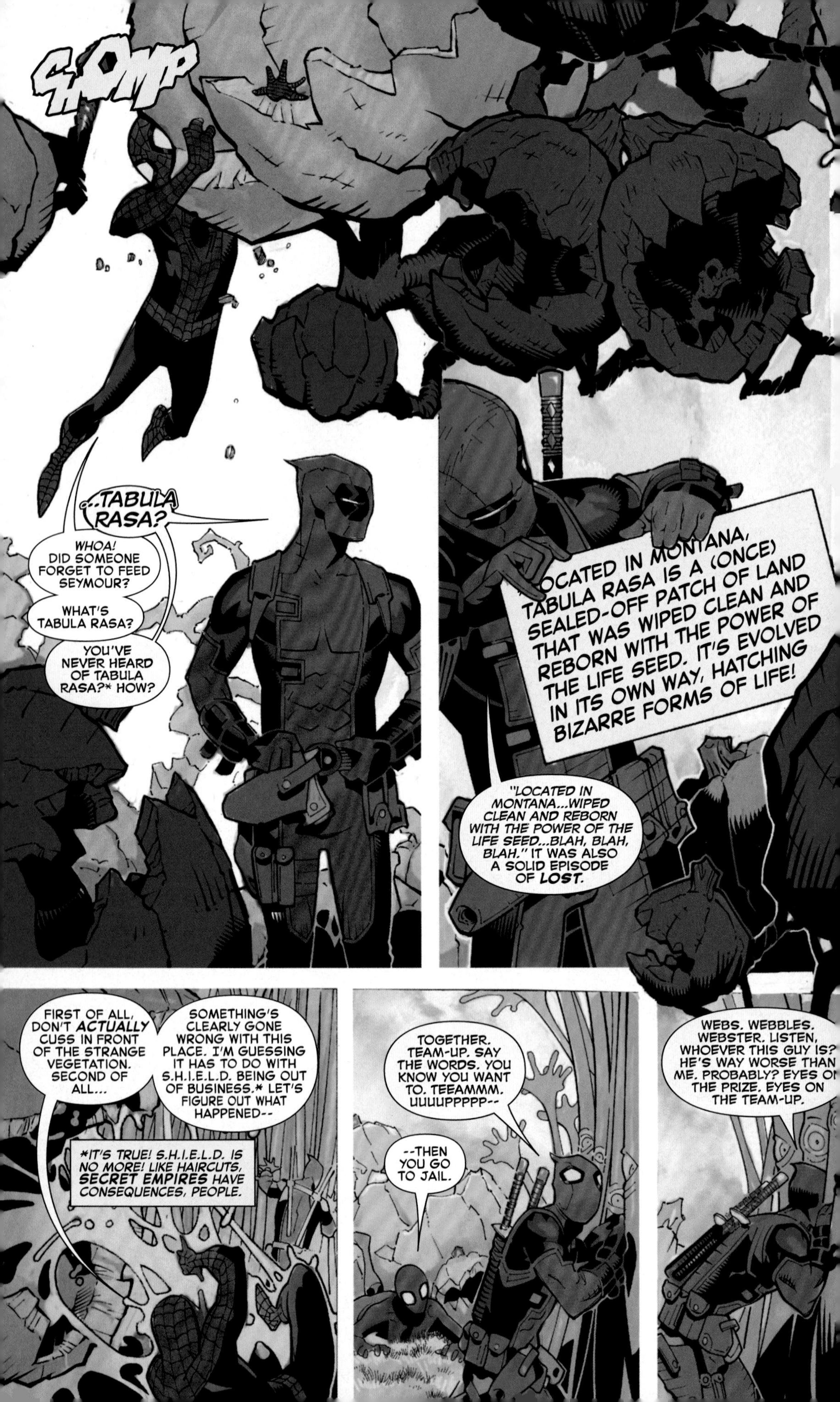

SHOMP
WHOA! DID SOMEONE FORGET TO FEED SEYMOUR?
...TABULA RASA?
WHAT'S TABULA RASA?
YOU'VE NEVER HEARD OF TABULA RASA?* HOW?
LOCATED IN MONTANA, TABULA RASA IS A (ONCE) SEALED-OFF PATCH OF LAND THAT WAS WIPED CLEAN AND REBORN WITH THE POWER OF THE LIFE SEED. IT'S EVOLVED IN ITS OWN WAY, HATCHING BIZARRE FORMS OF LIFE!
"LOCATED IN MONTANA...WIPED CLEAN AND REBORN WITH THE POWER OF THE LIFE SEED...BLAH, BLAH, BLAH." IT WAS ALSO A SOLID EPISODE OF **LOST**.
FIRST OF ALL, DON'T **ACTUALLY** CUSS IN FRONT OF THE STRANGE VEGETATION. SECOND OF ALL...
SOMETHING'S CLEARLY GONE WRONG WITH THIS PLACE. I'M GUESSING IT HAS TO DO WITH S.H.I.E.L.D. BEING OUT OF BUSINESS.* LET'S FIGURE OUT WHAT HAPPENED--
*IT'S TRUE! S.H.I.E.L.D. IS NO MORE! LIKE HAIRCUTS, **SECRET EMPIRES** HAVE CONSEQUENCES, PEOPLE.
TOGETHER. TEAM-UP. SAY THE WORDS. YOU KNOW YOU WANT TO. TEEAMMM. UUUUPPPPP--
--THEN YOU GO TO JAIL.
WEBS. WEBBLES. WEBSTER. LISTEN, WHOEVER THIS GUY IS? HE'S WAY WORSE THAN ME. PROBABLY? EYES ON THE PRIZE. EYES ON THE TEAM-UP.

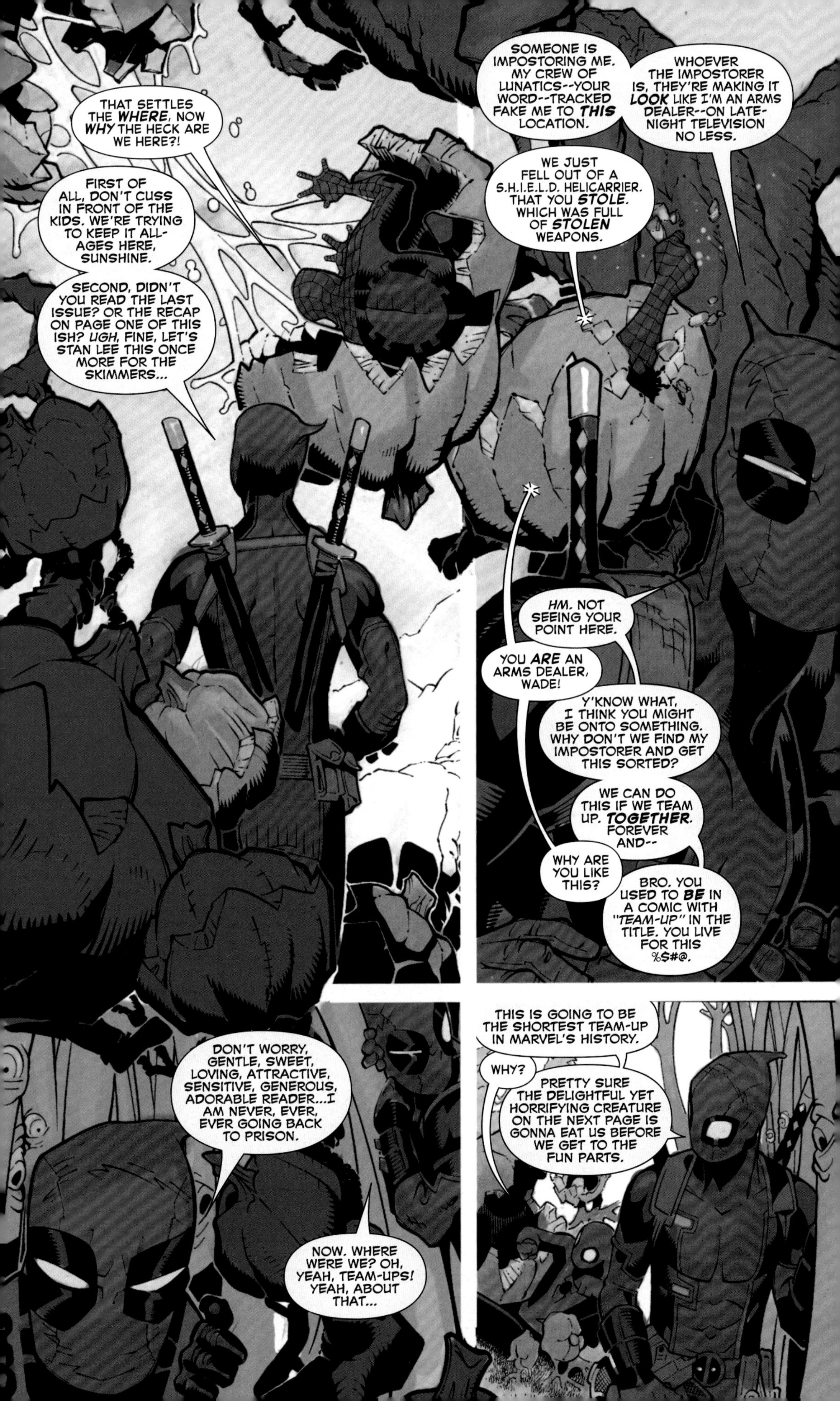

THAT SETTLES THE *WHERE*, NOW *WHY* THE HECK ARE WE HERE?!
FIRST OF ALL, DON'T CUSS IN FRONT OF THE KIDS. WE'RE TRYING TO KEEP IT ALL-AGES HERE, SUNSHINE.
SECOND, DIDN'T YOU READ THE LAST ISSUE? OR THE RECAP ON PAGE ONE OF THIS ISH? *UGH*, FINE, LET'S STAN LEE THIS ONCE MORE FOR THE SKIMMERS...
SOMEONE IS IMPOSTORING ME. MY CREW OF LUNATICS--YOUR WORD--TRACKED FAKE ME TO *THIS* LOCATION.
WHOEVER THE IMPOSTORER IS, THEY'RE MAKING IT *LOOK* LIKE I'M AN ARMS DEALER--ON LATE-NIGHT TELEVISION NO LESS.
WE JUST FELL OUT OF A S.H.I.E.L.D. HELICARRIER. THAT YOU *STOLE*. WHICH WAS FULL OF *STOLEN* WEAPONS.
HM. NOT SEEING YOUR POINT HERE.
YOU *ARE* AN ARMS DEALER, WADE!
Y'KNOW WHAT, I THINK YOU MIGHT BE ONTO SOMETHING. WHY DON'T WE FIND MY IMPOSTORER AND GET THIS SORTED?
WE CAN DO THIS IF WE TEAM UP. *TOGETHER*. FOREVER AND--
WHY ARE YOU LIKE THIS?
BRO. YOU USED TO *BE* IN A COMIC WITH "*TEAM-UP*" IN THE TITLE. YOU LIVE FOR THIS %$#@.
DON'T WORRY, GENTLE, SWEET, LOVING, ATTRACTIVE, SENSITIVE, GENEROUS, ADORABLE READER...I AM NEVER, EVER, EVER GOING BACK TO PRISON.
NOW. WHERE WERE WE? OH, YEAH, TEAM-UPS! YEAH, ABOUT THAT...
THIS IS GOING TO BE THE SHORTEST TEAM-UP IN MARVEL'S HISTORY.
WHY?
PRETTY SURE THE DELIGHTFUL YET HORRIFYING CREATURE ON THE NEXT PAGE IS GONNA EAT US BEFORE WE GET TO THE FUN PARTS.

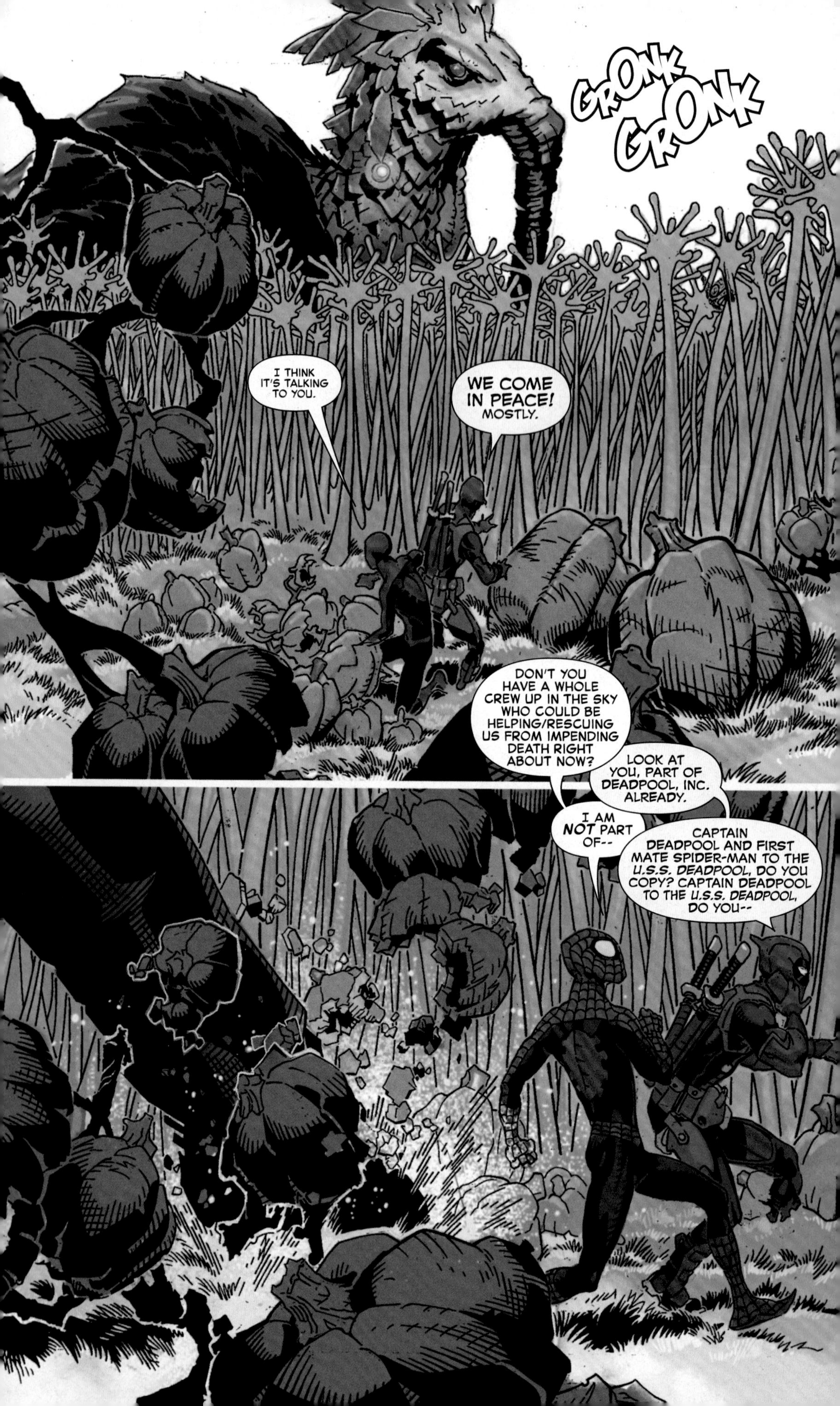
GRONK GRONK
I THINK IT'S TALKING TO YOU.
WE COME IN PEACE! MOSTLY.
DON'T YOU HAVE A WHOLE CREW UP IN THE SKY WHO COULD BE HELPING/RESCUING US FROM IMPENDING DEATH RIGHT ABOUT NOW?
LOOK AT YOU, PART OF DEADPOOL, INC. ALREADY.
I AM NOT PART OF--
CAPTAIN DEADPOOL AND FIRST MATE SPIDER-MAN TO THE U.S.S. DEADPOOL, DO YOU COPY? CAPTAIN DEADPOOL TO THE U.S.S. DEADPOOL, DO YOU--

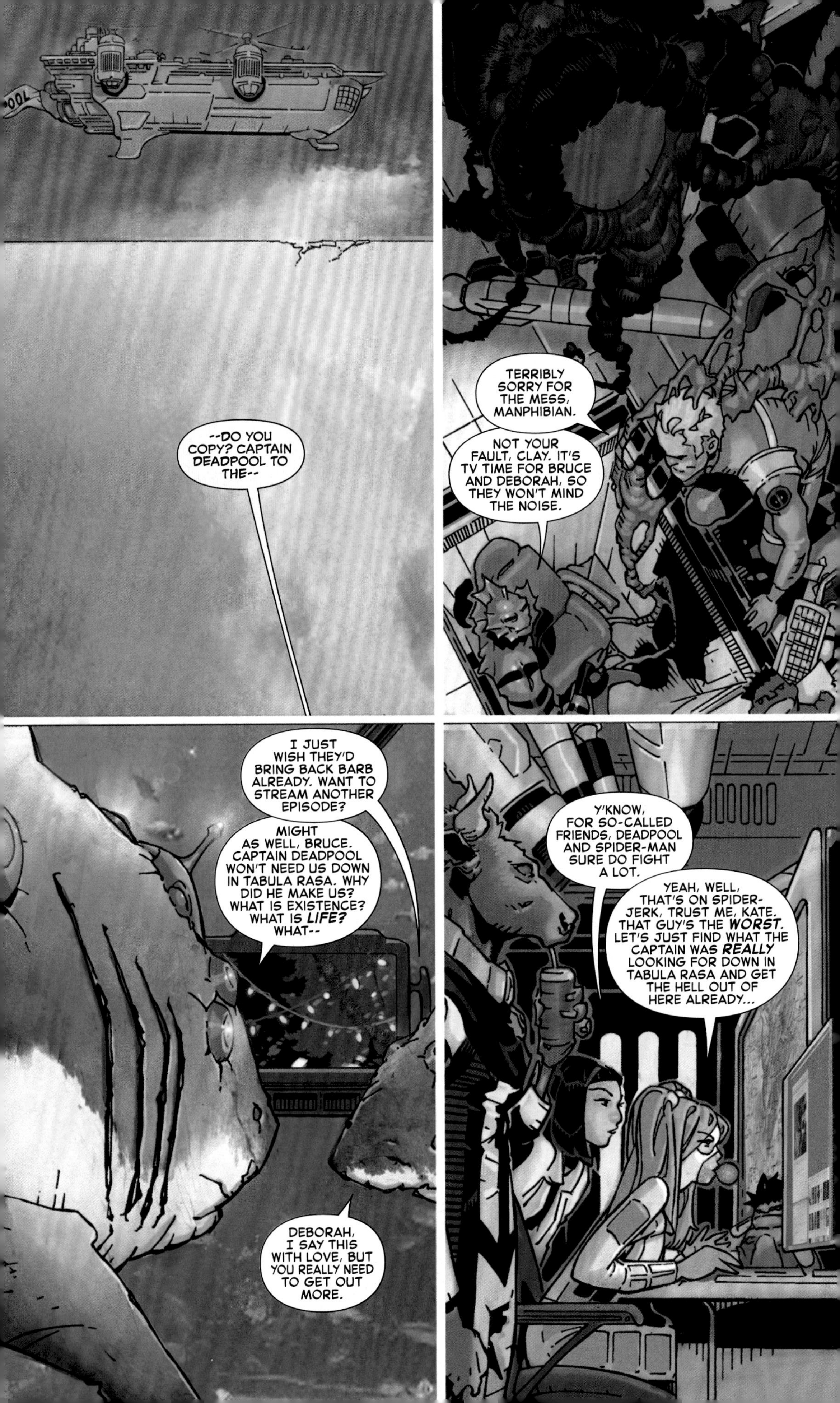
--DO YOU COPY? CAPTAIN DEADPOOL TO THE--
TERRIBLY SORRY FOR THE MESS, MANPHIBIAN.
NOT YOUR FAULT, CLAY. IT'S TV TIME FOR BRUCE AND DEBORAH, SO THEY WON'T MIND THE NOISE.
I JUST WISH THEY'D BRING BACK BARB ALREADY. WANT TO STREAM ANOTHER EPISODE?
MIGHT AS WELL, BRUCE. CAPTAIN DEADPOOL WON'T NEED US DOWN IN TABULA RASA. WHY DID HE MAKE US? WHAT IS EXISTENCE? WHAT IS LIFE? WHAT--
DEBORAH, I SAY THIS WITH LOVE, BUT YOU REALLY NEED TO GET OUT MORE.
Y'KNOW, FOR SO-CALLED FRIENDS, DEADPOOL AND SPIDER-MAN SURE DO FIGHT A LOT.
YEAH, WELL, THAT'S ON SPIDER-JERK, TRUST ME, KATE. THAT GUY'S THE WORST. LET'S JUST FIND WHAT THE CAPTAIN WAS REALLY LOOKING FOR DOWN IN TABULA RASA AND GET THE HELL OUT OF HERE ALREADY...

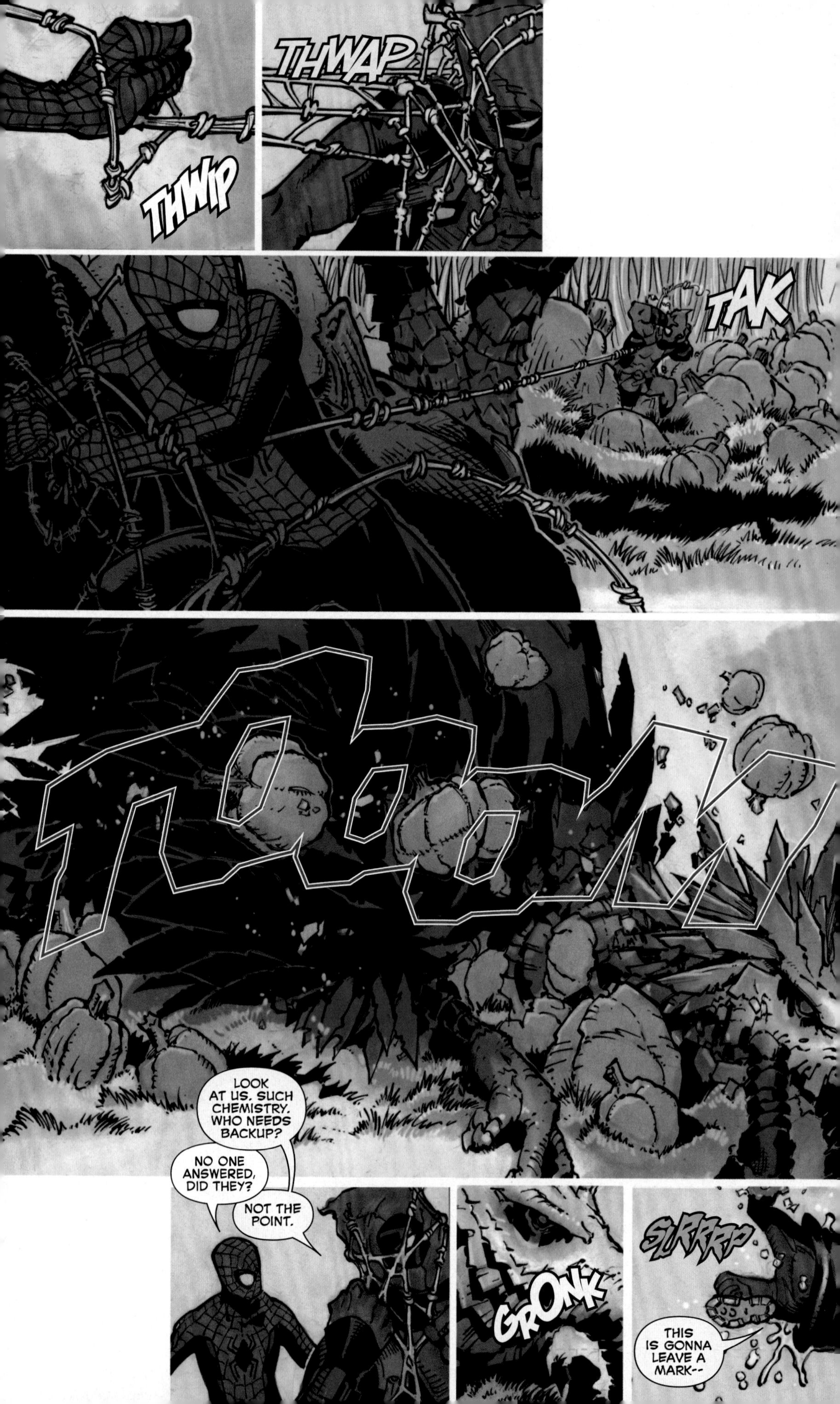
THWIP
THWAP
TAK
THOOM
LOOK AT US. SUCH CHEMISTRY. WHO NEEDS BACKUP?
NO ONE ANSWERED, DID THEY?
NOT THE POINT.
GRONK
SLRRRP
THIS IS GONNA LEAVE A MARK--

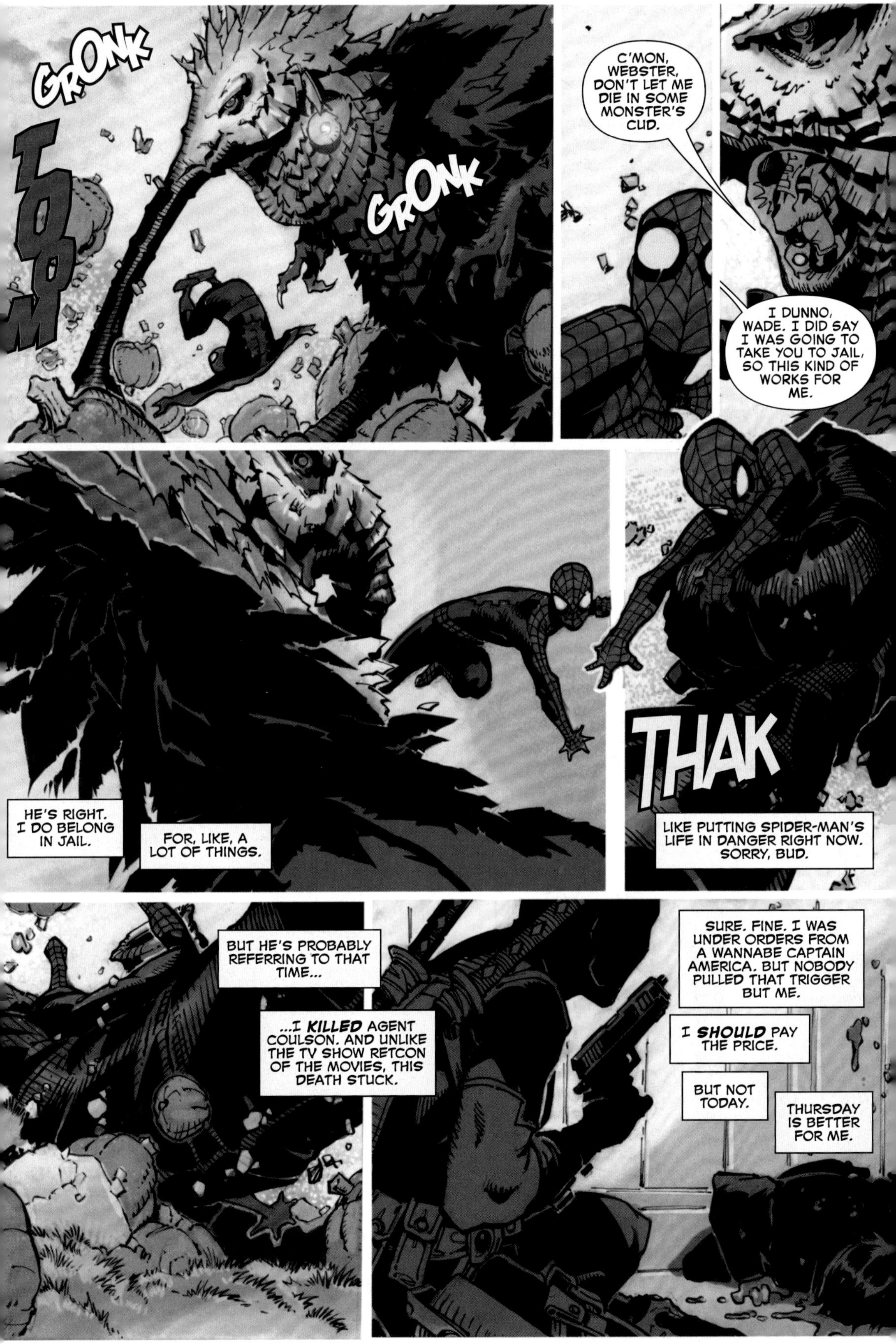
GRONK
TOOOM
GRONK
C'MON, WEBSTER, DON'T LET ME DIE IN SOME MONSTER'S CUD.
I DUNNO, WADE. I DID SAY I WAS GOING TO TAKE YOU TO JAIL, SO THIS KIND OF WORKS FOR ME.
HE'S RIGHT. I DO BELONG IN JAIL.
FOR, LIKE, A LOT OF THINGS.
THAK
LIKE PUTTING SPIDER-MAN'S LIFE IN DANGER RIGHT NOW. SORRY, BUD.
BUT HE'S PROBABLY REFERRING TO THAT TIME...
...I KILLED AGENT COULSON. AND UNLIKE THE TV SHOW RETCON OF THE MOVIES, THIS DEATH STUCK.
SURE. FINE. I WAS UNDER ORDERS FROM A WANNABE CAPTAIN AMERICA. BUT NOBODY PULLED THAT TRIGGER BUT ME.
I SHOULD PAY THE PRICE.
BUT NOT TODAY.
THURSDAY IS BETTER FOR ME.

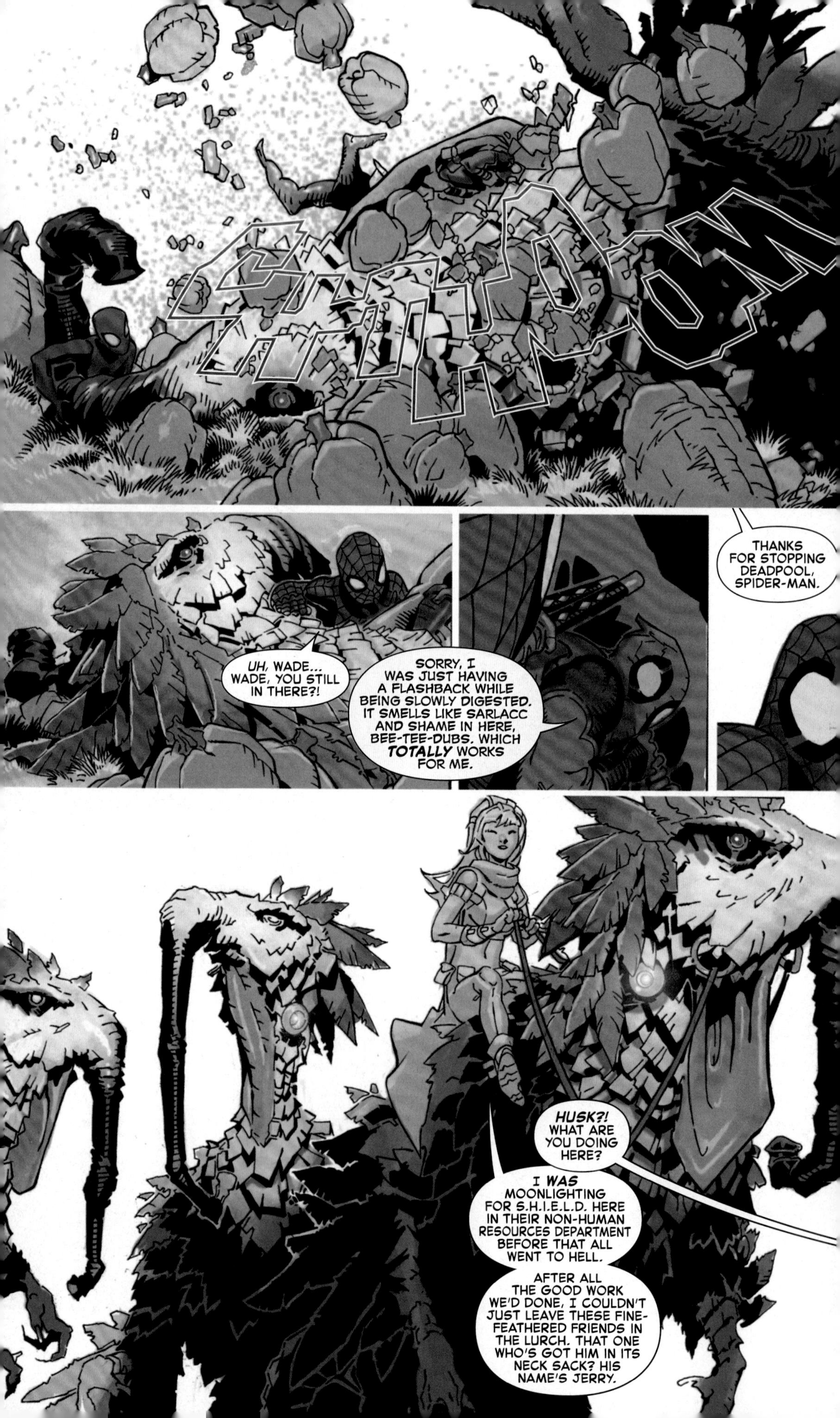

SHTHOOM
UH, WADE... WADE, YOU STILL IN THERE?!
SORRY, I WAS JUST HAVING A FLASHBACK WHILE BEING SLOWLY DIGESTED. IT SMELLS LIKE SARLACC AND SHAME IN HERE, BEE-TEE-DUBS. WHICH TOTALLY WORKS FOR ME.
THANKS FOR STOPPING DEADPOOL, SPIDER-MAN.
HUSK?! WHAT ARE YOU DOING HERE?
I WAS MOONLIGHTING FOR S.H.I.E.L.D. HERE IN THEIR NON-HUMAN RESOURCES DEPARTMENT BEFORE THAT ALL WENT TO HELL.
AFTER ALL THE GOOD WORK WE'D DONE, I COULDN'T JUST LEAVE THESE FINE-FEATHERED FRIENDS IN THE LURCH. THAT ONE WHO'S GOT HIM IN ITS NECK SACK? HIS NAME'S JERRY.

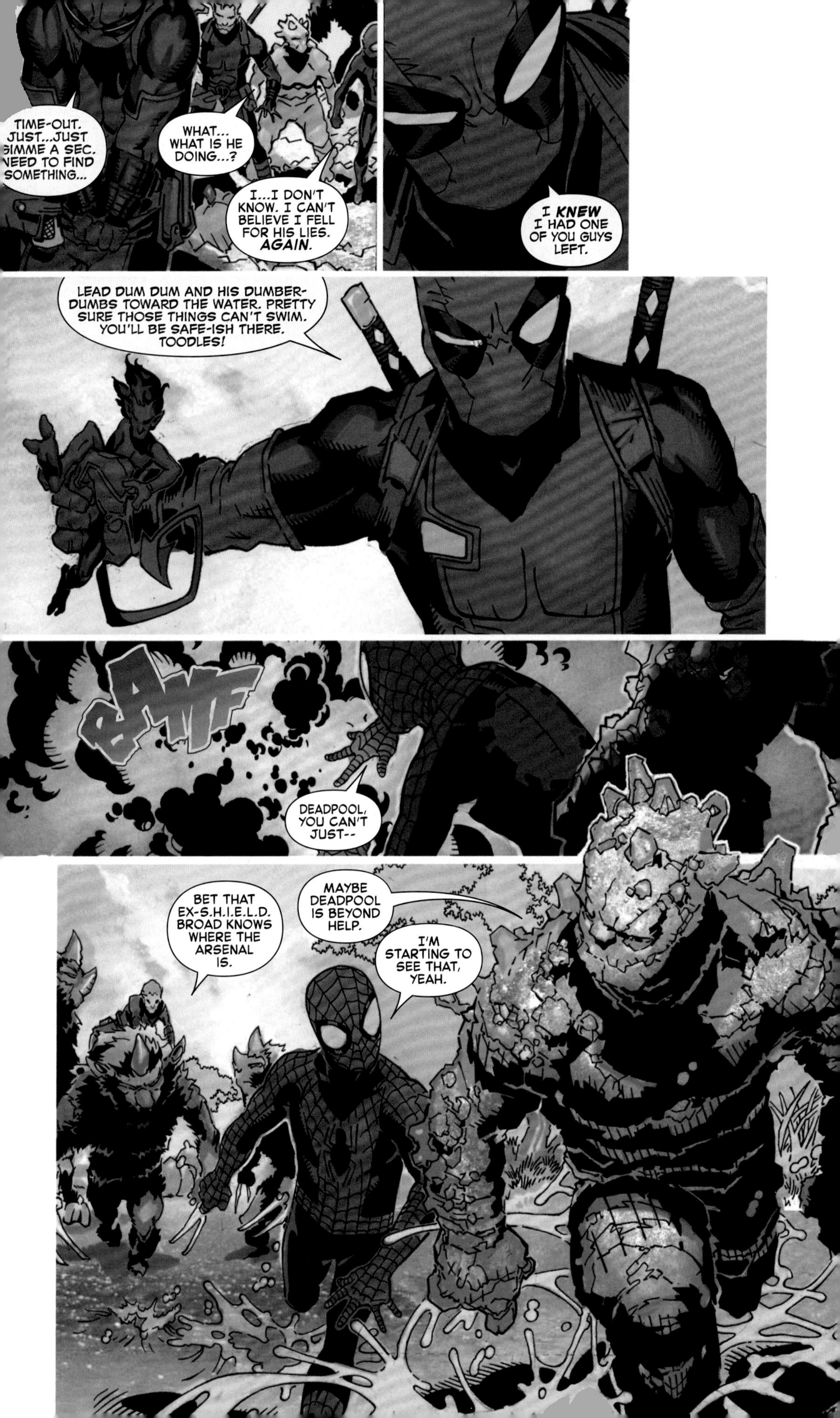
TIME-OUT. JUST...JUST GIMME A SEC. NEED TO FIND SOMETHING...
WHAT... WHAT IS HE DOING...?
I...I DON'T KNOW. I CAN'T BELIEVE I FELL FOR HIS LIES. AGAIN.
I KNEW I HAD ONE OF YOU GUYS LEFT.
LEAD DUM DUM AND HIS DUMBER-DUMBS TOWARD THE WATER. PRETTY SURE THOSE THINGS CAN'T SWIM. YOU'LL BE SAFE-ISH THERE. TOODLES!
BAMF
DEADPOOL, YOU CAN'T JUST--
BET THAT EX-S.H.I.E.L.D. BROAD KNOWS WHERE THE ARSENAL IS.
MAYBE DEADPOOL IS BEYOND HELP.
I'M STARTING TO SEE THAT, YEAH.

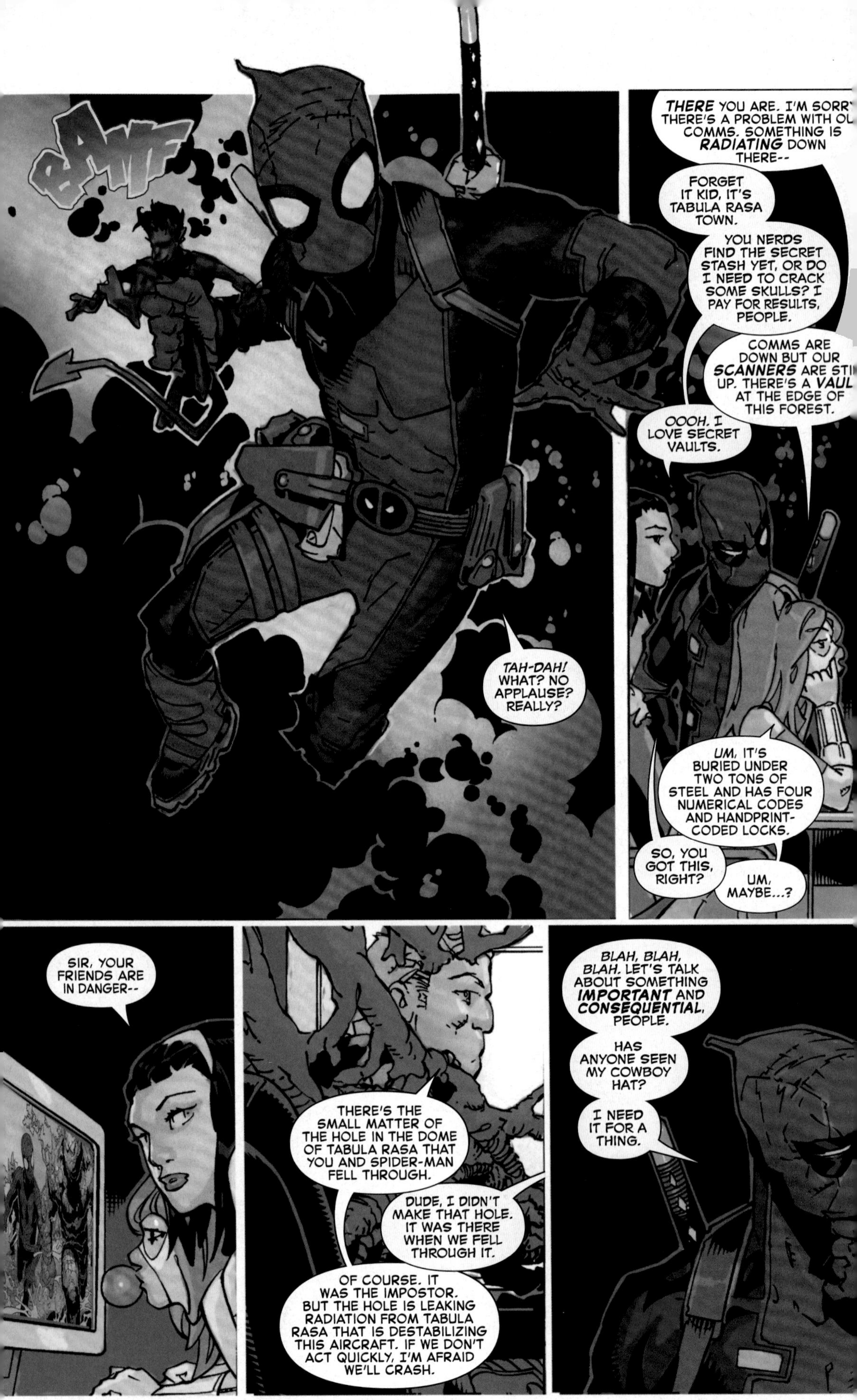
BAMF
TAH-DAH! WHAT? NO APPLAUSE? REALLY?
THERE YOU ARE. I'M SORR THERE'S A PROBLEM WITH OU COMMS. SOMETHING IS RADIATING DOWN THERE--
FORGET IT KID, IT'S TABULA RASA TOWN.
YOU NERDS FIND THE SECRET STASH YET, OR DO I NEED TO CRACK SOME SKULLS? I PAY FOR RESULTS, PEOPLE.
COMMS ARE DOWN BUT OUR SCANNERS ARE STI UP. THERE'S A VAUL AT THE EDGE OF THIS FOREST.
OOOH. I LOVE SECRET VAULTS.
UM, IT'S BURIED UNDER TWO TONS OF STEEL AND HAS FOUR NUMERICAL CODES AND HANDPRINT-CODED LOCKS.
SO, YOU GOT THIS, RIGHT?
UM, MAYBE...?
SIR, YOUR FRIENDS ARE IN DANGER--
THERE'S THE SMALL MATTER OF THE HOLE IN THE DOME OF TABULA RASA THAT YOU AND SPIDER-MAN FELL THROUGH.
DUDE, I DIDN'T MAKE THAT HOLE. IT WAS THERE WHEN WE FELL THROUGH IT.
OF COURSE. IT WAS THE IMPOSTOR. BUT THE HOLE IS LEAKING RADIATION FROM TABULA RASA THAT IS DESTABILIZING THIS AIRCRAFT. IF WE DON'T ACT QUICKLY, I'M AFRAID WE'LL CRASH.
BLAH, BLAH, BLAH. LET'S TALK ABOUT SOMETHING IMPORTANT AND CONSEQUENTIAL, PEOPLE.
HAS ANYONE SEEN MY COWBOY HAT?
I NEED IT FOR A THING.

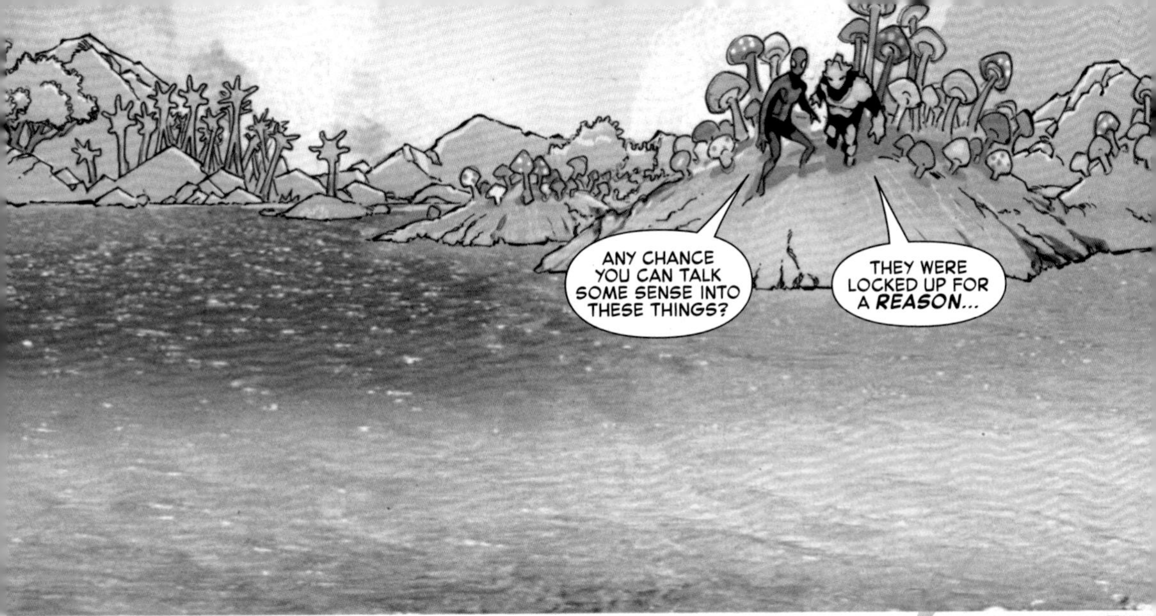
ANY CHANCE YOU CAN TALK SOME SENSE INTO THESE THINGS?
THEY WERE LOCKED UP FOR A *REASON*...

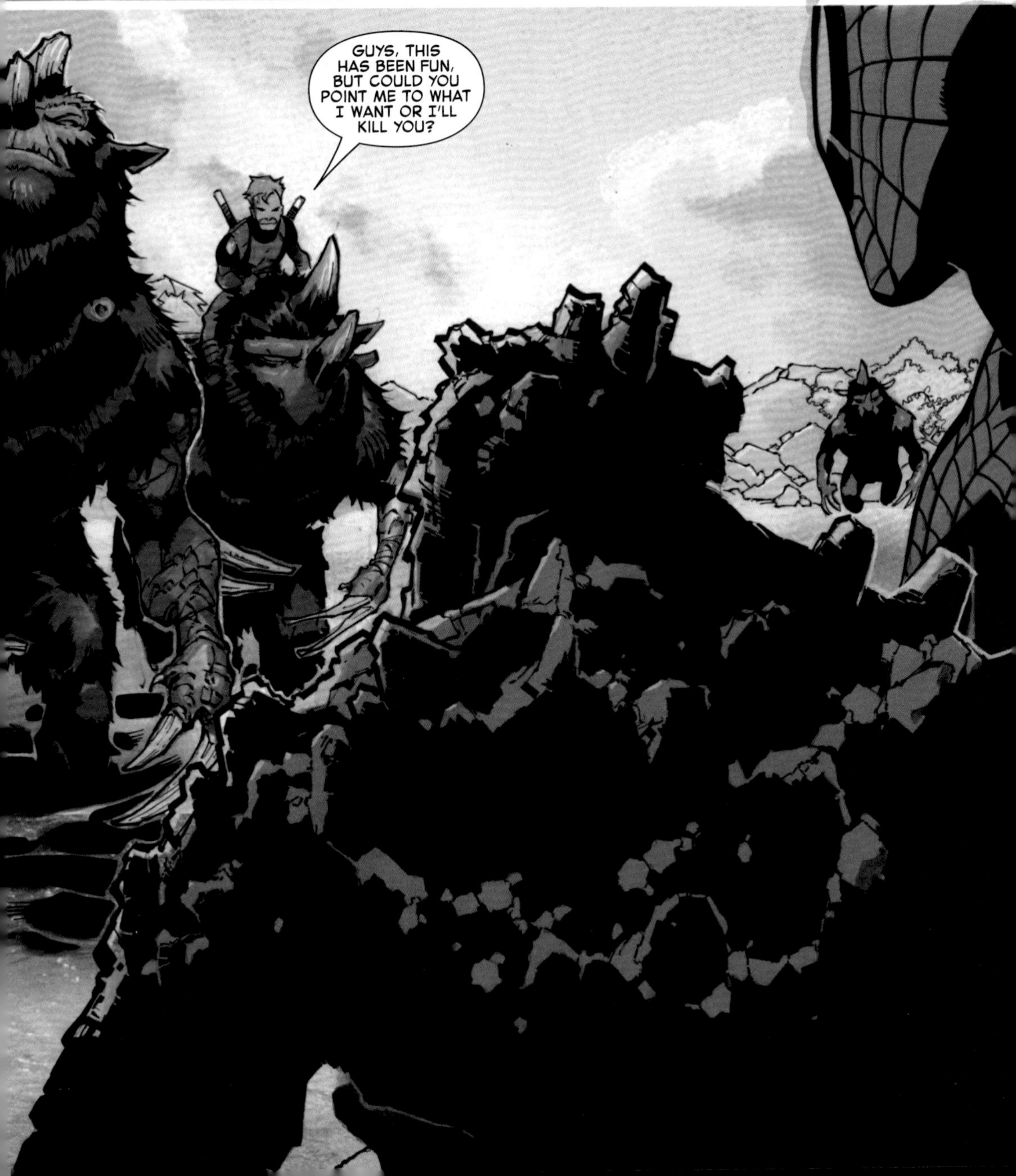
GUYS, THIS HAS BEEN FUN, BUT COULD YOU POINT ME TO WHAT I WANT OR I'LL KILL YOU?

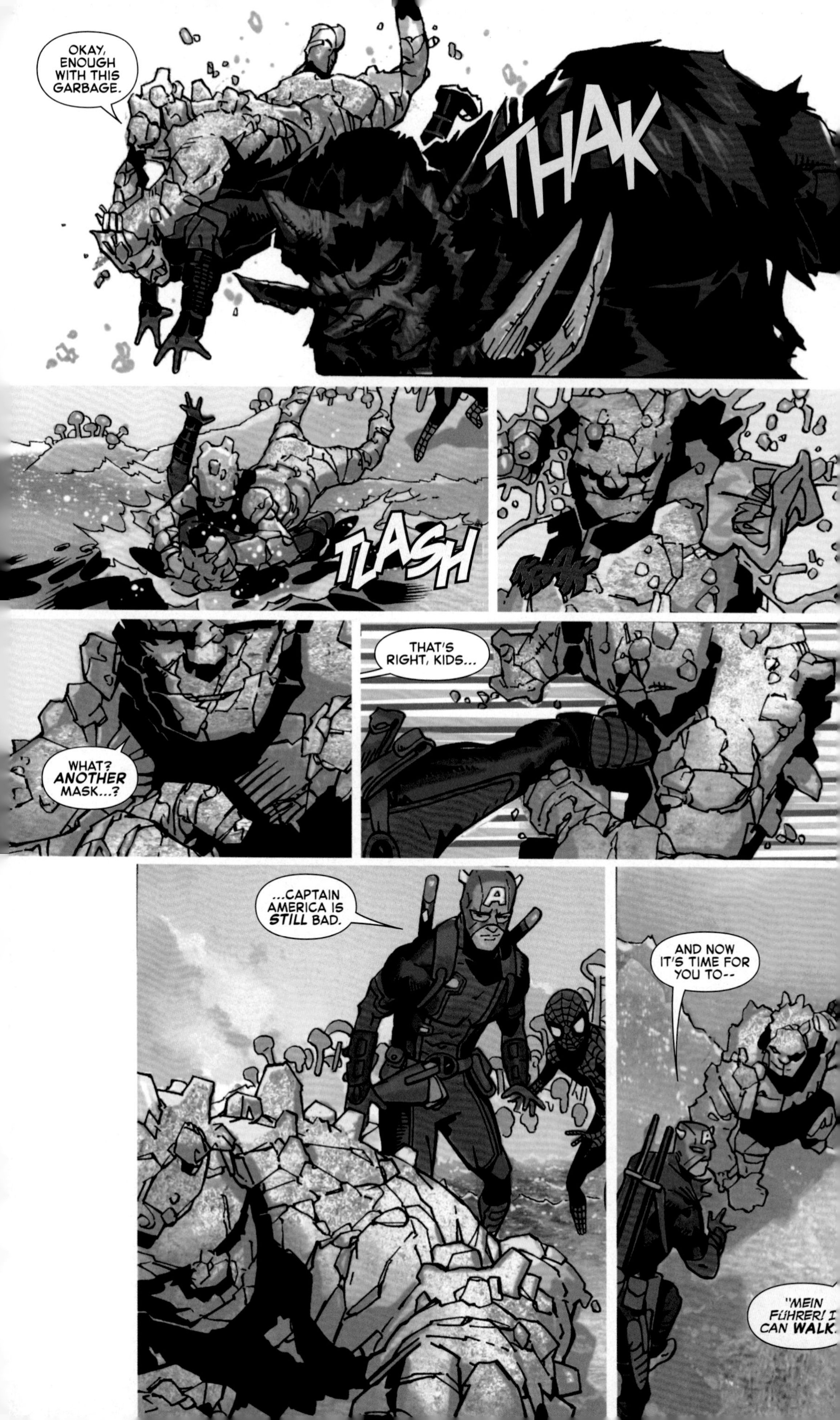
OKAY, ENOUGH WITH THIS GARBAGE.
THAK
TLASH
WHAT? ANOTHER MASK...?
THAT'S RIGHT, KIDS...
...CAPTAIN AMERICA IS STILL BAD.
AND NOW IT'S TIME FOR YOU TO--
"MEIN FÜHRER! I CAN WALK.

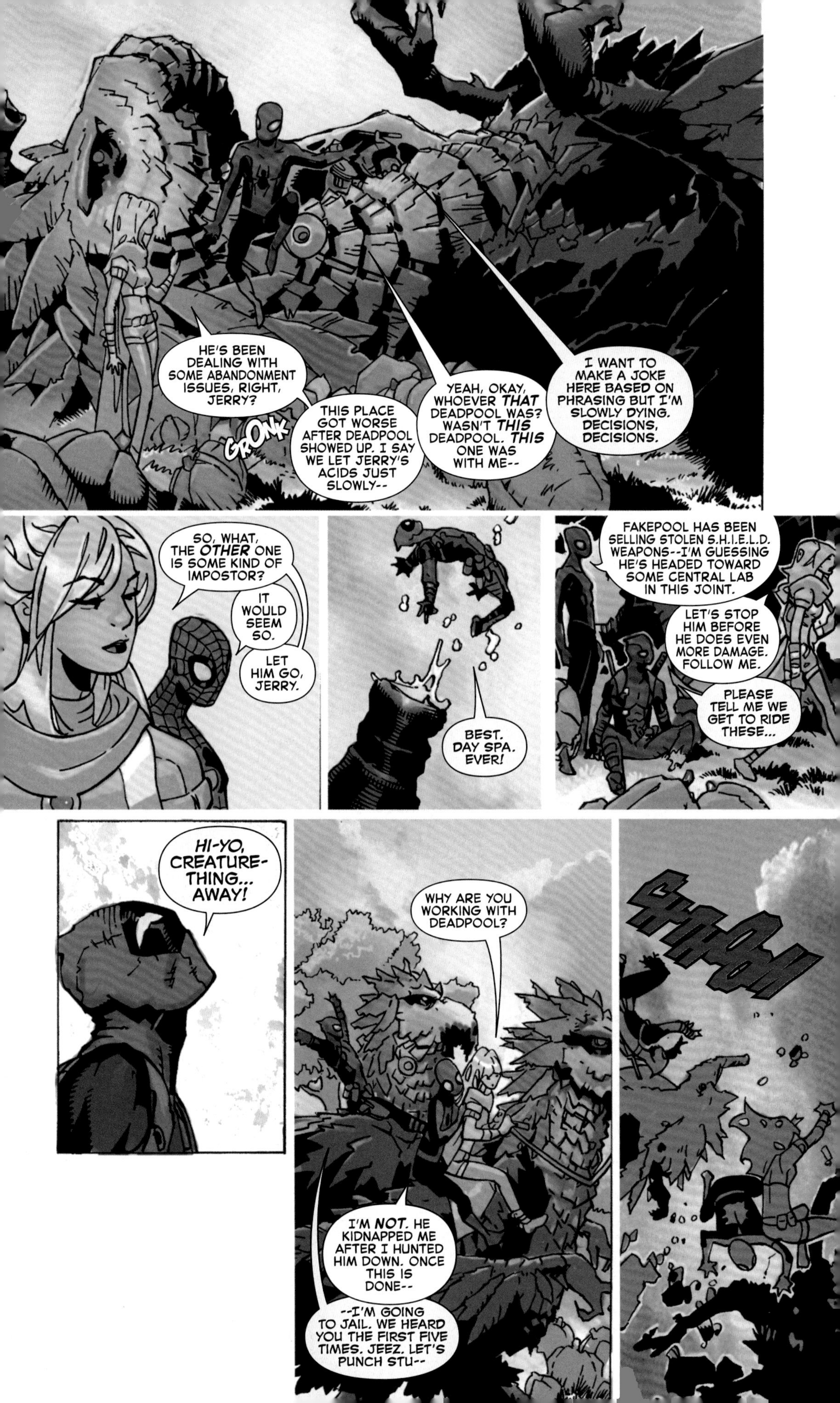
HE'S BEEN DEALING WITH SOME ABANDONMENT ISSUES, RIGHT, JERRY?
GRONK
THIS PLACE GOT WORSE AFTER DEADPOOL SHOWED UP. I SAY WE LET JERRY'S ACIDS JUST SLOWLY--
YEAH, OKAY, WHOEVER THAT DEADPOOL WAS? WASN'T THIS DEADPOOL. THIS ONE WAS WITH ME--
I WANT TO MAKE A JOKE HERE BASED ON PHRASING BUT I'M SLOWLY DYING. DECISIONS, DECISIONS.
SO, WHAT, THE OTHER ONE IS SOME KIND OF IMPOSTOR?
IT WOULD SEEM SO.
LET HIM GO, JERRY.
BEST. DAY SPA. EVER!
FAKEPOOL HAS BEEN SELLING STOLEN S.H.I.E.L.D. WEAPONS--I'M GUESSING HE'S HEADED TOWARD SOME CENTRAL LAB IN THIS JOINT.
LET'S STOP HIM BEFORE HE DOES EVEN MORE DAMAGE. FOLLOW ME.
PLEASE TELL ME WE GET TO RIDE THESE...
HI-YO, CREATURE-THING... AWAY!
WHY ARE YOU WORKING WITH DEADPOOL?
I'M NOT. HE KIDNAPPED ME AFTER I HUNTED HIM DOWN. ONCE THIS IS DONE--
--I'M GOING TO JAIL. WE HEARD YOU THE FIRST FIVE TIMES. JEEZ. LET'S PUNCH STU--
SHOOM

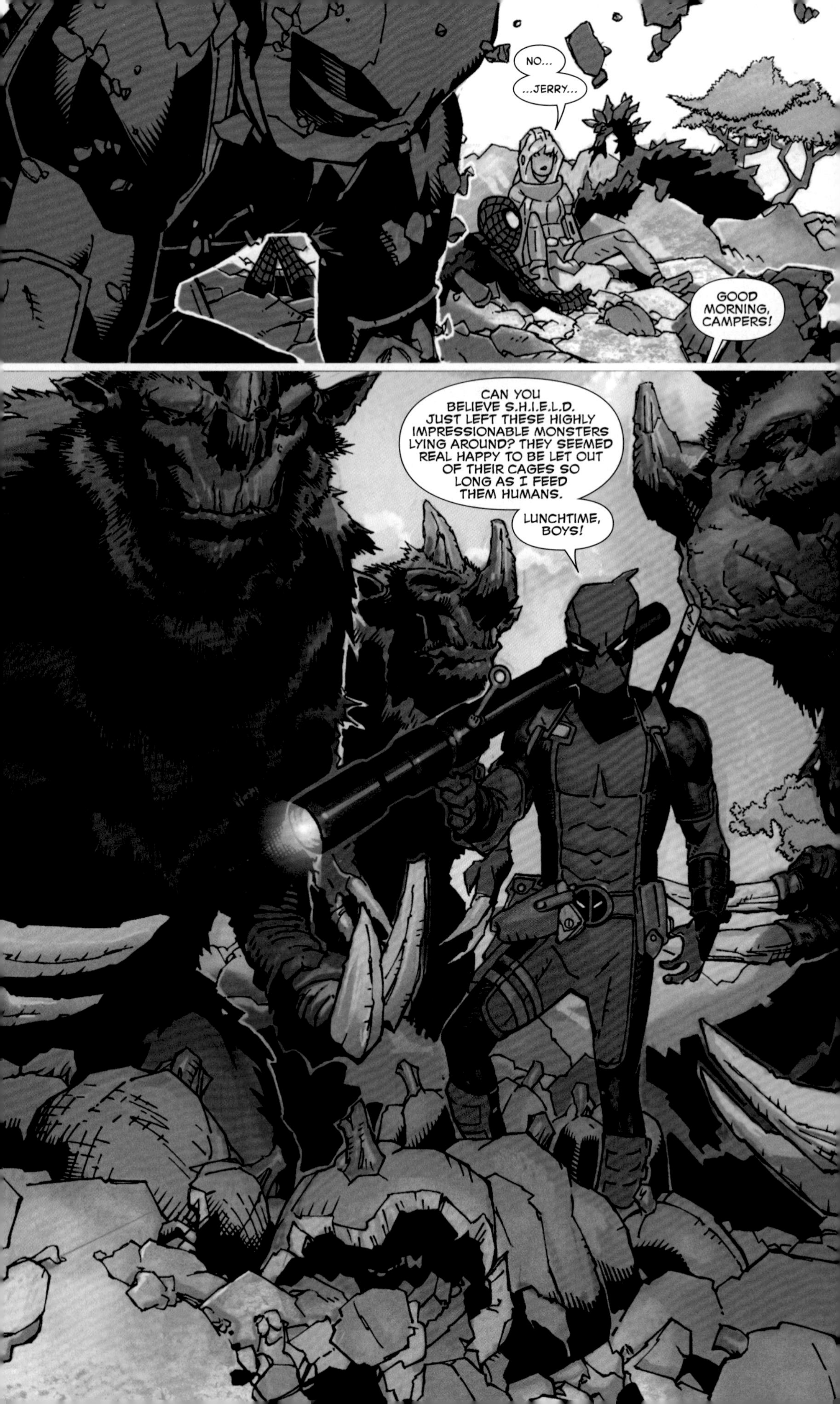
NO...
...JERRY...
GOOD MORNING, CAMPERS!
CAN YOU BELIEVE S.H.I.E.L.D. JUST LEFT THESE HIGHLY IMPRESSIONABLE MONSTERS LYING AROUND? THEY SEEMED REAL HAPPY TO BE LET OUT OF THEIR CAGES SO LONG AS I FEED THEM HUMANS.
LUNCHTIME, BOYS!

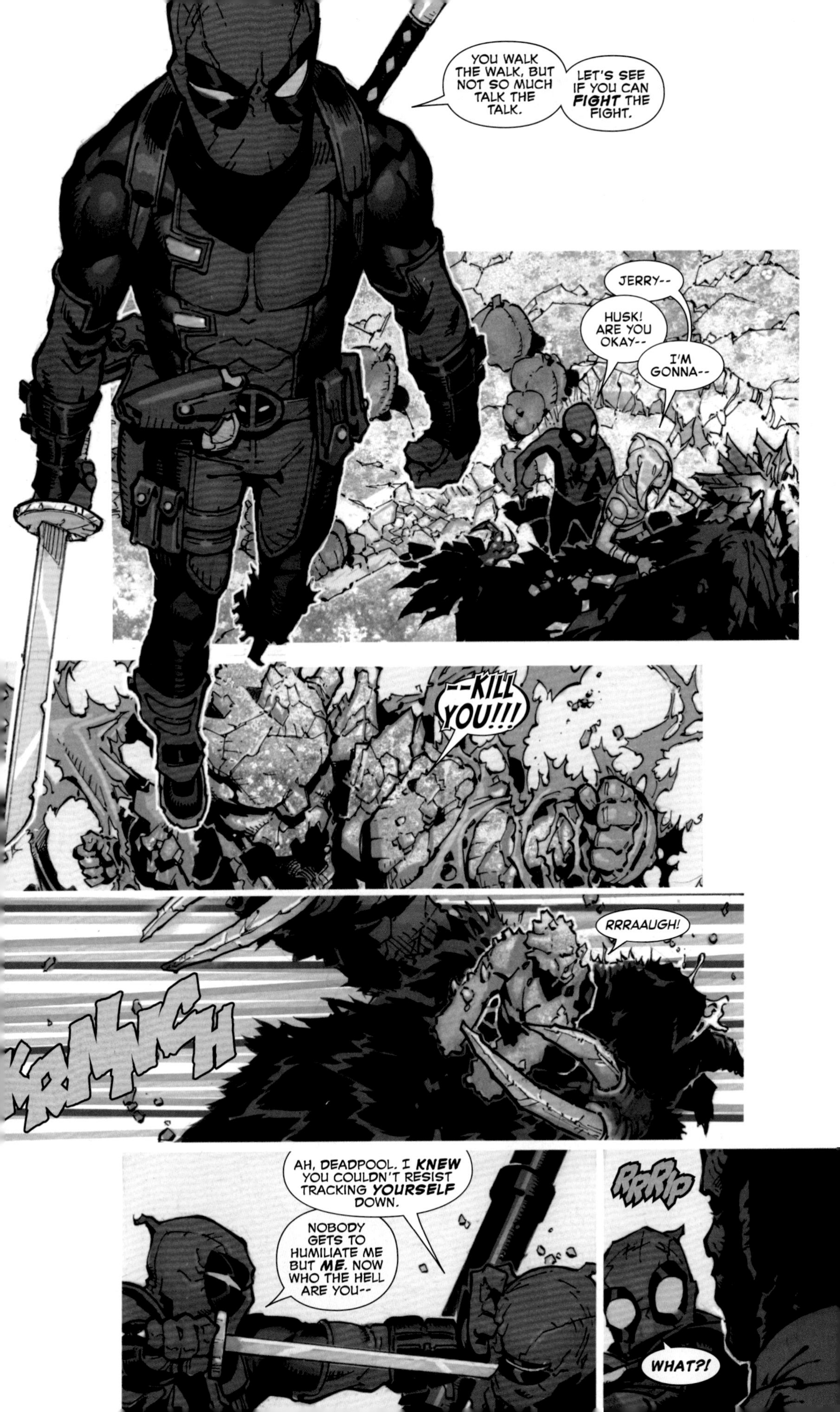
YOU WALK THE WALK, BUT NOT SO MUCH TALK THE TALK.
LET'S SEE IF YOU CAN FIGHT THE FIGHT.
JERRY--
HUSK! ARE YOU OKAY--
I'M GONNA--
--KILL YOU!!!
RRRAAUGH!
KRUNCH
AH, DEADPOOL. I KNEW YOU COULDN'T RESIST TRACKING YOURSELF DOWN.
NOBODY GETS TO HUMILIATE ME BUT ME. NOW WHO THE HELL ARE YOU--
RRRIP
WHAT?!

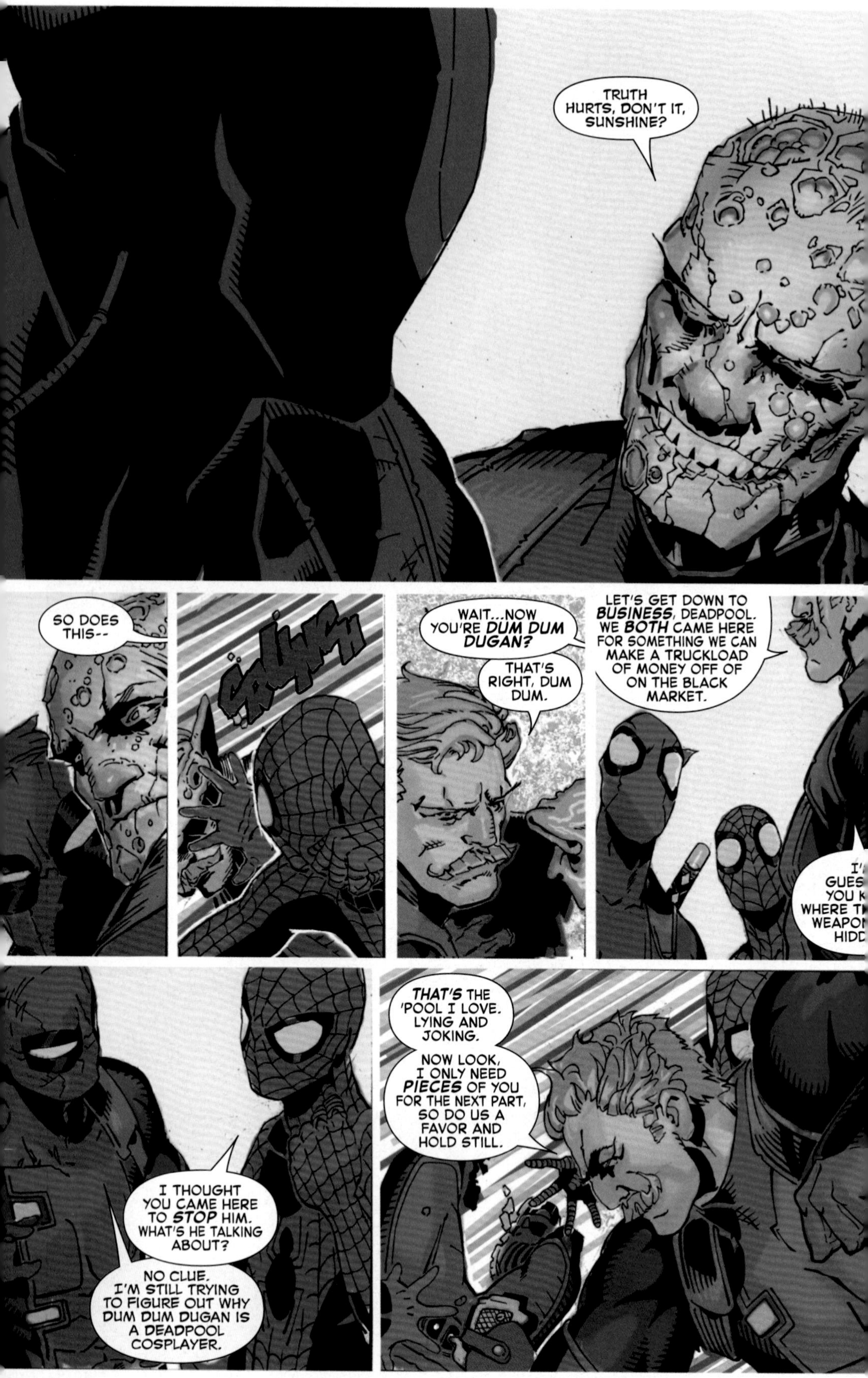

TRUTH HURTS, DON'T IT, SUNSHINE?
SO DOES THIS--
WAIT...NOW YOU'RE *DUM DUM DUGAN?*
THAT'S RIGHT, DUM DUM.
LET'S GET DOWN TO *BUSINESS*, DEADPOOL. WE *BOTH* CAME HERE FOR SOMETHING WE CAN MAKE A TRUCKLOAD OF MONEY OFF OF ON THE BLACK MARKET.
I THOUGHT YOU CAME HERE TO *STOP* HIM. WHAT'S HE TALKING ABOUT?
NO CLUE. I'M STILL TRYING TO FIGURE OUT WHY DUM DUM DUGAN IS A DEADPOOL COSPLAYER.
THAT'S THE 'POOL I LOVE. LYING AND JOKING.
NOW LOOK, I ONLY NEED *PIECES* OF YOU FOR THE NEXT PART, SO DO US A FAVOR AND HOLD STILL.

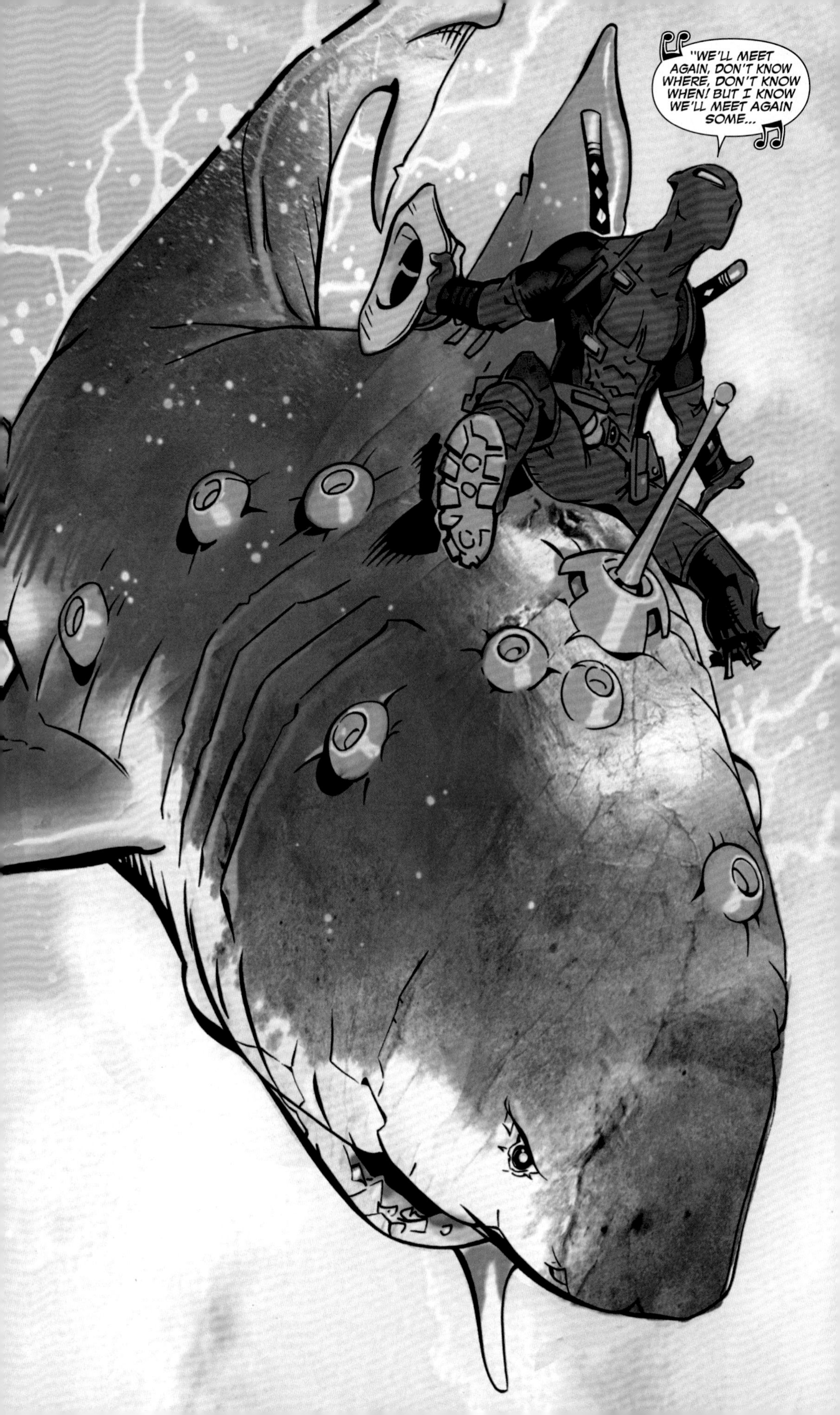
"WE'LL MEET AGAIN, DON'T KNOW WHERE, DON'T KNOW WHEN! BUT I KNOW WE'LL MEET AGAIN SOME...

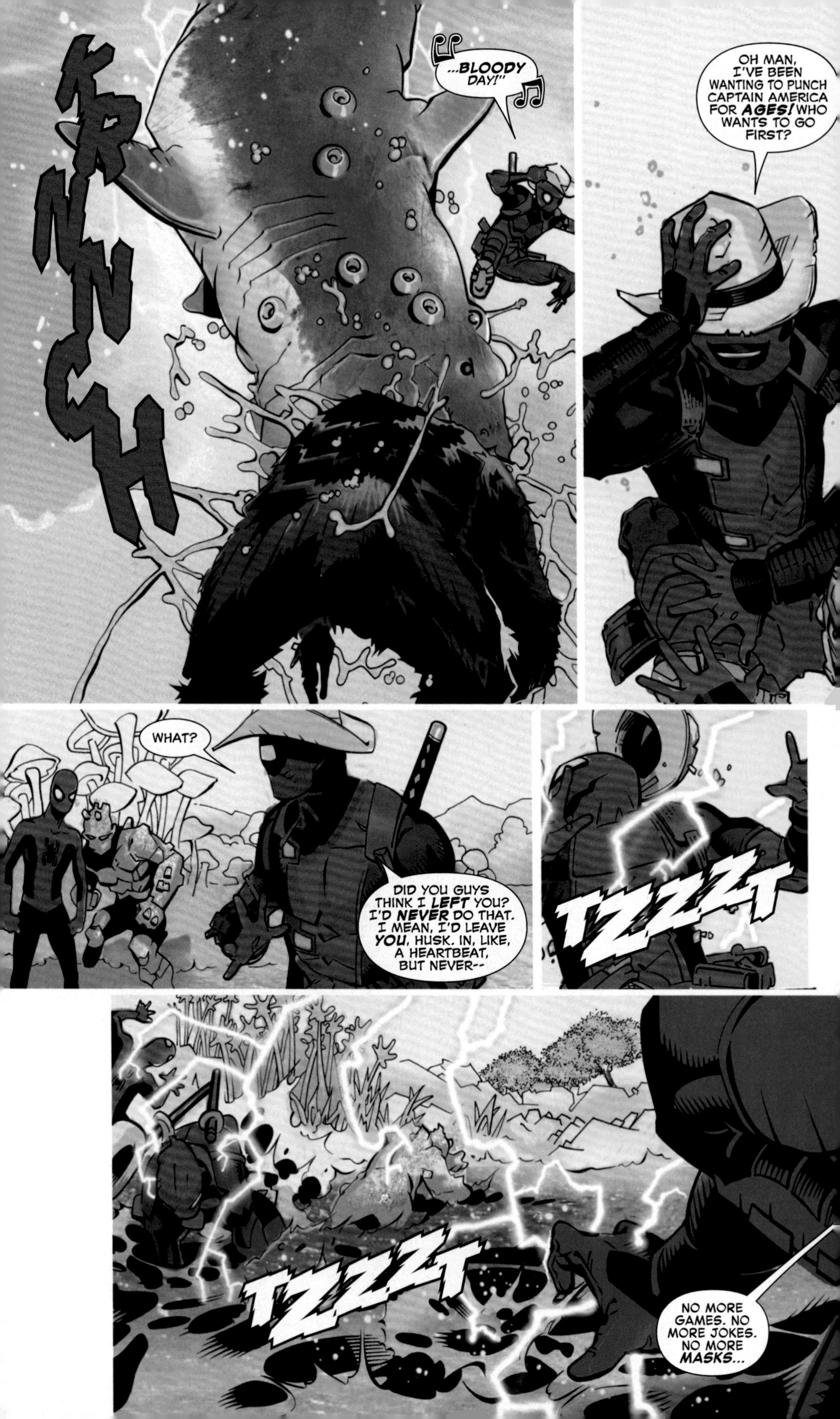
KRNNNCH
"...BLOODY DAY!"
OH MAN, I'VE BEEN WANTING TO PUNCH CAPTAIN AMERICA FOR AGES! WHO WANTS TO GO FIRST?
WHAT?
DID YOU GUYS THINK I LEFT YOU? I'D NEVER DO THAT. I MEAN, I'D LEAVE YOU, HUSK. IN, LIKE, A HEARTBEAT, BUT NEVER--
TZZZT
TZZZT
NO MORE GAMES. NO MORE JOKES. NO MORE MASKS...

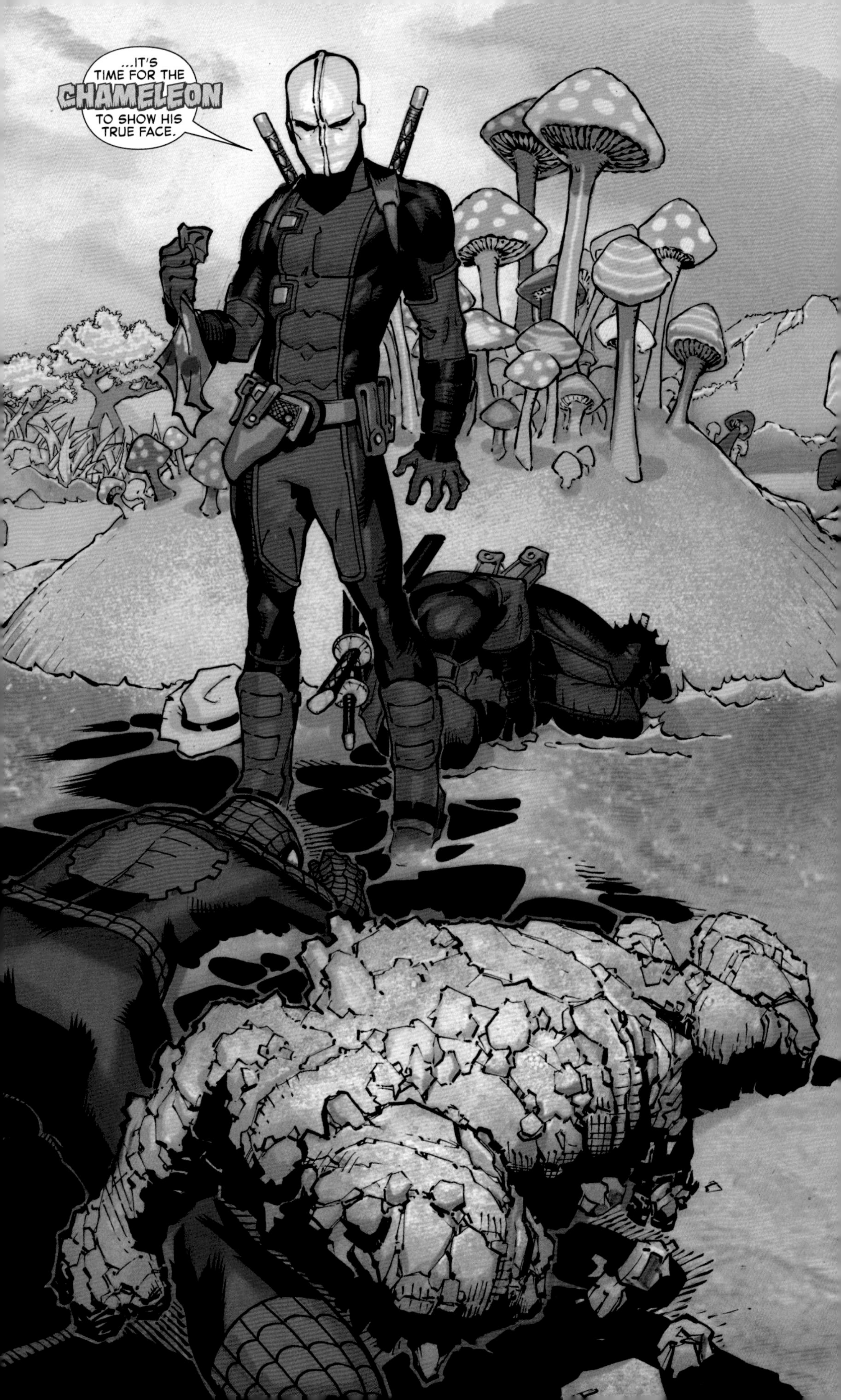
...IT'S TIME FOR THE CHAMELEON TO SHOW HIS TRUE FACE.

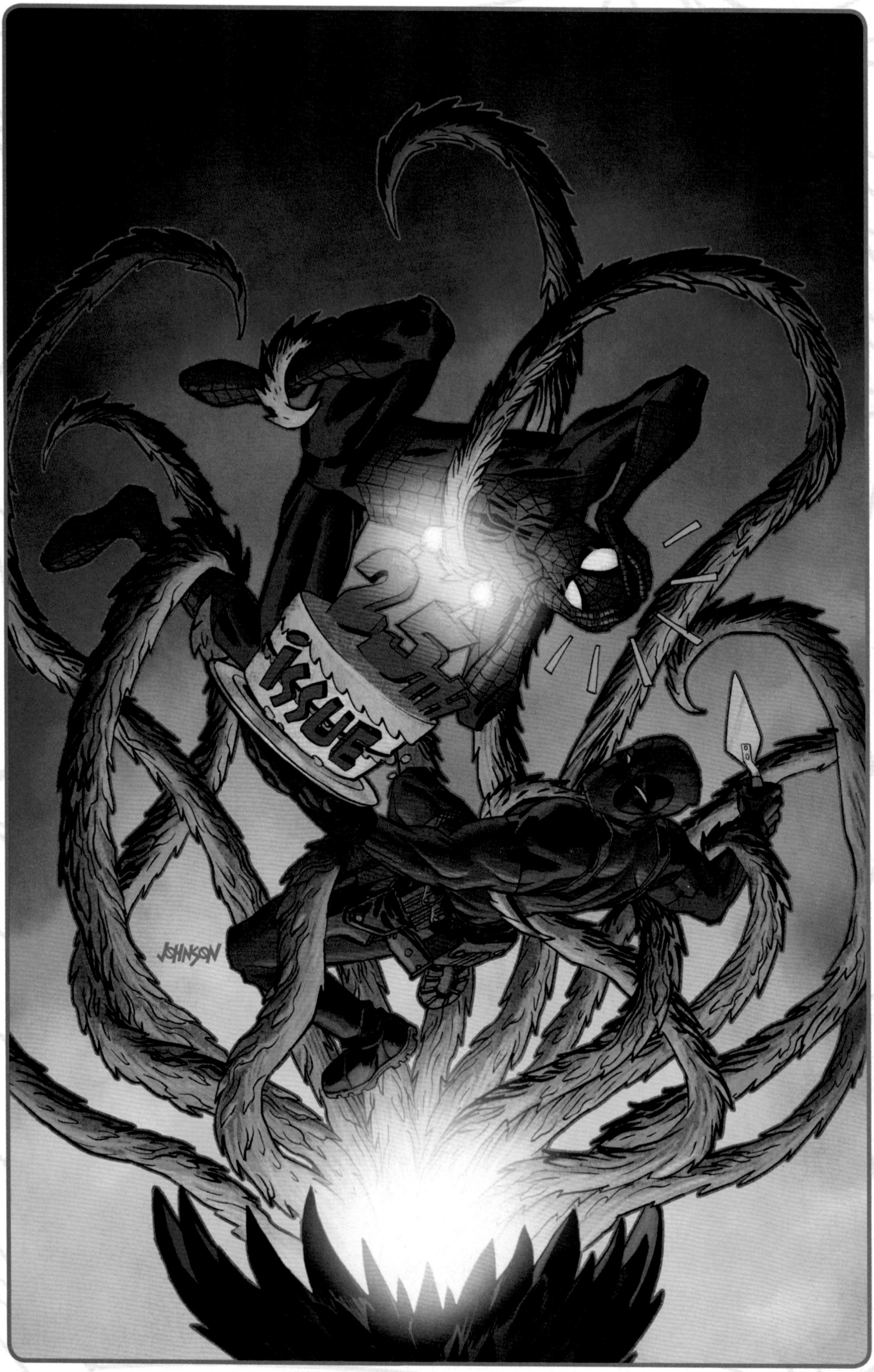
ISSUE
JOHNSON

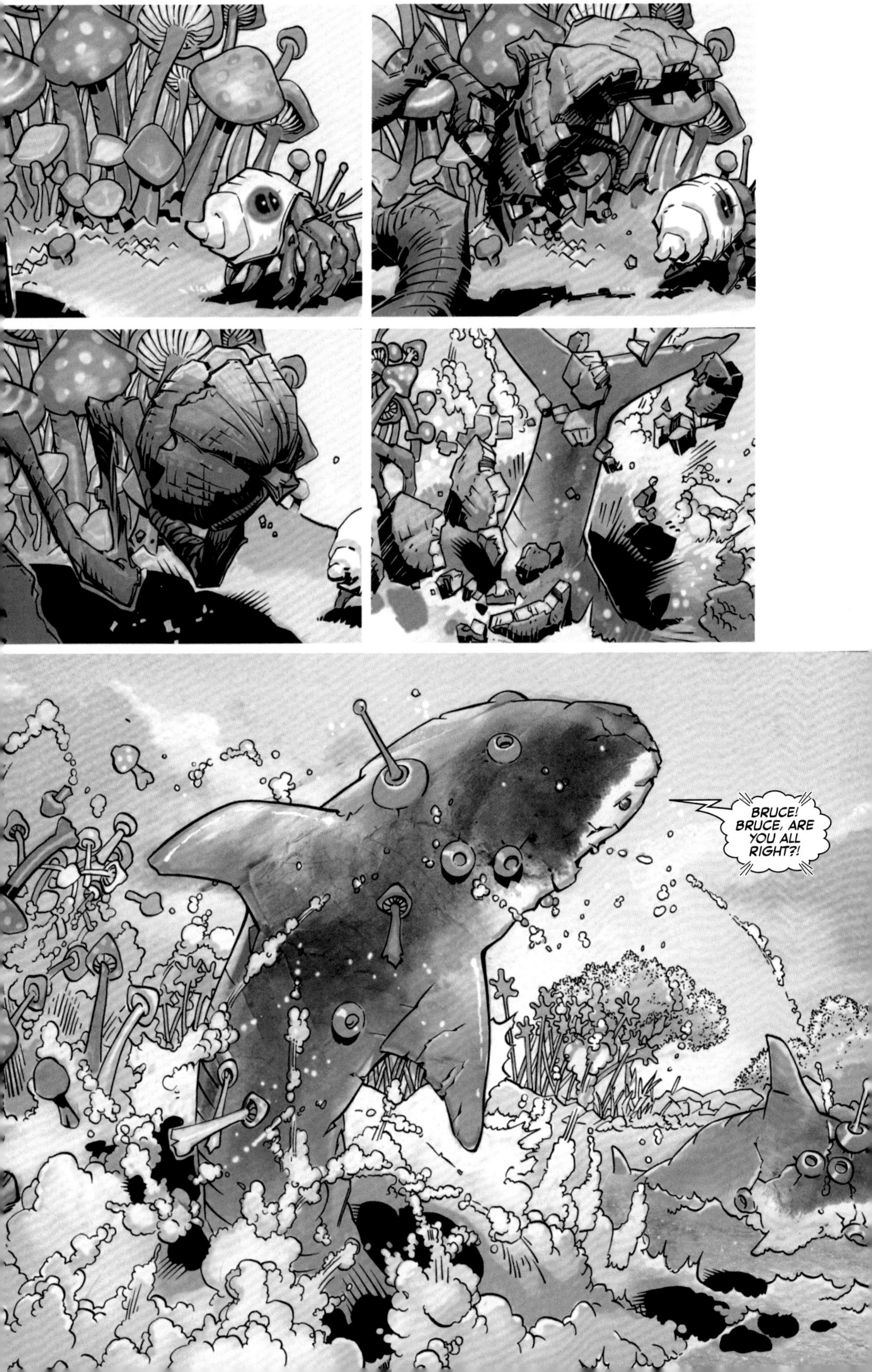
BRUCE! BRUCE, ARE YOU ALL RIGHT?!

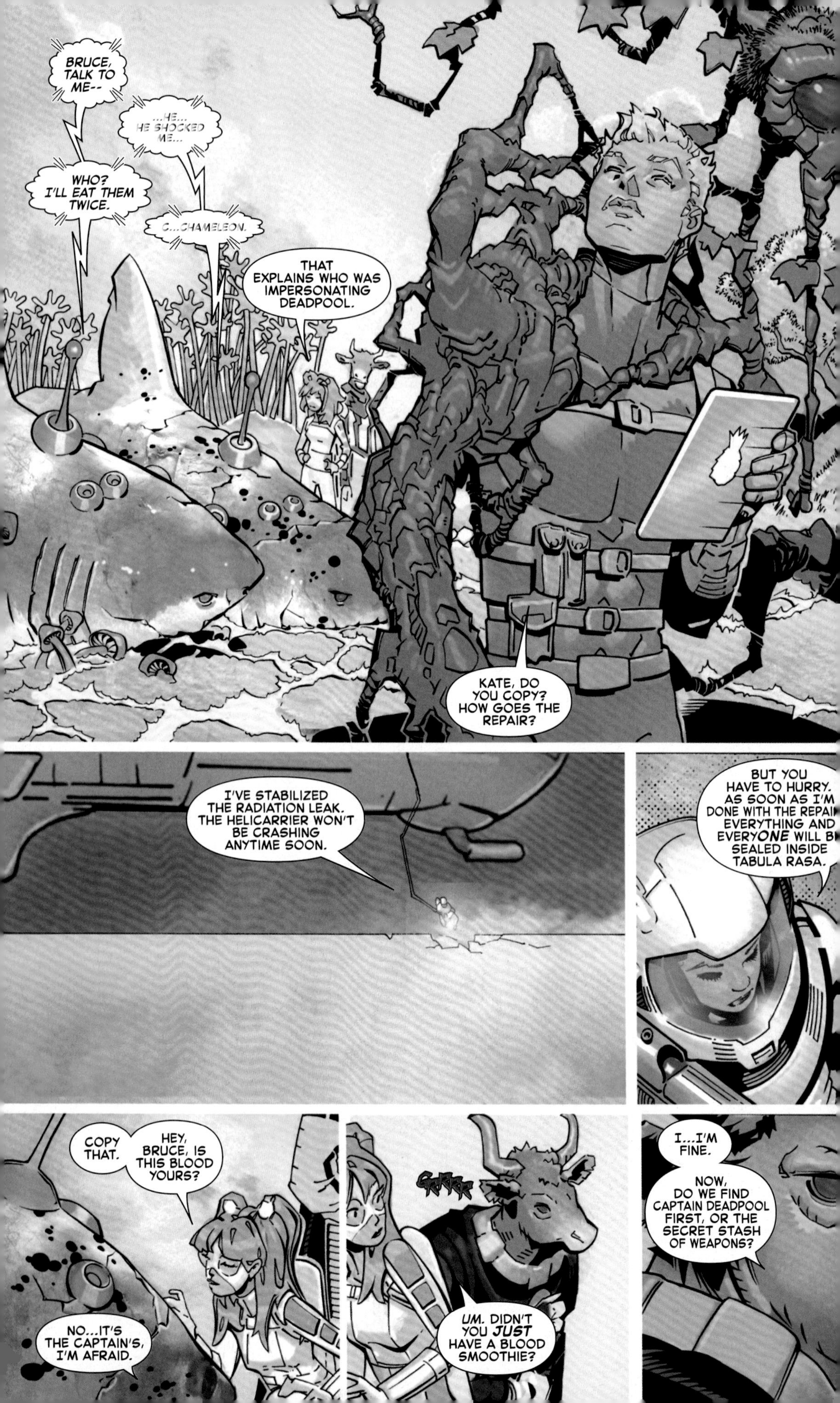

BRUCE, TALK TO ME--
...HE... HE SHOCKED ME...
WHO? I'LL EAT THEM TWICE.
C...CHAMELEON.
THAT EXPLAINS WHO WAS IMPERSONATING DEADPOOL.
KATE, DO YOU COPY? HOW GOES THE REPAIR?
I'VE STABILIZED THE RADIATION LEAK. THE HELICARRIER WON'T BE CRASHING ANYTIME SOON.
BUT YOU HAVE TO HURRY. AS SOON AS I'M DONE WITH THE REPAI
EVERYTHING AND EVERYONE WILL B
SEALED INSIDE TABULA RASA.
COPY THAT.
HEY, BRUCE, IS THIS BLOOD YOURS?
NO...IT'S THE CAPTAIN'S, I'M AFRAID.
GRRRR
UM. DIDN'T YOU JUST HAVE A BLOOD SMOOTHIE?
I...I'M FINE.
NOW, DO WE FIND CAPTAIN DEADPOOL FIRST, OR THE SECRET STASH OF WEAPONS?

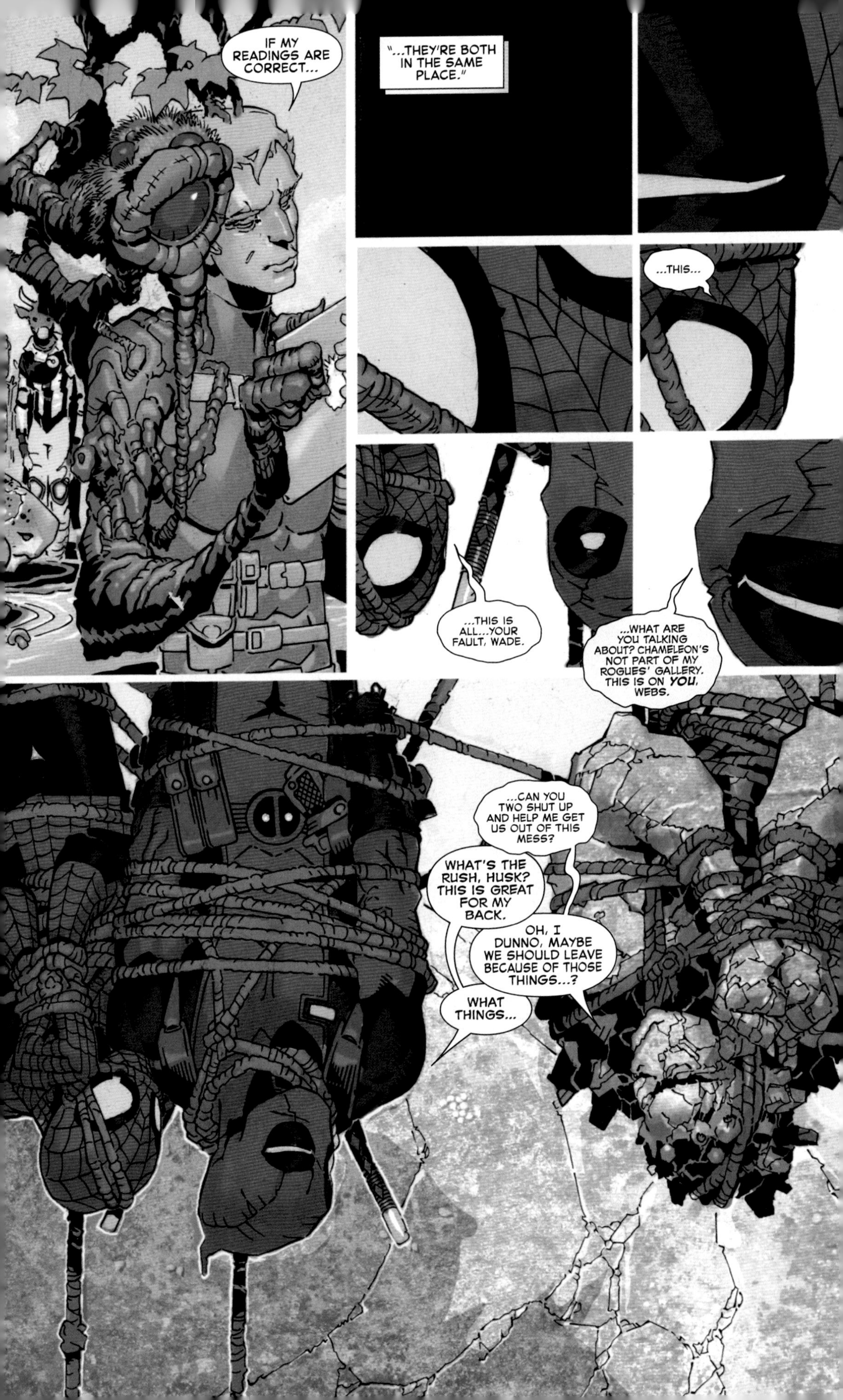
IF MY READINGS ARE CORRECT...
"...THEY'RE BOTH IN THE SAME PLACE."
...THIS...
...THIS IS ALL...YOUR FAULT, WADE.
...WHAT ARE YOU TALKING ABOUT? CHAMELEON'S NOT PART OF MY ROGUES' GALLERY. THIS IS ON YOU, WEBS.
...CAN YOU TWO SHUT UP AND HELP ME GET US OUT OF THIS MESS?
WHAT'S THE RUSH, HUSK? THIS IS GREAT FOR MY BACK.
OH, I DUNNO, MAYBE WE SHOULD LEAVE BECAUSE OF THOSE THINGS...?
WHAT THINGS...

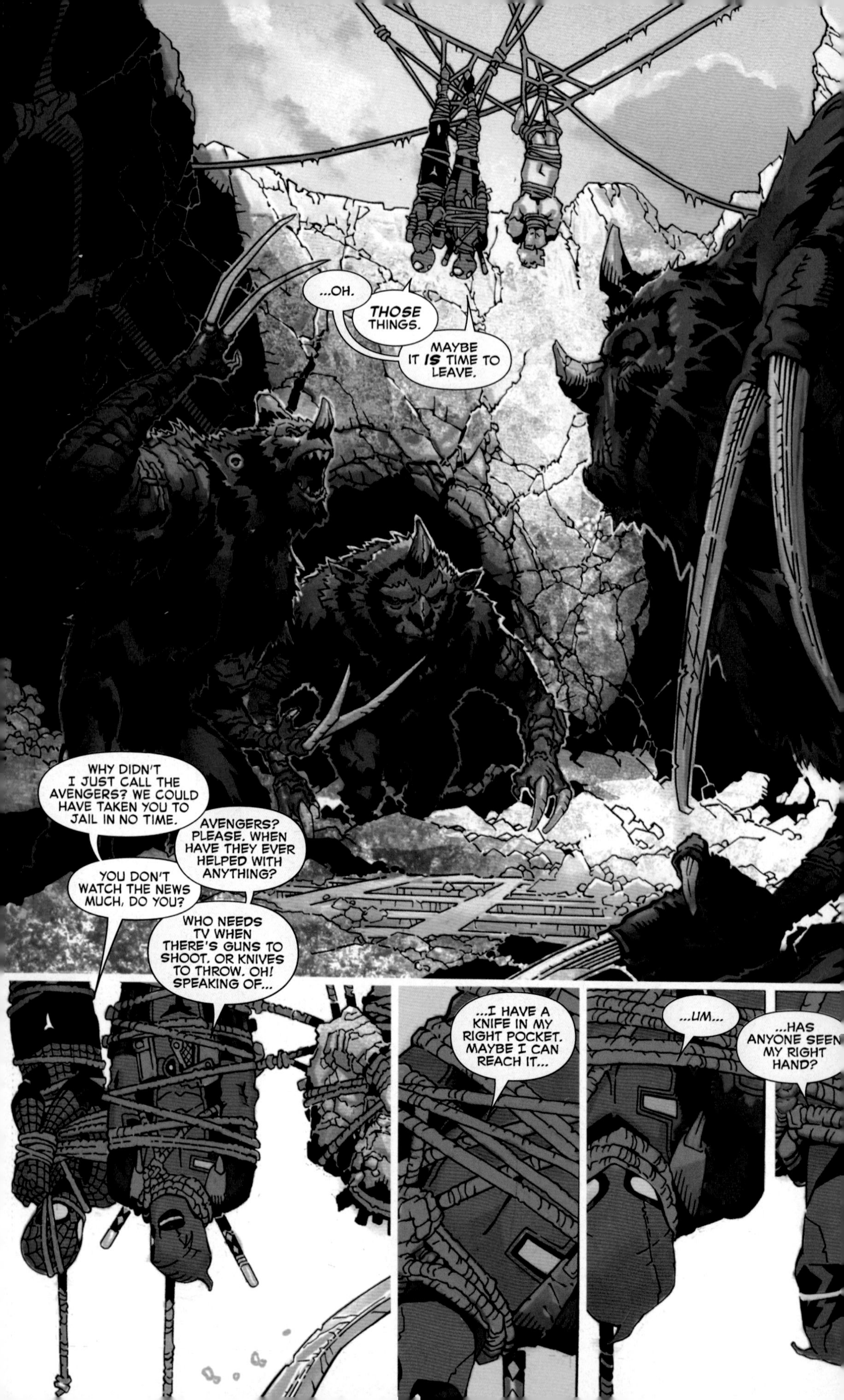
...OH.
THOSE THINGS.
MAYBE IT IS TIME TO LEAVE.
WHY DIDN'T I JUST CALL THE AVENGERS? WE COULD HAVE TAKEN YOU TO JAIL IN NO TIME.
AVENGERS? PLEASE. WHEN HAVE THEY EVER HELPED WITH ANYTHING?
YOU DON'T WATCH THE NEWS MUCH, DO YOU?
WHO NEEDS TV WHEN THERE'S GUNS TO SHOOT. OR KNIVES TO THROW. OH! SPEAKING OF...
...I HAVE A KNIFE IN MY RIGHT POCKET. MAYBE I CAN REACH IT...
...UM...
...HAS ANYONE SEEN MY RIGHT HAND?

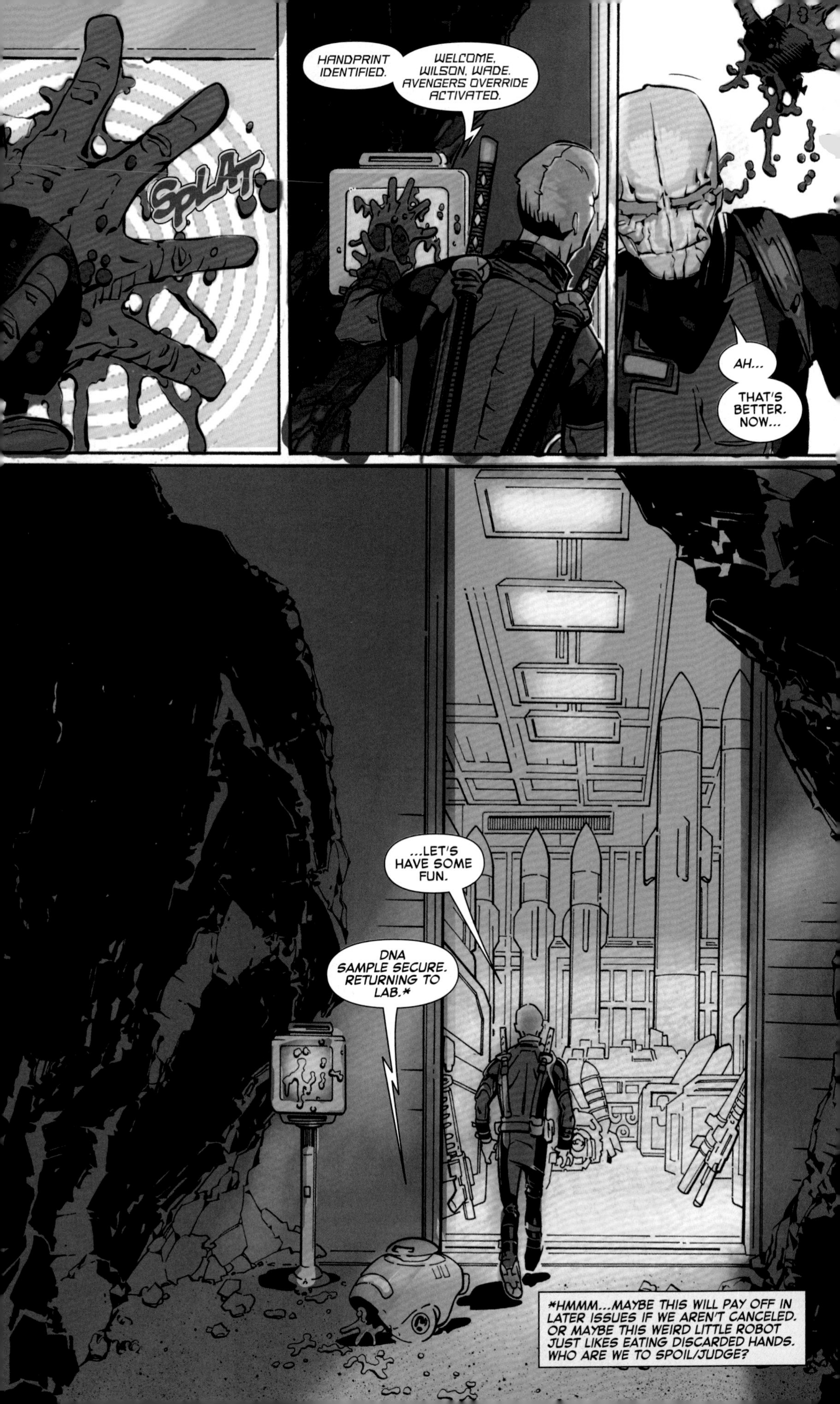
SPLAT
HANDPRINT IDENTIFIED.
WELCOME, WILSON, WADE. AVENGERS OVERRIDE ACTIVATED.
AH...
THAT'S BETTER. NOW...
...LET'S HAVE SOME FUN.
DNA SAMPLE SECURE. RETURNING TO LAB.*
*HMMM...MAYBE THIS WILL PAY OFF IN LATER ISSUES IF WE AREN'T CANCELED. OR MAYBE THIS WEIRD LITTLE ROBOT JUST LIKES EATING DISCARDED HANDS. WHO ARE WE TO SPOIL/JUDGE?

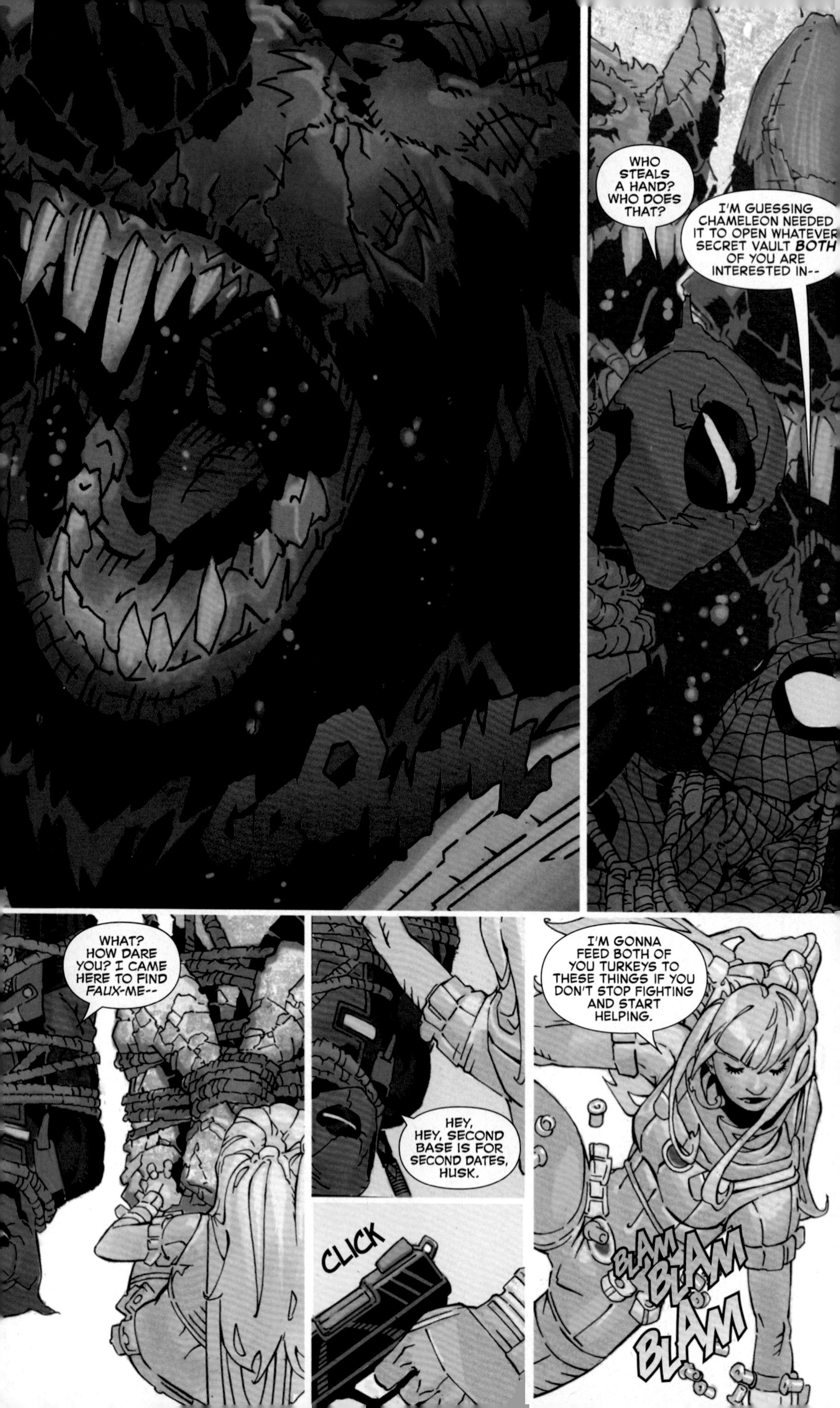
GROWL
WHO STEALS A HAND? WHO DOES THAT?
I'M GUESSING CHAMELEON NEEDED IT TO OPEN WHATEVER SECRET VAULT BOTH OF YOU ARE INTERESTED IN--
WHAT? HOW DARE YOU? I CAME HERE TO FIND FAUX-ME--
HEY, HEY, SECOND BASE IS FOR SECOND DATES, HUSK.
CLICK
I'M GONNA FEED BOTH OF YOU TURKEYS TO THESE THINGS IF YOU DON'T STOP FIGHTING AND START HELPING.
BLAM BLAM BLAM BLAM

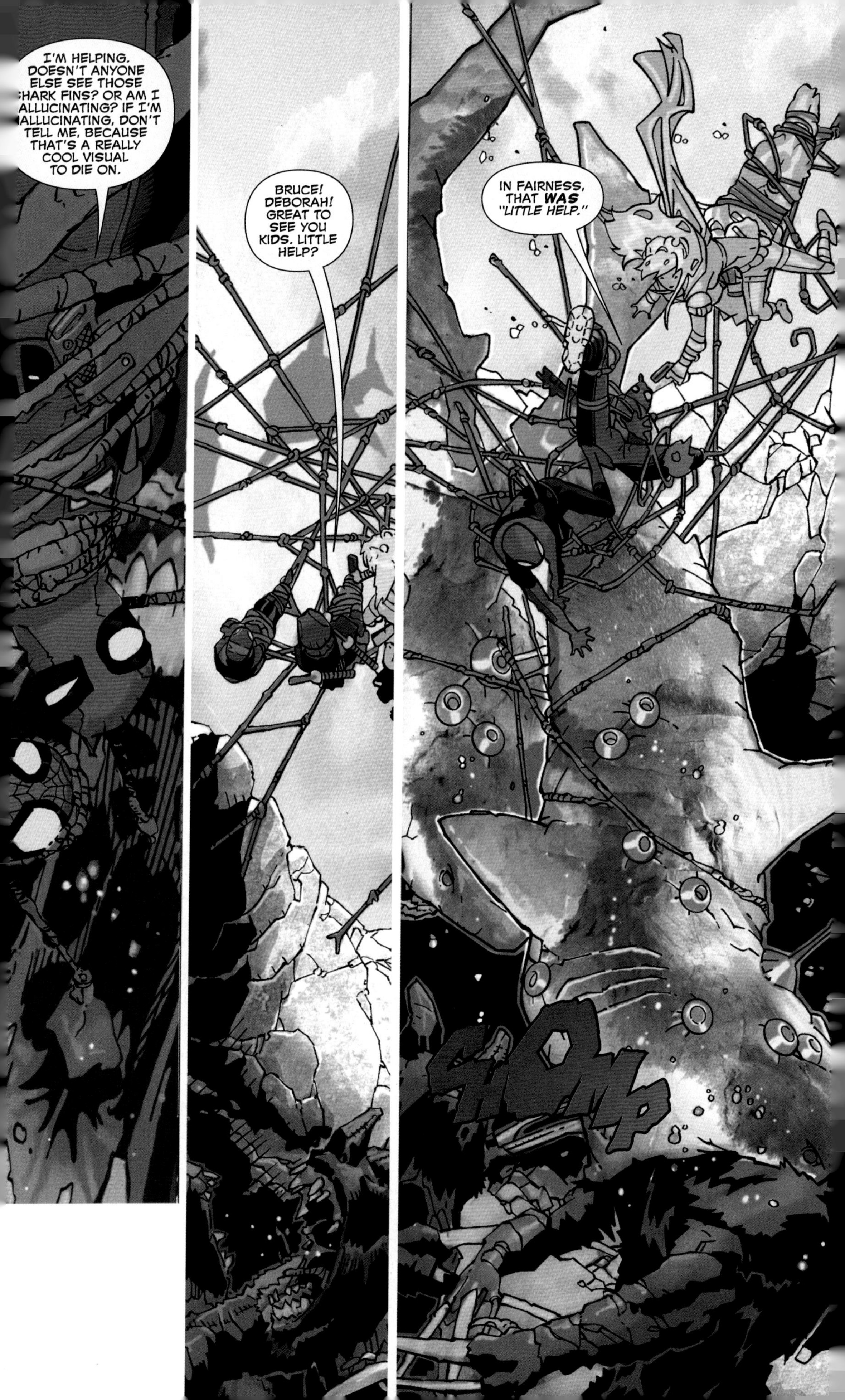
I'M HELPING. DOESN'T ANYONE ELSE SEE THOSE HARK FINS? OR AM I ALLUCINATING? IF I'M ALLUCINATING, DON'T TELL ME, BECAUSE THAT'S A REALLY COOL VISUAL TO DIE ON.
BRUCE! DEBORAH! GREAT TO SEE YOU KIDS. LITTLE HELP?
IN FAIRNESS, THAT **WAS** "LITTLE HELP."
CHOMP

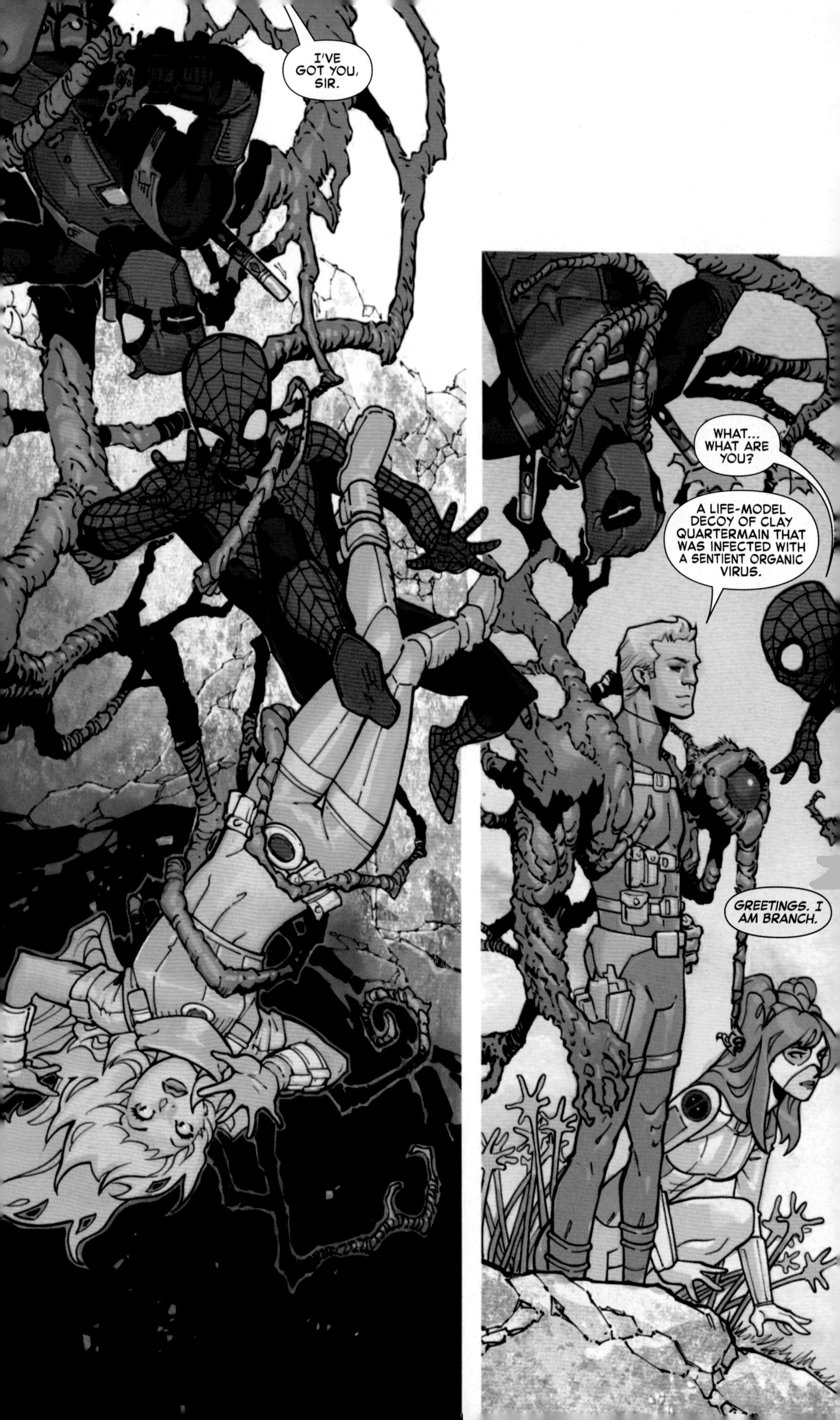
I'VE GOT YOU, SIR.
WHAT... WHAT ARE YOU?
A LIFE-MODEL DECOY OF CLAY QUARTERMAIN THAT WAS INFECTED WITH A SENTIENT ORGANIC VIRUS.
GREETINGS. I AM BRANCH.

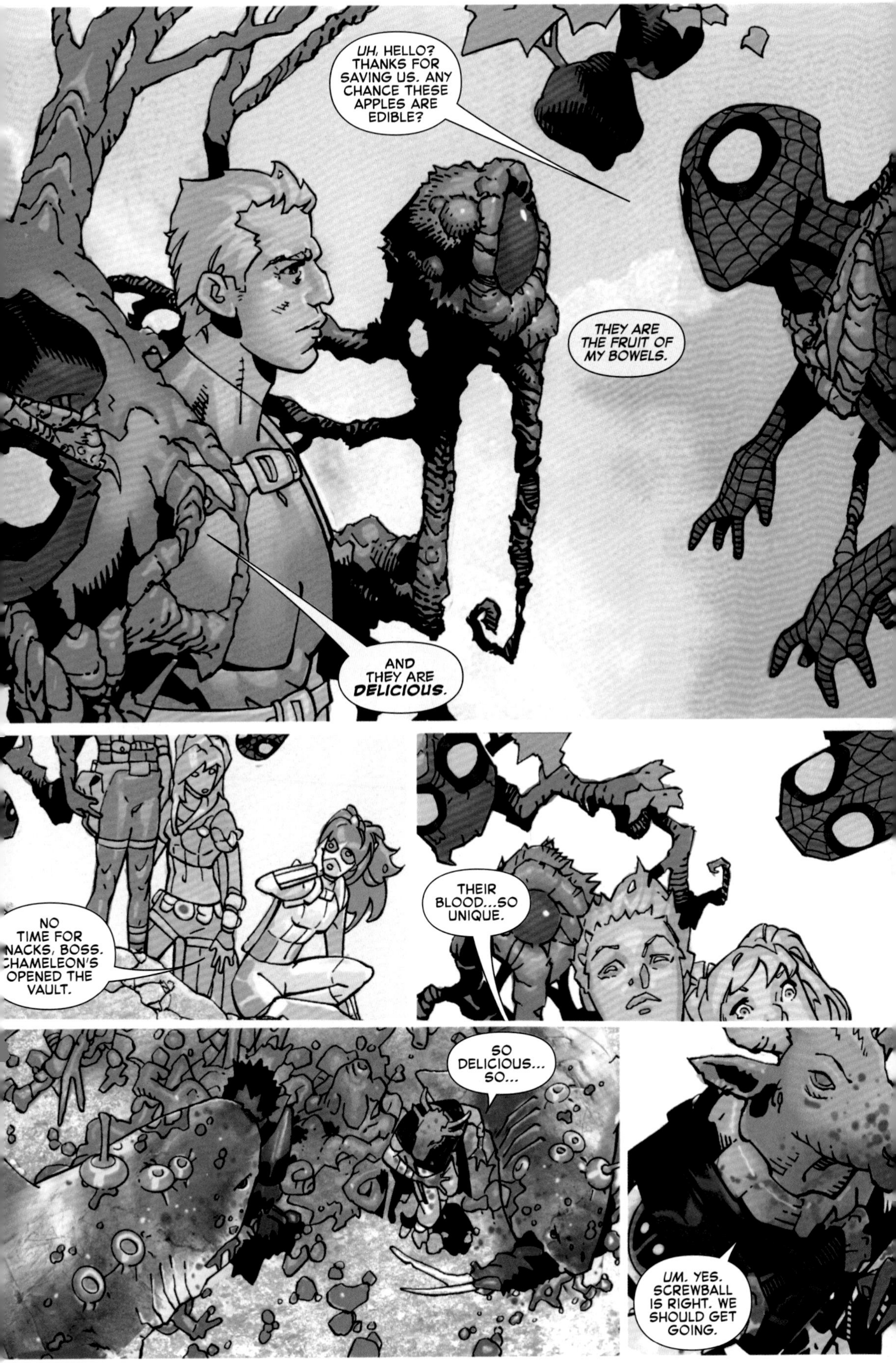
UH, HELLO? THANKS FOR SAVING US. ANY CHANCE THESE APPLES ARE EDIBLE?
THEY ARE THE FRUIT OF MY BOWELS.
AND THEY ARE DELICIOUS.
NO TIME FOR NACKS, BOSS. CHAMELEON'S OPENED THE VAULT.
THEIR BLOOD...SO UNIQUE.
SO DELICIOUS... SO...
UM. YES. SCREWBALL IS RIGHT. WE SHOULD GET GOING.

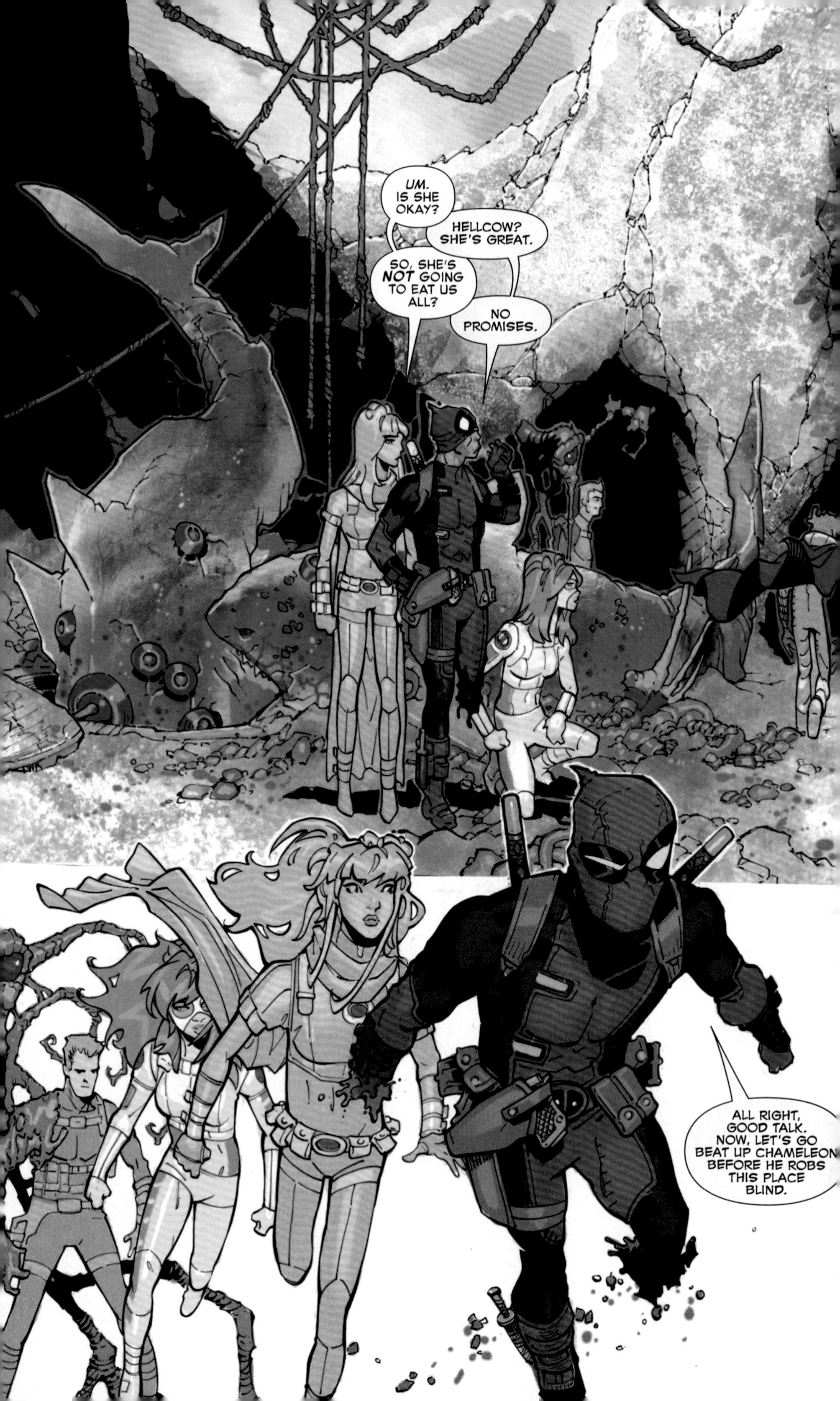
UM. IS SHE OKAY?
HELLCOW? SHE'S GREAT.
SO, SHE'S *NOT* GOING TO EAT US ALL?
NO PROMISES.
ALL RIGHT, GOOD TALK. NOW, LET'S GO BEAT UP CHAMELEON BEFORE HE ROBS THIS PLACE BLIND.

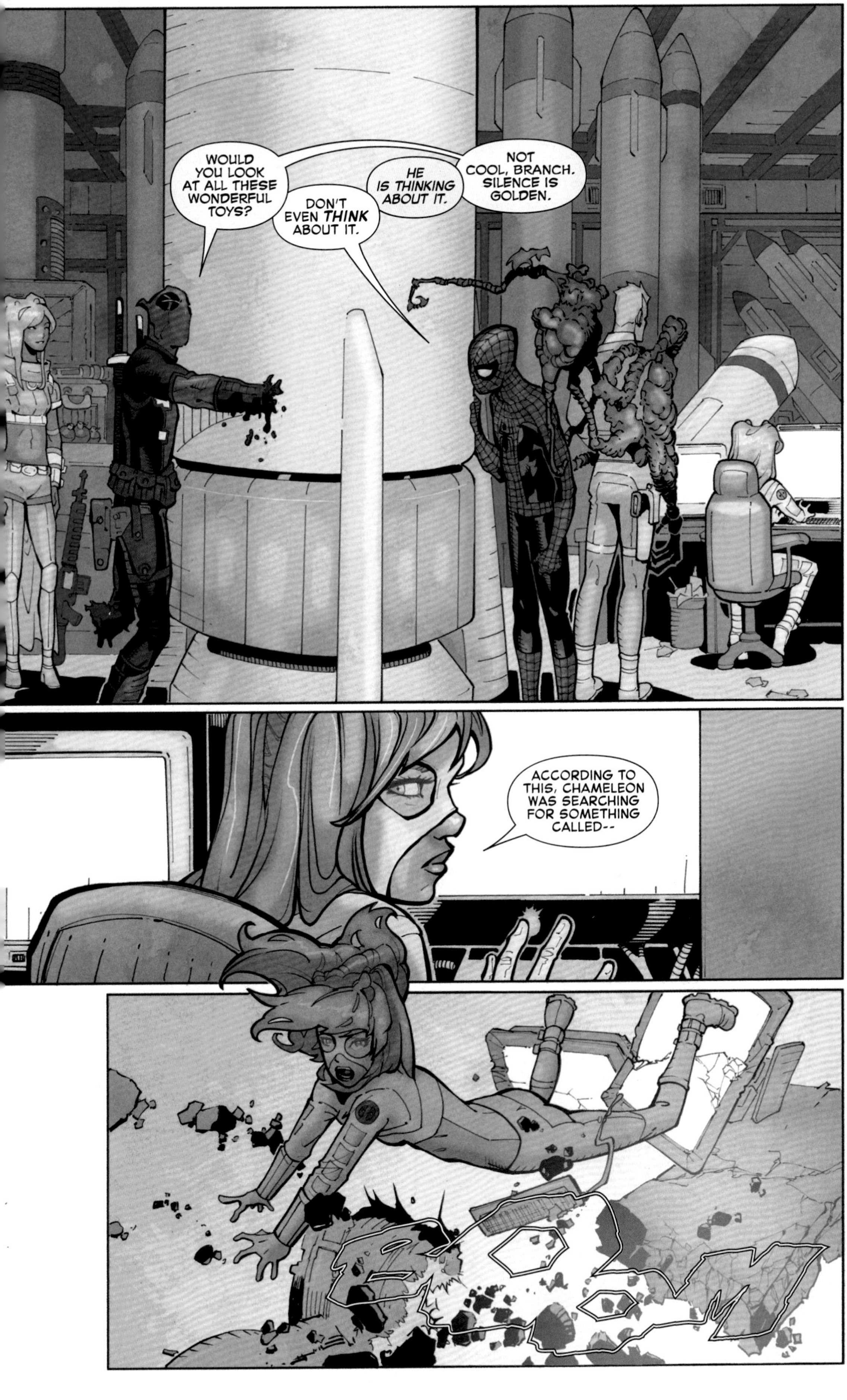
WOULD YOU LOOK AT ALL THESE WONDERFUL TOYS?
DON'T EVEN THINK ABOUT IT.
HE IS THINKING ABOUT IT.
NOT COOL, BRANCH. SILENCE IS GOLDEN.
ACCORDING TO THIS, CHAMELEON WAS SEARCHING FOR SOMETHING CALLED--
BOOM

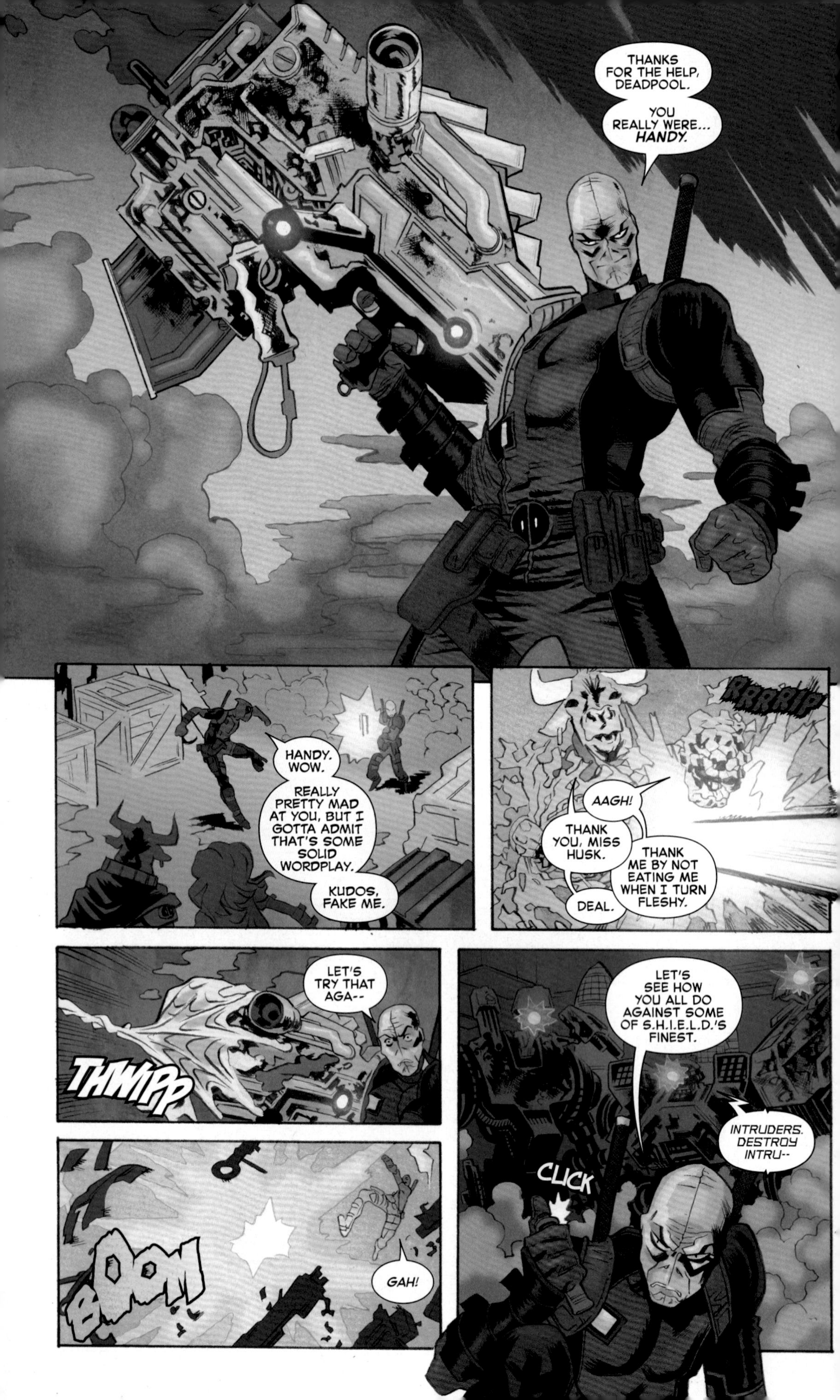

THANKS FOR THE HELP, DEADPOOL.
YOU REALLY WERE... HANDY.
HANDY. WOW.
REALLY PRETTY MAD AT YOU, BUT I GOTTA ADMIT THAT'S SOME SOLID WORDPLAY.
KUDOS, FAKE ME.
RRRRIP
AAGH!
THANK YOU, MISS HUSK.
THANK ME BY NOT EATING ME WHEN I TURN FLESHY.
DEAL.
LET'S TRY THAT AGA--
THWIPP
BOOM
GAH!
LET'S SEE HOW YOU ALL DO AGAINST SOME OF S.H.I.E.L.D.'S FINEST.
INTRUDERS. DESTROY INTRU--
CLICK

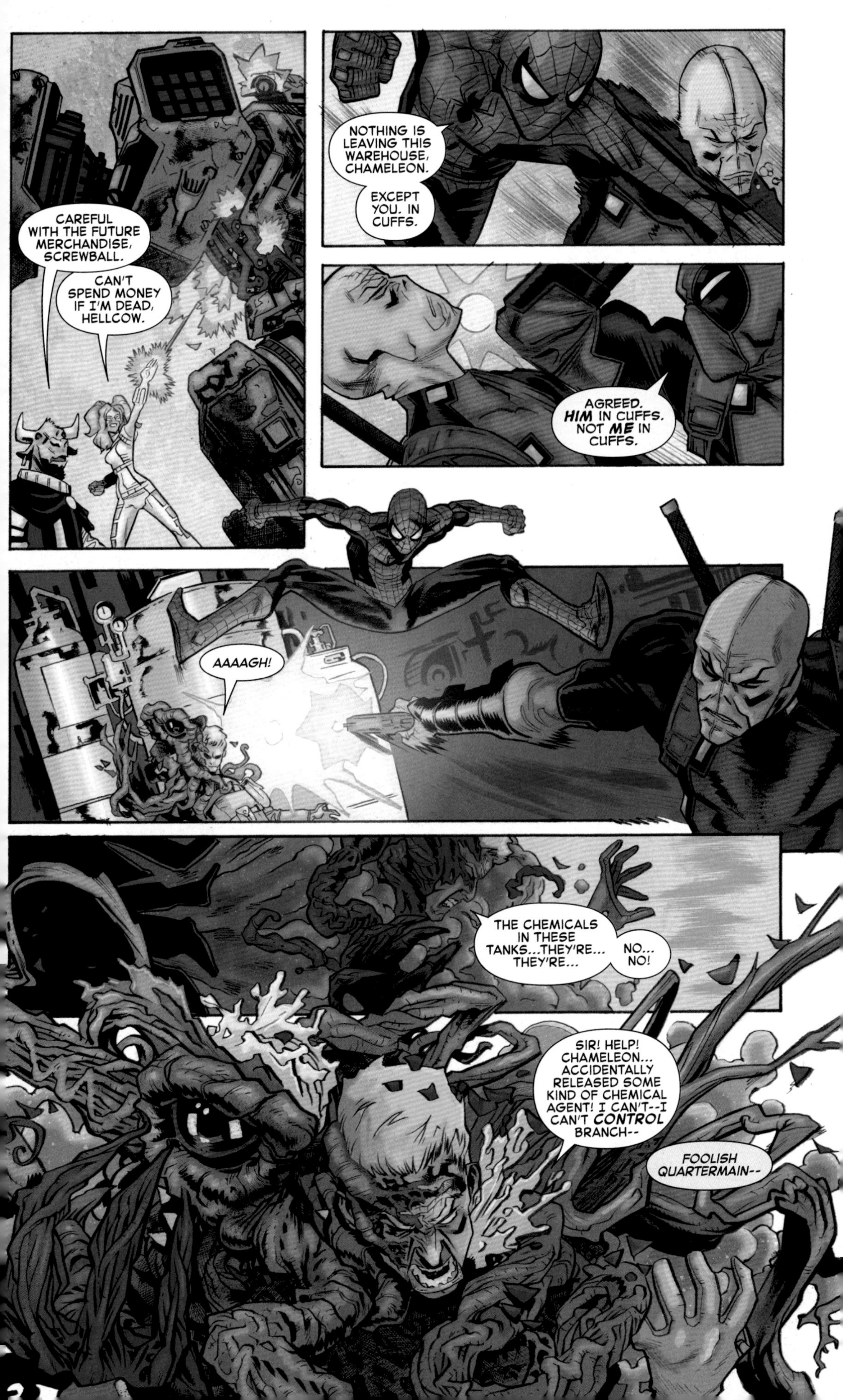
CAREFUL WITH THE FUTURE MERCHANDISE, SCREWBALL.
CAN'T SPEND MONEY IF I'M DEAD, HELLCOW.
NOTHING IS LEAVING THIS WAREHOUSE, CHAMELEON.
EXCEPT YOU. IN CUFFS.
AGREED. HIM IN CUFFS. NOT ME IN CUFFS.
AAAAGH!
THE CHEMICALS IN THESE TANKS...THEY'RE... THEY'RE...
NO... NO!
SIR! HELP! CHAMELEON... ACCIDENTALLY RELEASED SOME KIND OF CHEMICAL AGENT! I CAN'T--I CAN'T CONTROL BRANCH--
FOOLISH QUARTERMAIN--

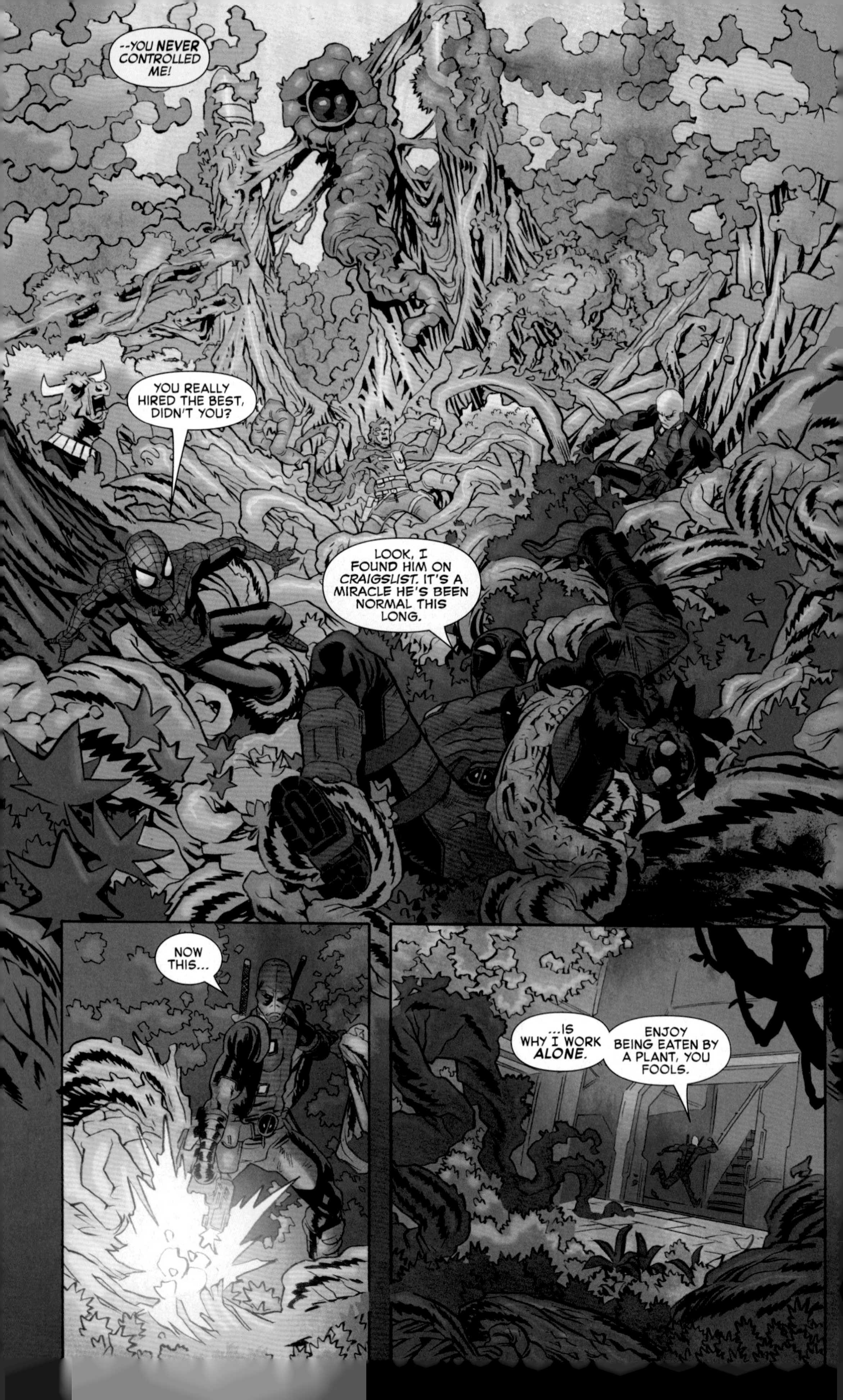
--YOU NEVER CONTROLLED ME!
YOU REALLY HIRED THE BEST, DIDN'T YOU?
LOOK, I FOUND HIM ON CRAIGSLIST. IT'S A MIRACLE HE'S BEEN NORMAL THIS LONG.
NOW THIS...
...IS WHY I WORK ALONE.
ENJOY BEING EATEN BY A PLANT, YOU FOOLS.

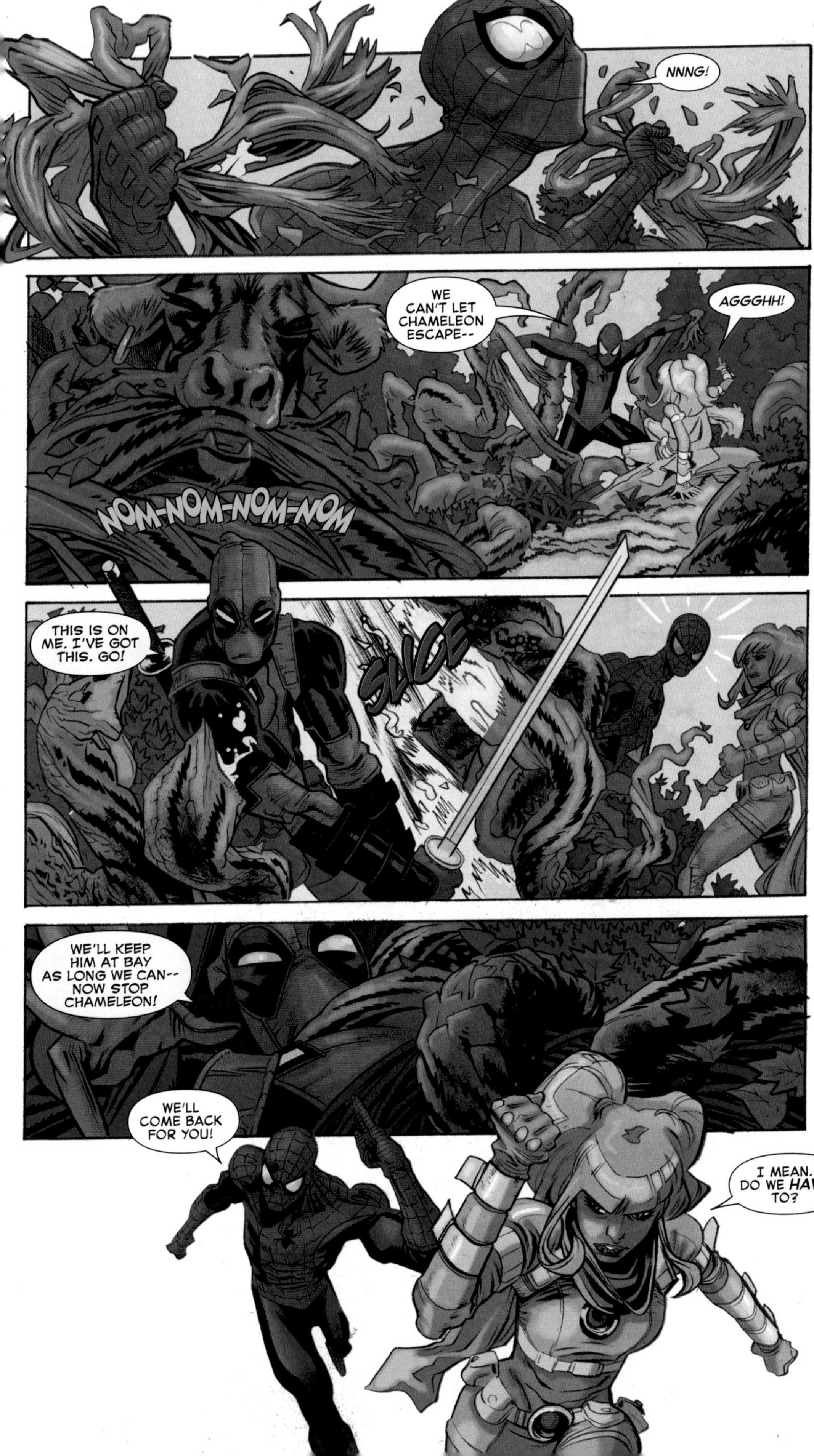
NNNG!
WE CAN'T LET CHAMELEON ESCAPE--
AGGGHH!
NOM-NOM-NOM-NOM
THIS IS ON ME. I'VE GOT THIS. GO!
SLICE
WE'LL KEEP HIM AT BAY AS LONG WE CAN--NOW STOP CHAMELEON!
WE'LL COME BACK FOR YOU!
I MEAN. DO WE *HAVE* TO?

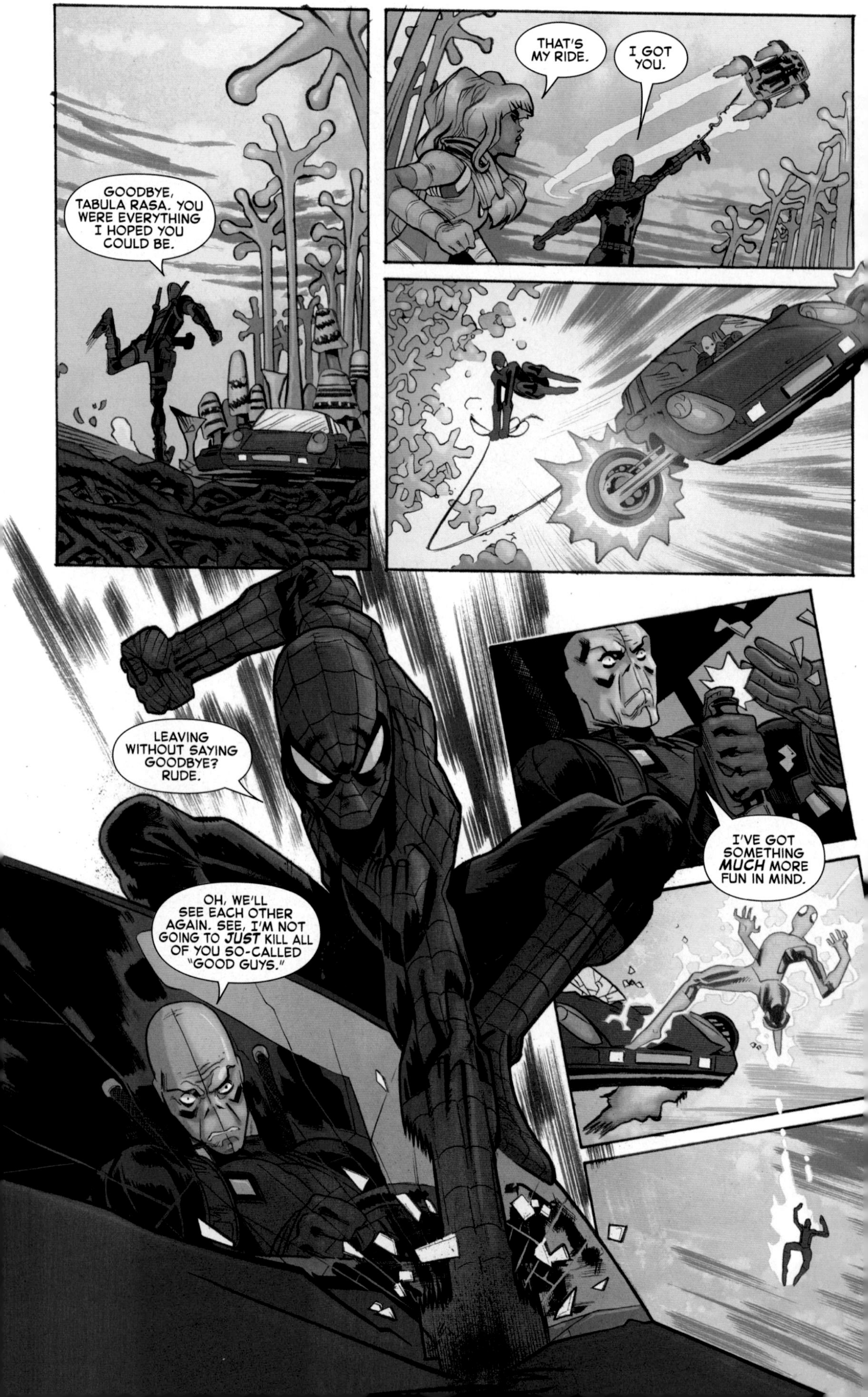
GOODBYE, TABULA RASA. YOU WERE EVERYTHING I HOPED YOU COULD BE.
THAT'S MY RIDE.
I GOT YOU.
LEAVING WITHOUT SAYING GOODBYE? RUDE.
OH, WE'LL SEE EACH OTHER AGAIN. SEE, I'M NOT GOING TO JUST KILL ALL OF YOU SO-CALLED "GOOD GUYS."
I'VE GOT SOMETHING MUCH MORE FUN IN MIND.

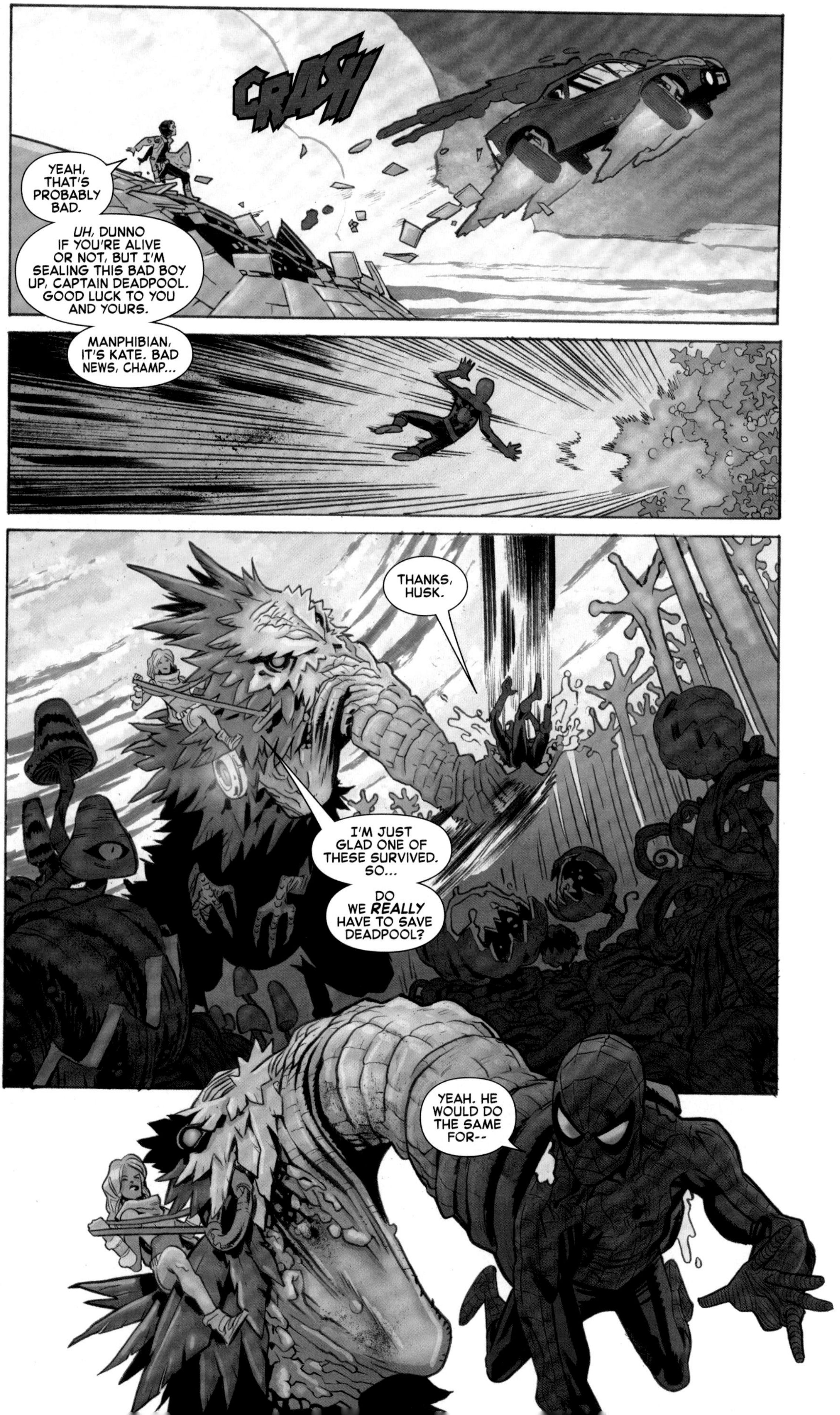
CRASH
YEAH, THAT'S PROBABLY BAD.
UH, DUNNO IF YOU'RE ALIVE OR NOT, BUT I'M SEALING THIS BAD BOY UP, CAPTAIN DEADPOOL. GOOD LUCK TO YOU AND YOURS.
MANPHIBIAN, IT'S KATE. BAD NEWS, CHAMP...
THANKS, HUSK.
I'M JUST GLAD ONE OF THESE SURVIVED. SO...
DO WE *REALLY* HAVE TO SAVE DEADPOOL?
YEAH. HE WOULD DO THE SAME FOR--

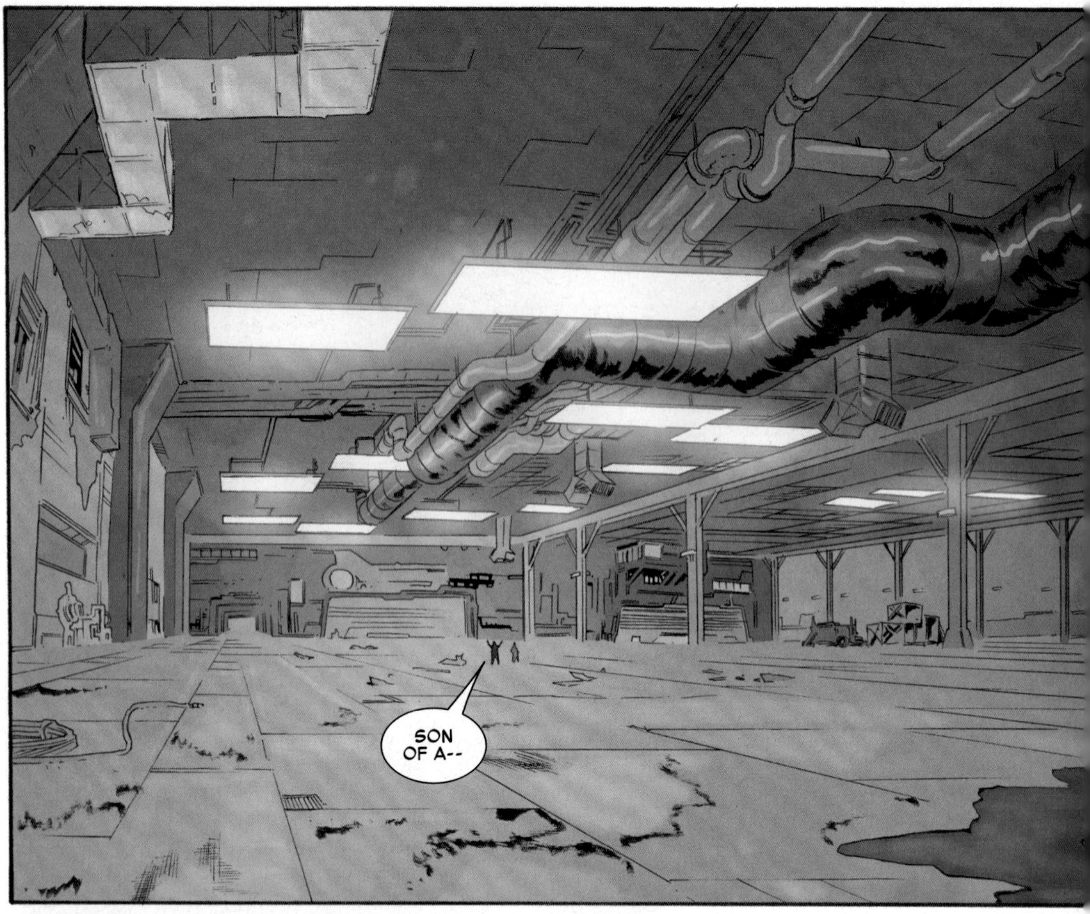
SON OF A--

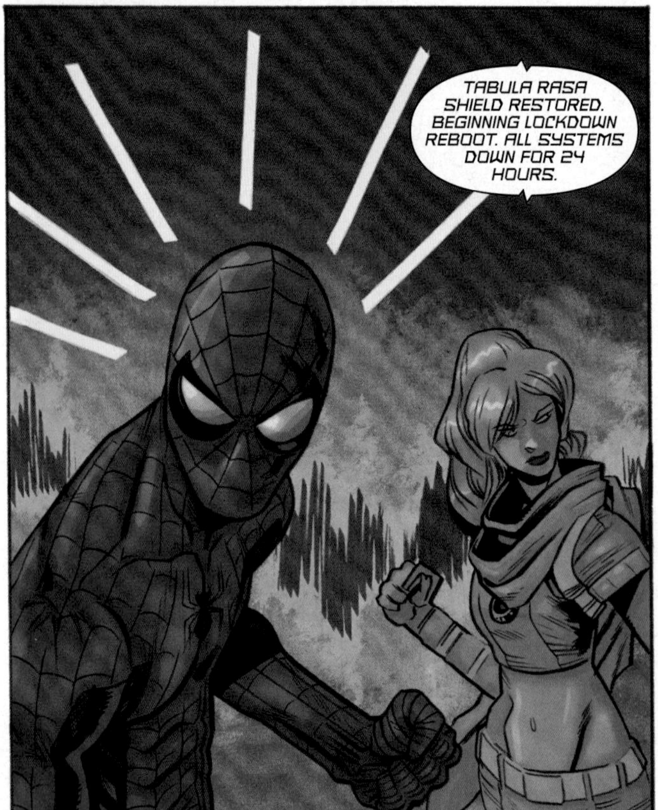
TABULA RASA SHIELD RESTORED. BEGINNING LOCKDOWN REBOOT. ALL SYSTEMS DOWN FOR 24 HOURS.

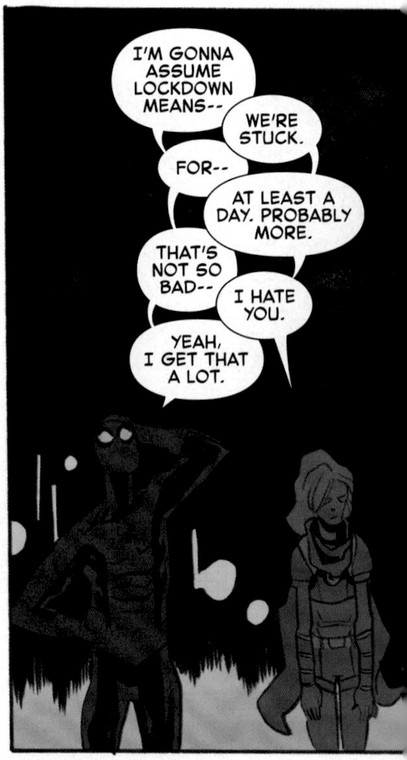
I'M GONNA ASSUME LOCKDOWN MEANS--
WE'RE STUCK.
FOR--
AT LEAST A DAY. PROBABLY MORE.
THAT'S NOT SO BAD--
I HATE YOU.
YEAH, I GET THAT A LOT.

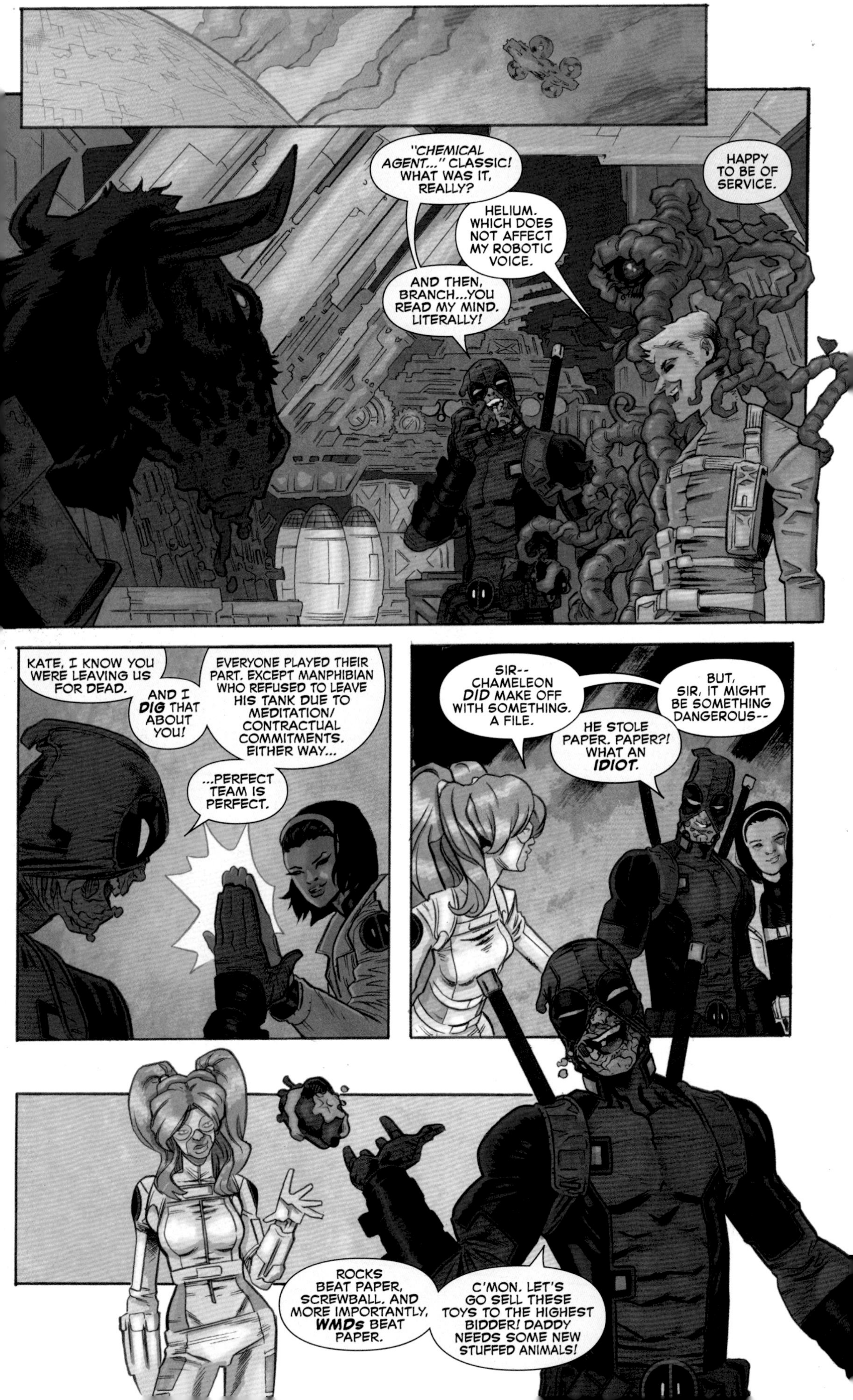

"CHEMICAL AGENT..." CLASSIC! WHAT WAS IT, REALLY?
HELIUM. WHICH DOES NOT AFFECT MY ROBOTIC VOICE.
AND THEN, BRANCH...YOU READ MY MIND. LITERALLY!
HAPPY TO BE OF SERVICE.
KATE, I KNOW YOU WERE LEAVING US FOR DEAD.
AND I DIG THAT ABOUT YOU!
EVERYONE PLAYED THEIR PART. EXCEPT MANPHIBIAN WHO REFUSED TO LEAVE HIS TANK DUE TO MEDITATION/ CONTRACTUAL COMMITMENTS. EITHER WAY...
...PERFECT TEAM IS PERFECT.
SIR-- CHAMELEON DID MAKE OFF WITH SOMETHING. A FILE.
HE STOLE PAPER. PAPER?! WHAT AN IDIOT.
BUT, SIR, IT MIGHT BE SOMETHING DANGEROUS--
ROCKS BEAT PAPER, SCREWBALL. AND MORE IMPORTANTLY, WMDs BEAT PAPER.
C'MON. LET'S GO SELL THESE TOYS TO THE HIGHEST BIDDER! DADDY NEEDS SOME NEW STUFFED ANIMALS!

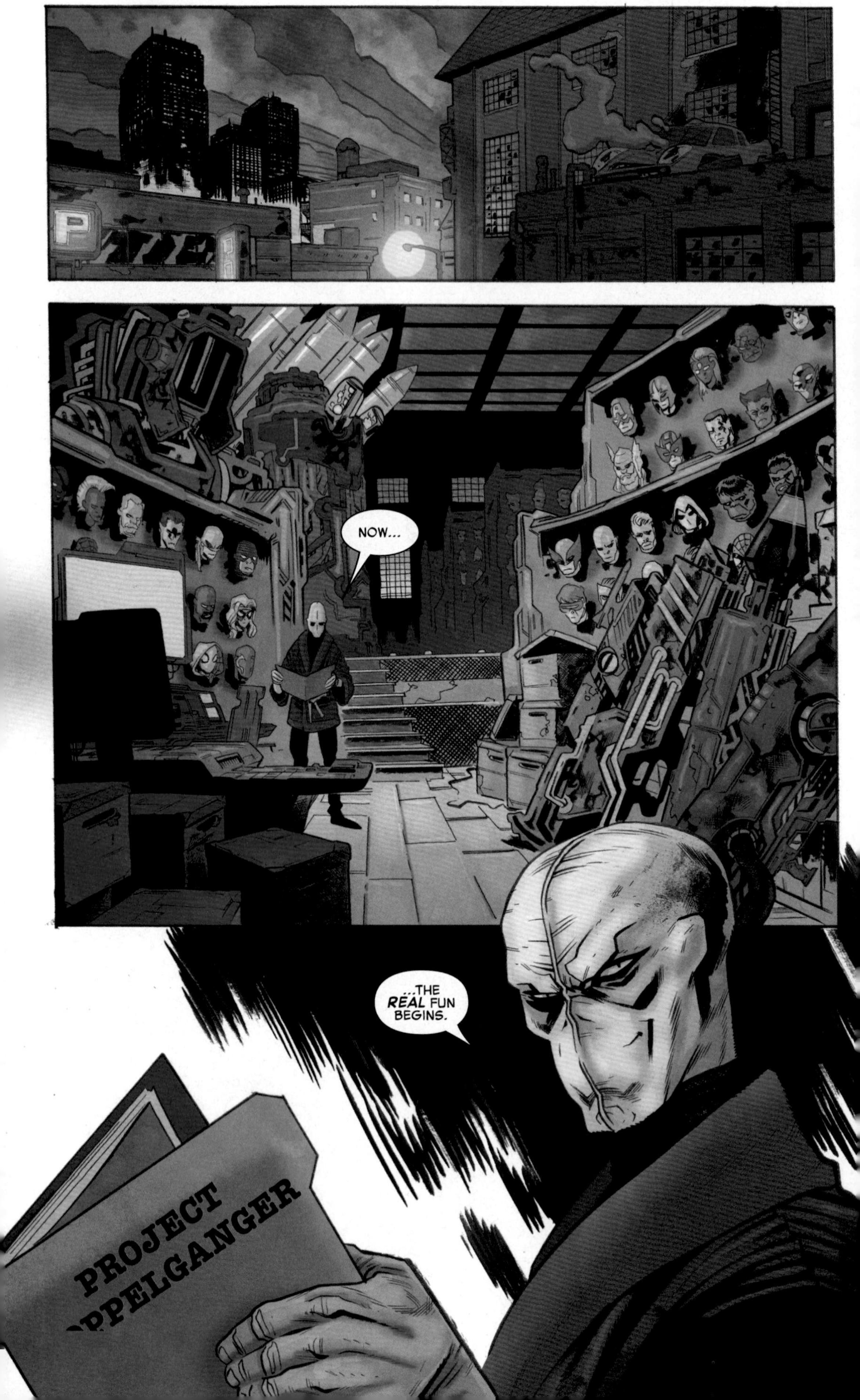
NOW...
...THE REAL FUN BEGINS.
PROJECT
PPELGANGER

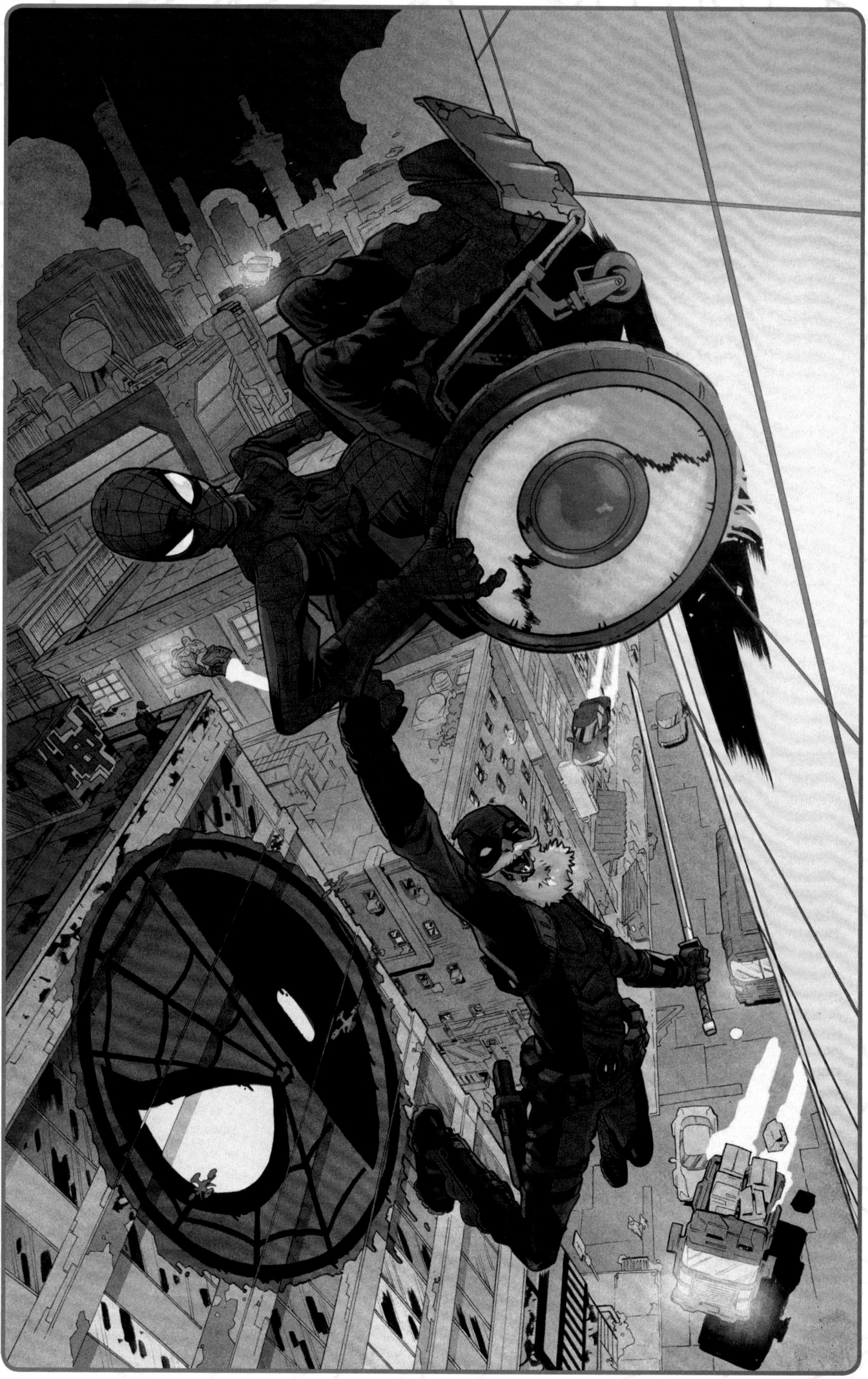

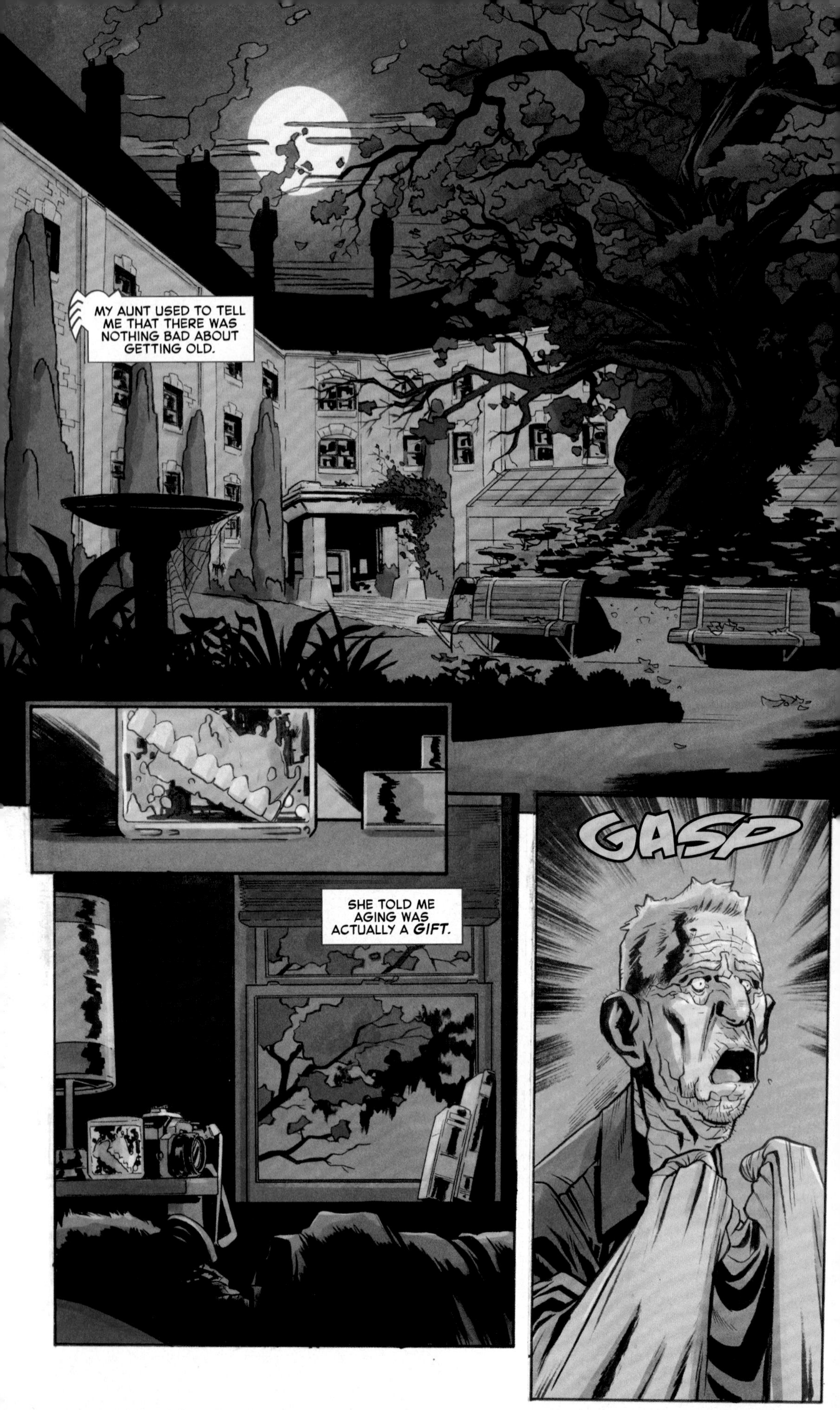

MY AUNT USED TO TELL ME THAT THERE WAS NOTHING BAD ABOUT GETTING OLD.
SHE TOLD ME AGING WAS ACTUALLY A *GIFT*.
GASP

"YOU **LEARN** THINGS ABOUT YOURSELF WITH EACH YEAR," SHE'D SAY. "AND WITH EACH YEAR YOU'RE LUCKY ENOUGH TO GET, YOU'VE GOT A NEW CHANCE TO **GROW.**

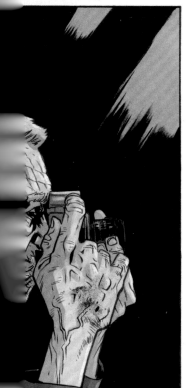

CLICK   CLICK

"GETTING OLD DOESN'T KILL YOU...

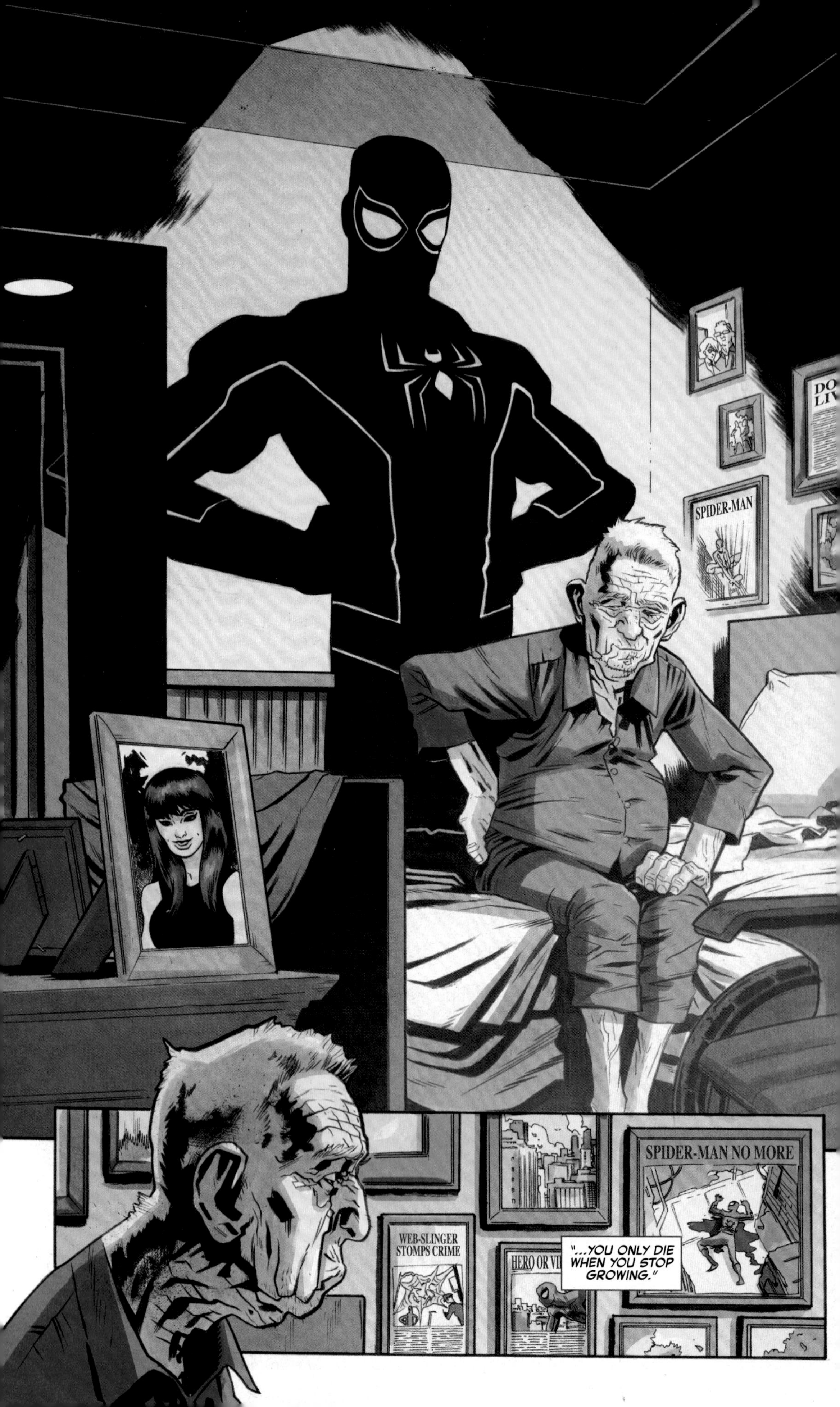
SPIDER-MAN
SPIDER-MAN NO MORE
WEB-SLINGER STOMPS CRIME
"...YOU ONLY DIE WHEN YOU STOP GROWING."

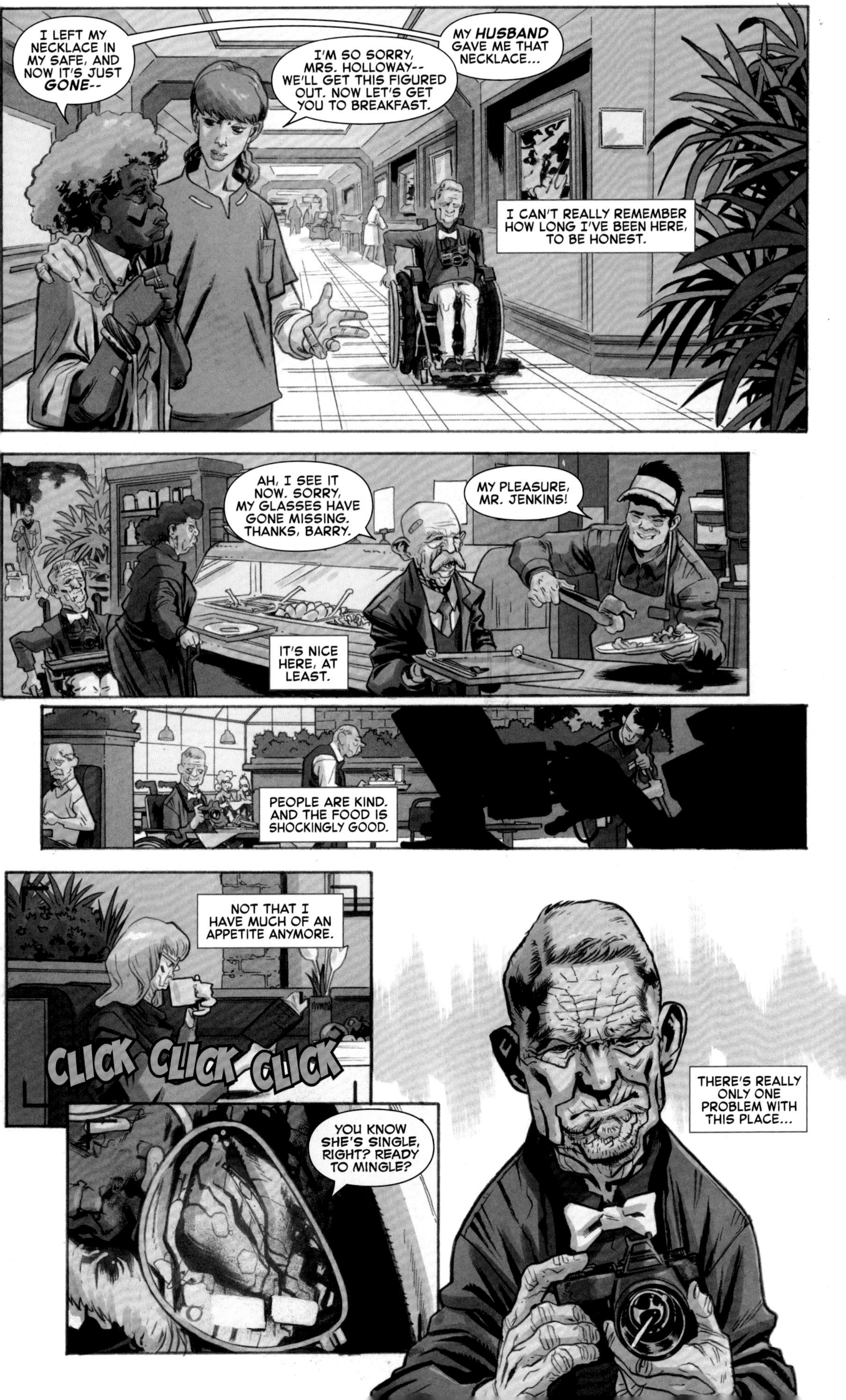
I LEFT MY NECKLACE IN MY SAFE, AND NOW IT'S JUST GONE--
I'M SO SORRY, MRS. HOLLOWAY-- WE'LL GET THIS FIGURED OUT. NOW LET'S GET YOU TO BREAKFAST.
MY HUSBAND GAVE ME THAT NECKLACE...
I CAN'T REALLY REMEMBER HOW LONG I'VE BEEN HERE, TO BE HONEST.
AH, I SEE IT NOW. SORRY, MY GLASSES HAVE GONE MISSING. THANKS, BARRY.
MY PLEASURE, MR. JENKINS!
IT'S NICE HERE, AT LEAST.
PEOPLE ARE KIND. AND THE FOOD IS SHOCKINGLY GOOD.
NOT THAT I HAVE MUCH OF AN APPETITE ANYMORE.
CLICK CLICK CLICK
YOU KNOW SHE'S SINGLE, RIGHT? READY TO MINGLE?
THERE'S REALLY ONLY ONE PROBLEM WITH THIS PLACE...

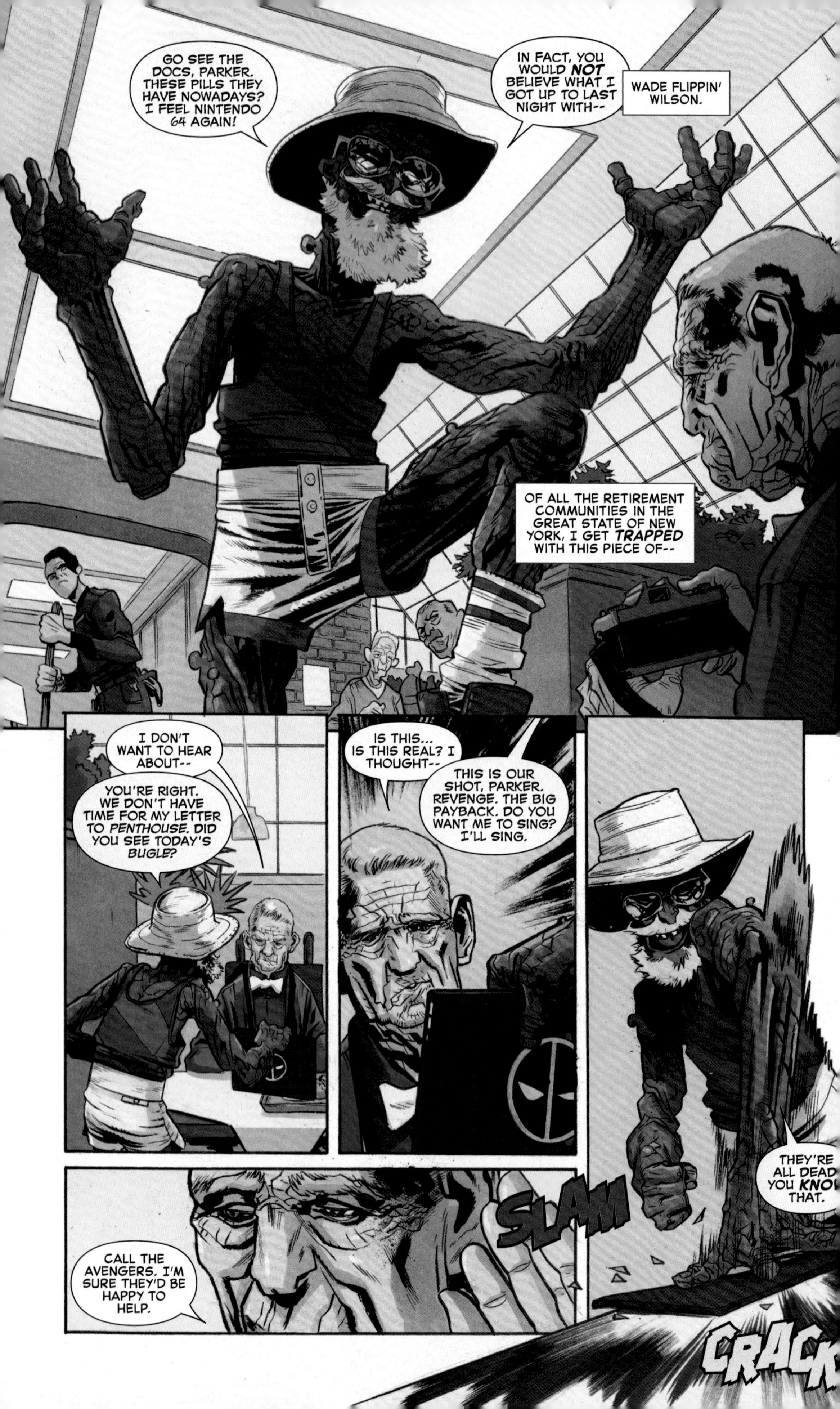
GO SEE THE DOCS, PARKER. THESE PILLS THEY HAVE NOWADAYS? I FEEL NINTENDO 64 AGAIN!
IN FACT, YOU WOULD **NOT** BELIEVE WHAT I GOT UP TO LAST NIGHT WITH--
WADE FLIPPIN' WILSON.
OF ALL THE RETIREMENT COMMUNITIES IN THE GREAT STATE OF NEW YORK, I GET ***TRAPPED*** WITH THIS PIECE OF--
I DON'T WANT TO HEAR ABOUT--
YOU'RE RIGHT. WE DON'T HAVE TIME FOR MY LETTER TO *PENTHOUSE*. DID YOU SEE TODAY'S *BUGLE?*
IS THIS... IS THIS REAL? I THOUGHT--
THIS IS OUR SHOT, PARKER. REVENGE. THE BIG PAYBACK. DO YOU WANT ME TO SING? I'LL SING.
CALL THE AVENGERS. I'M SURE THEY'D BE HAPPY TO HELP.
SLAM
THEY'RE ALL DEAD YOU **KNO** THAT.
CRACK

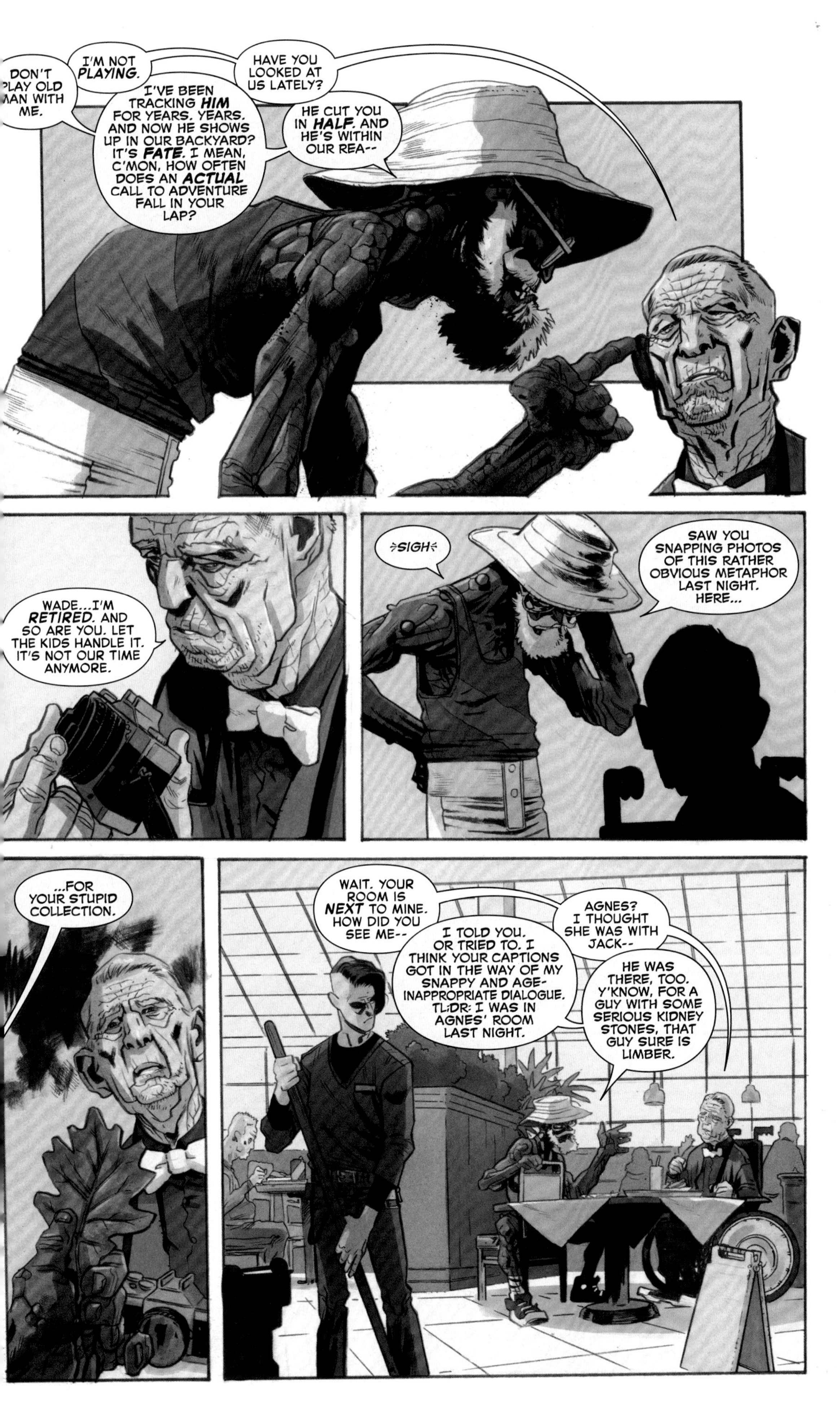

DON'T PLAY OLD MAN WITH ME.
I'M NOT PLAYING.
I'VE BEEN TRACKING HIM FOR YEARS. YEARS. AND NOW HE SHOWS UP IN OUR BACKYARD? IT'S FATE. I MEAN, C'MON, HOW OFTEN DOES AN ACTUAL CALL TO ADVENTURE FALL IN YOUR LAP?
HAVE YOU LOOKED AT US LATELY?
HE CUT YOU IN HALF. AND HE'S WITHIN OUR REA--
WADE...I'M RETIRED. AND SO ARE YOU. LET THE KIDS HANDLE IT. IT'S NOT OUR TIME ANYMORE.
SIGH
SAW YOU SNAPPING PHOTOS OF THIS RATHER OBVIOUS METAPHOR LAST NIGHT. HERE...
...FOR YOUR STUPID COLLECTION.
WAIT. YOUR ROOM IS NEXT TO MINE. HOW DID YOU SEE ME--
I TOLD YOU. OR TRIED TO. I THINK YOUR CAPTIONS GOT IN THE WAY OF MY SNAPPY AND AGE-INAPPROPRIATE DIALOGUE. TL;DR: I WAS IN AGNES' ROOM LAST NIGHT.
AGNES? I THOUGHT SHE WAS WITH JACK--
HE WAS THERE, TOO. Y'KNOW, FOR A GUY WITH SOME SERIOUS KIDNEY STONES, THAT GUY SURE IS LIMBER.

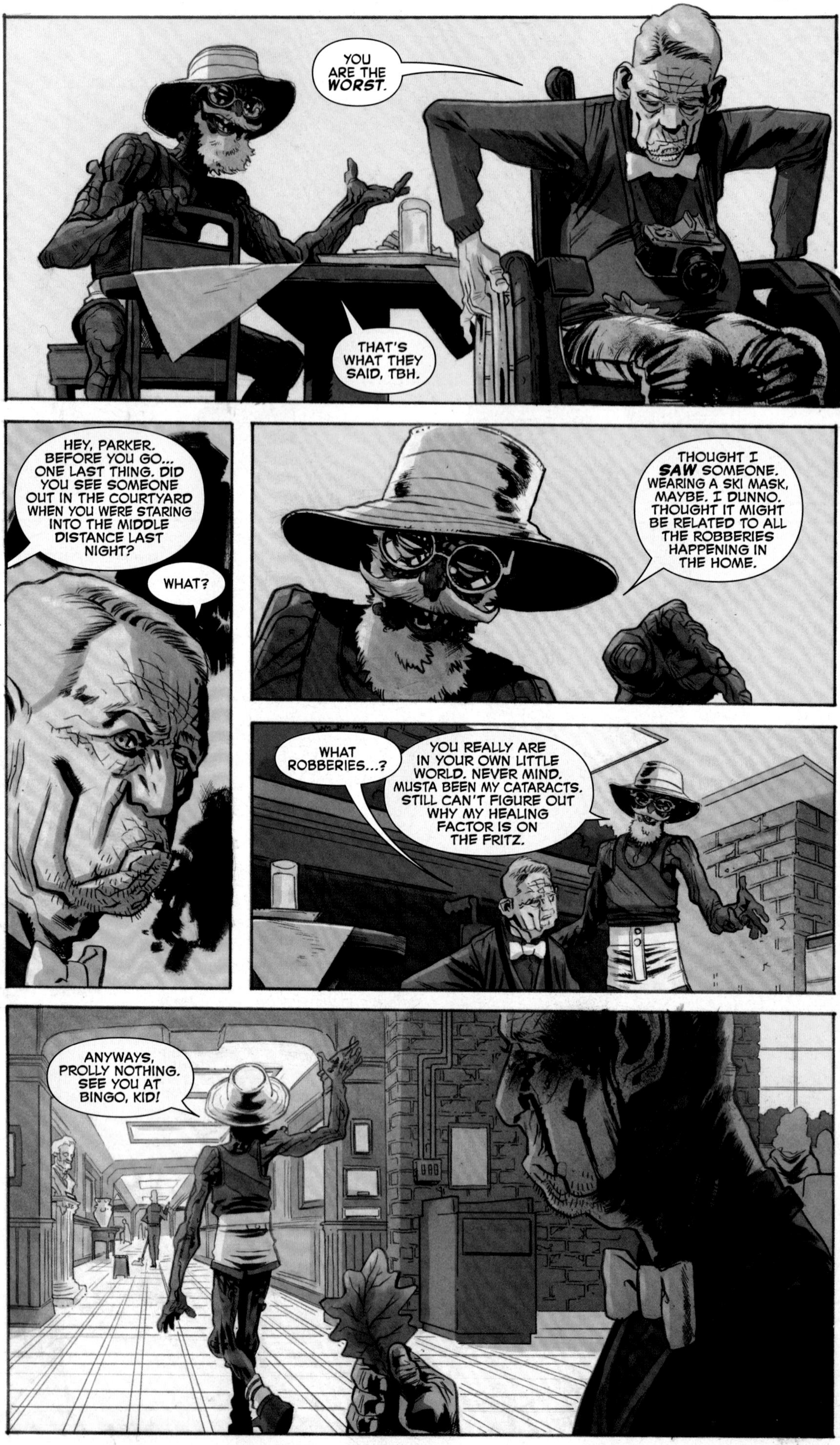
YOU ARE THE WORST.
THAT'S WHAT THEY SAID, TBH.
HEY, PARKER. BEFORE YOU GO... ONE LAST THING. DID YOU SEE SOMEONE OUT IN THE COURTYARD WHEN YOU WERE STARING INTO THE MIDDLE DISTANCE LAST NIGHT?
WHAT?
THOUGHT I SAW SOMEONE. WEARING A SKI MASK, MAYBE. I DUNNO. THOUGHT IT MIGHT BE RELATED TO ALL THE ROBBERIES HAPPENING IN THE HOME.
WHAT ROBBERIES...?
YOU REALLY ARE IN YOUR OWN LITTLE WORLD. NEVER MIND. MUSTA BEEN MY CATARACTS. STILL CAN'T FIGURE OUT WHY MY HEALING FACTOR IS ON THE FRITZ.
ANYWAYS, PROLLY NOTHING. SEE YOU AT BINGO, KID!

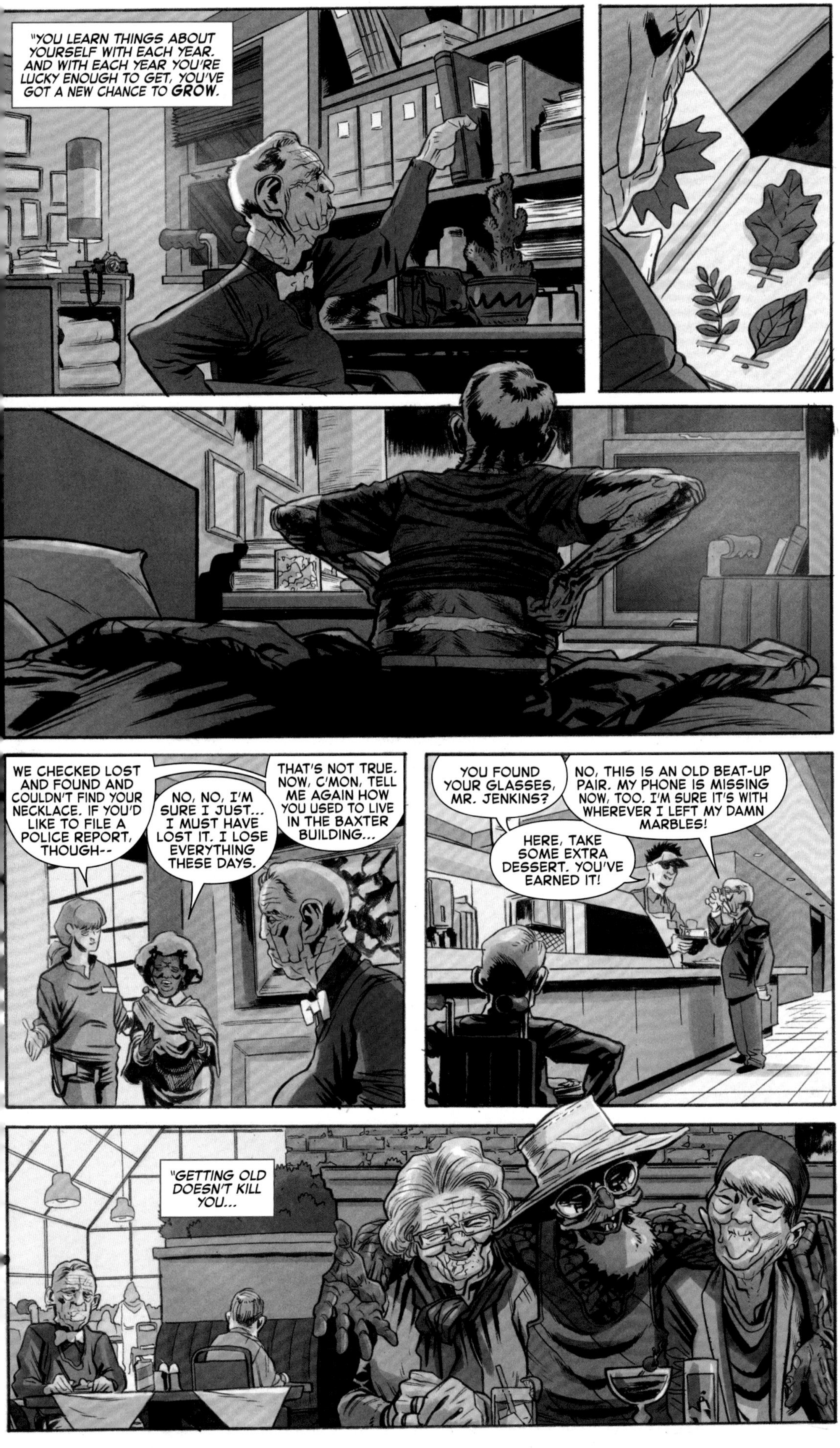
"YOU LEARN THINGS ABOUT YOURSELF WITH EACH YEAR. AND WITH EACH YEAR YOU'RE LUCKY ENOUGH TO GET, YOU'VE GOT A NEW CHANCE TO GROW.
WE CHECKED LOST AND FOUND AND COULDN'T FIND YOUR NECKLACE. IF YOU'D LIKE TO FILE A POLICE REPORT, THOUGH--
NO, NO, I'M SURE I JUST... I MUST HAVE LOST IT. I LOSE EVERYTHING THESE DAYS.
THAT'S NOT TRUE. NOW, C'MON, TELL ME AGAIN HOW YOU USED TO LIVE IN THE BAXTER BUILDING...
YOU FOUND YOUR GLASSES, MR. JENKINS?
NO, THIS IS AN OLD BEAT-UP PAIR. MY PHONE IS MISSING NOW, TOO. I'M SURE IT'S WITH WHEREVER I LEFT MY DAMN MARBLES!
HERE, TAKE SOME EXTRA DESSERT. YOU'VE EARNED IT!
"GETTING OLD DOESN'T KILL YOU...

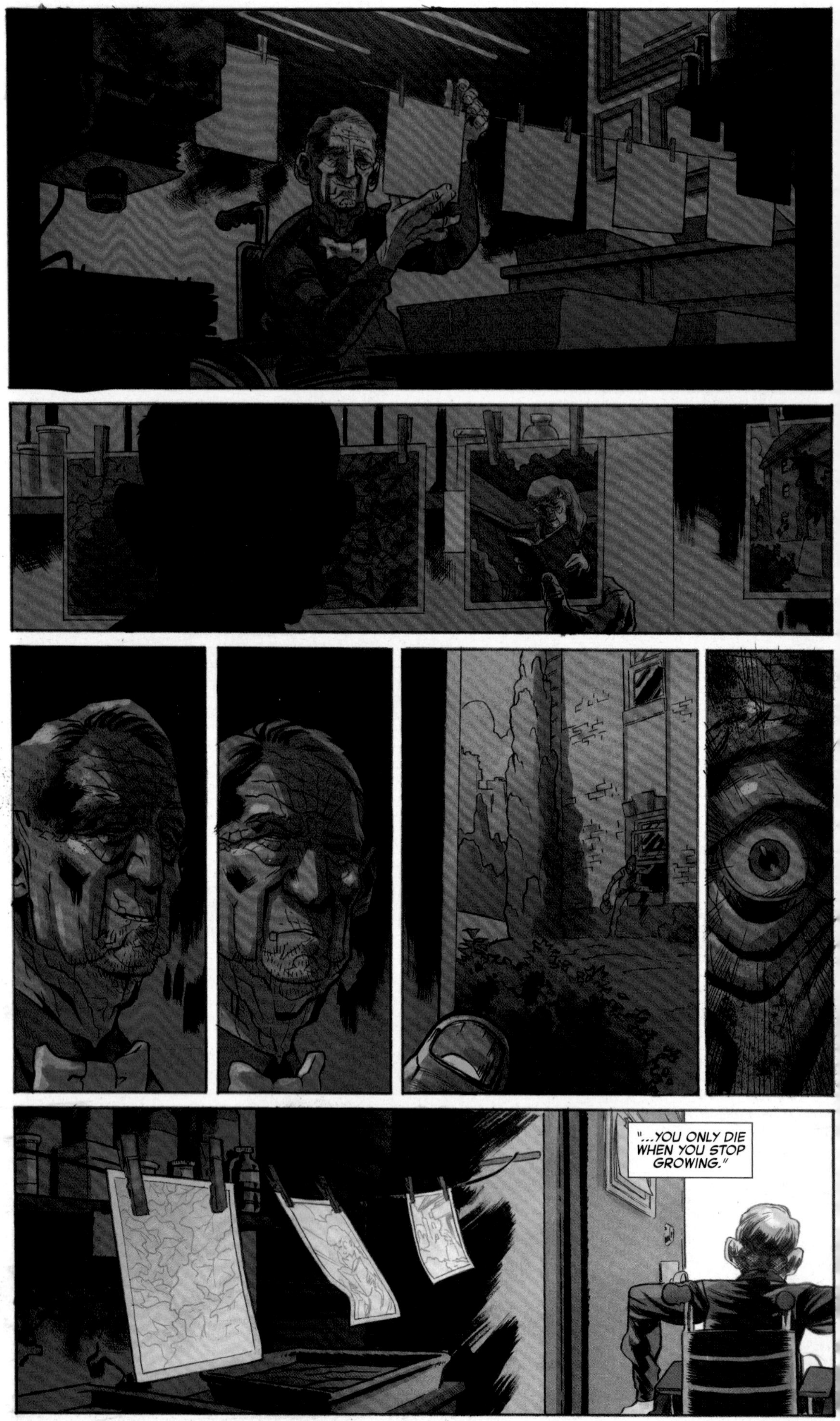
"...YOU ONLY DIE WHEN YOU STOP GROWING."

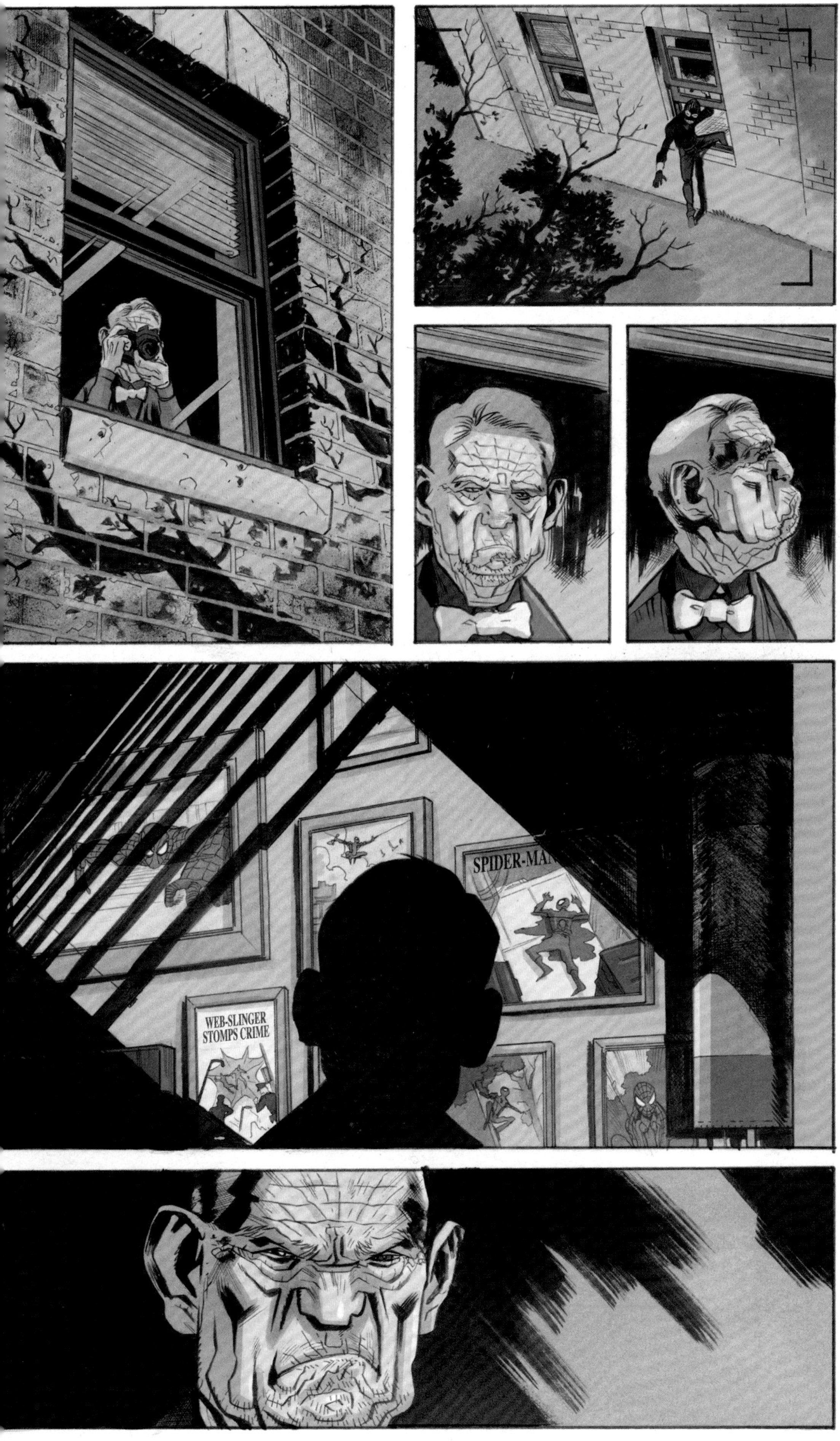
SPIDER-MAN
WEB-SLINGER
STOMPS CRIME

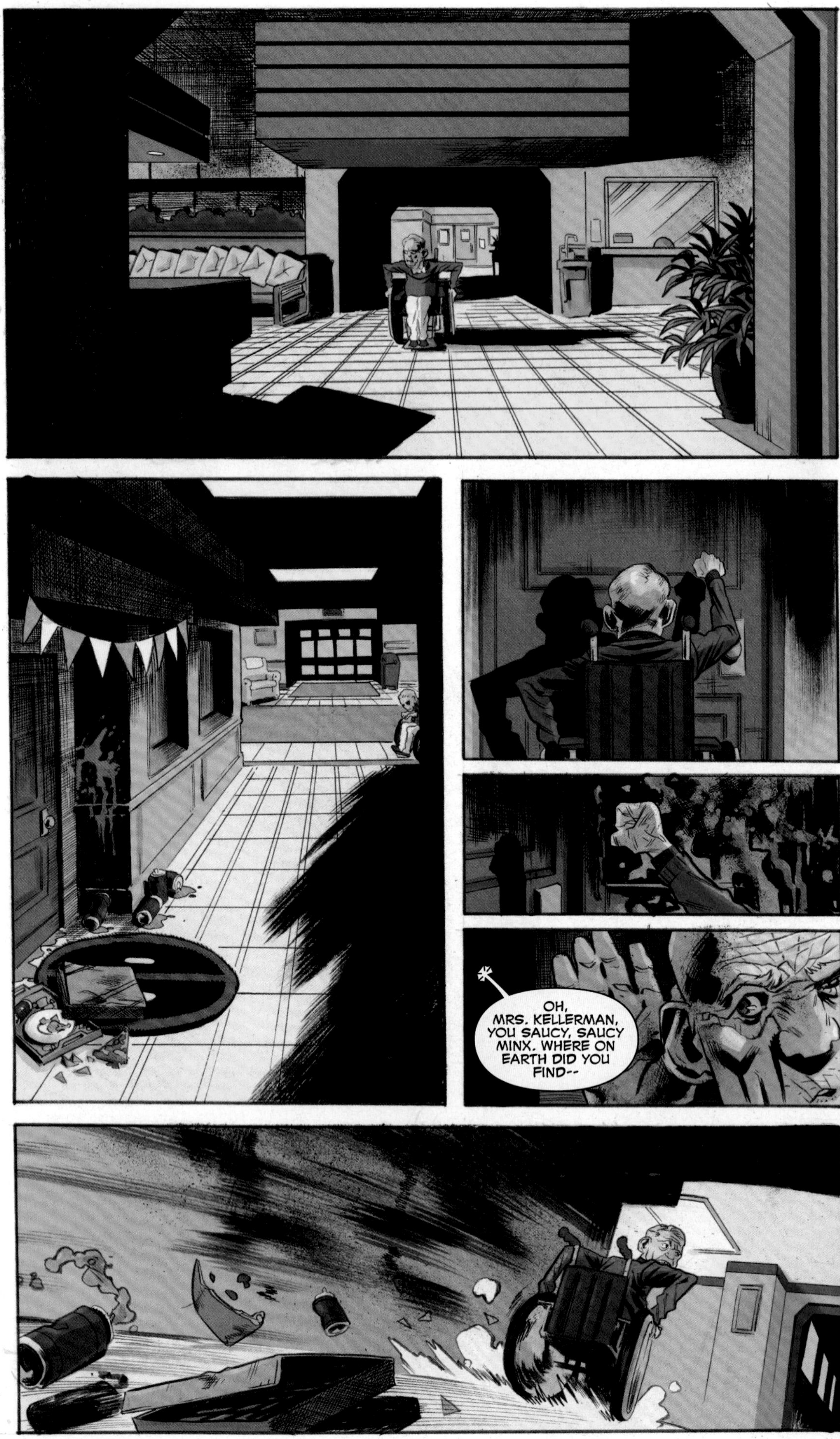
OH, MRS. KELLERMAN, YOU SAUCY, SAUCY MINX. WHERE ON EARTH DID YOU FIND--

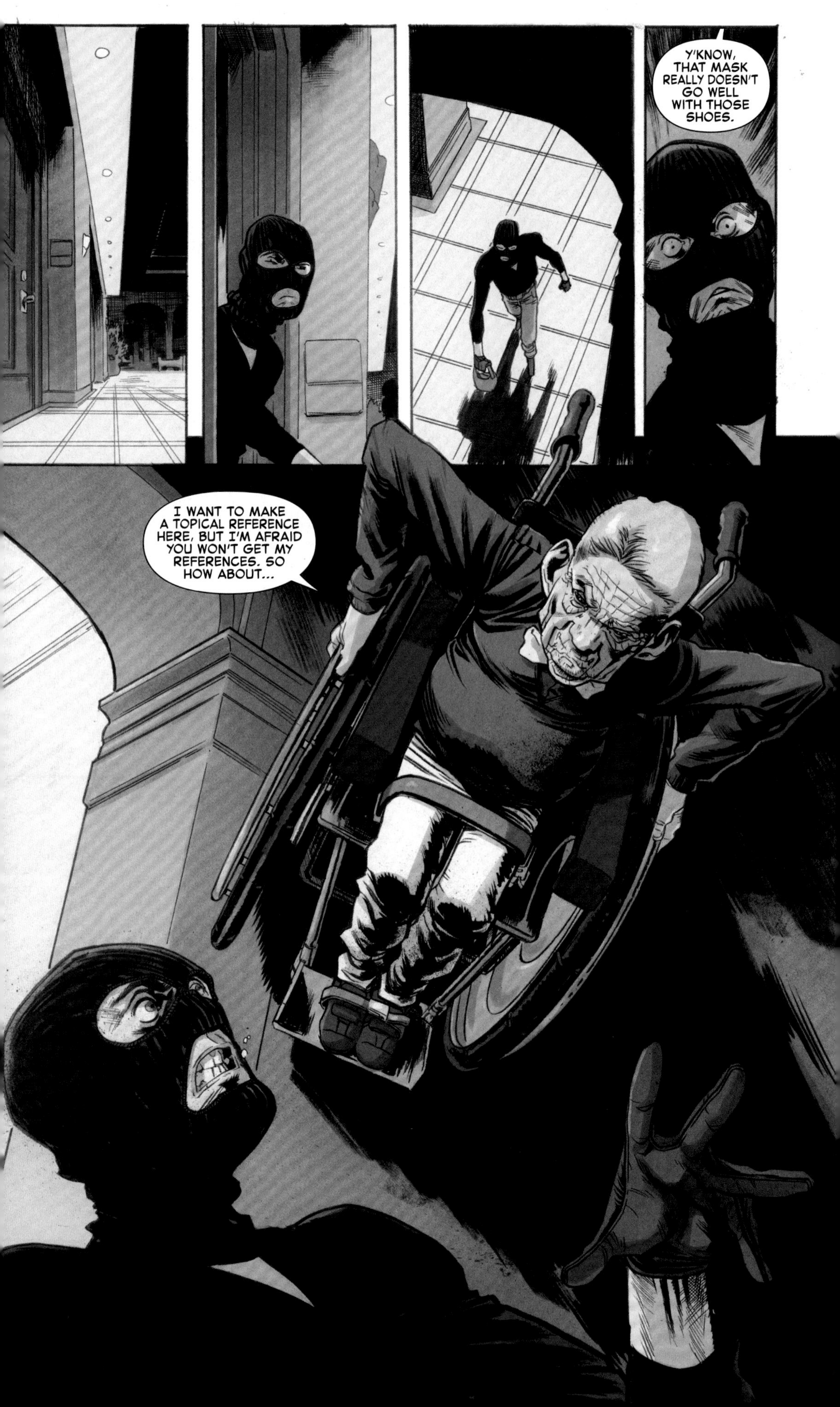
Y'KNOW, THAT MASK REALLY DOESN'T GO WELL WITH THOSE SHOES.
I WANT TO MAKE A TOPICAL REFERENCE HERE, BUT I'M AFRAID YOU WON'T GET MY REFERENCES. SO HOW ABOUT...

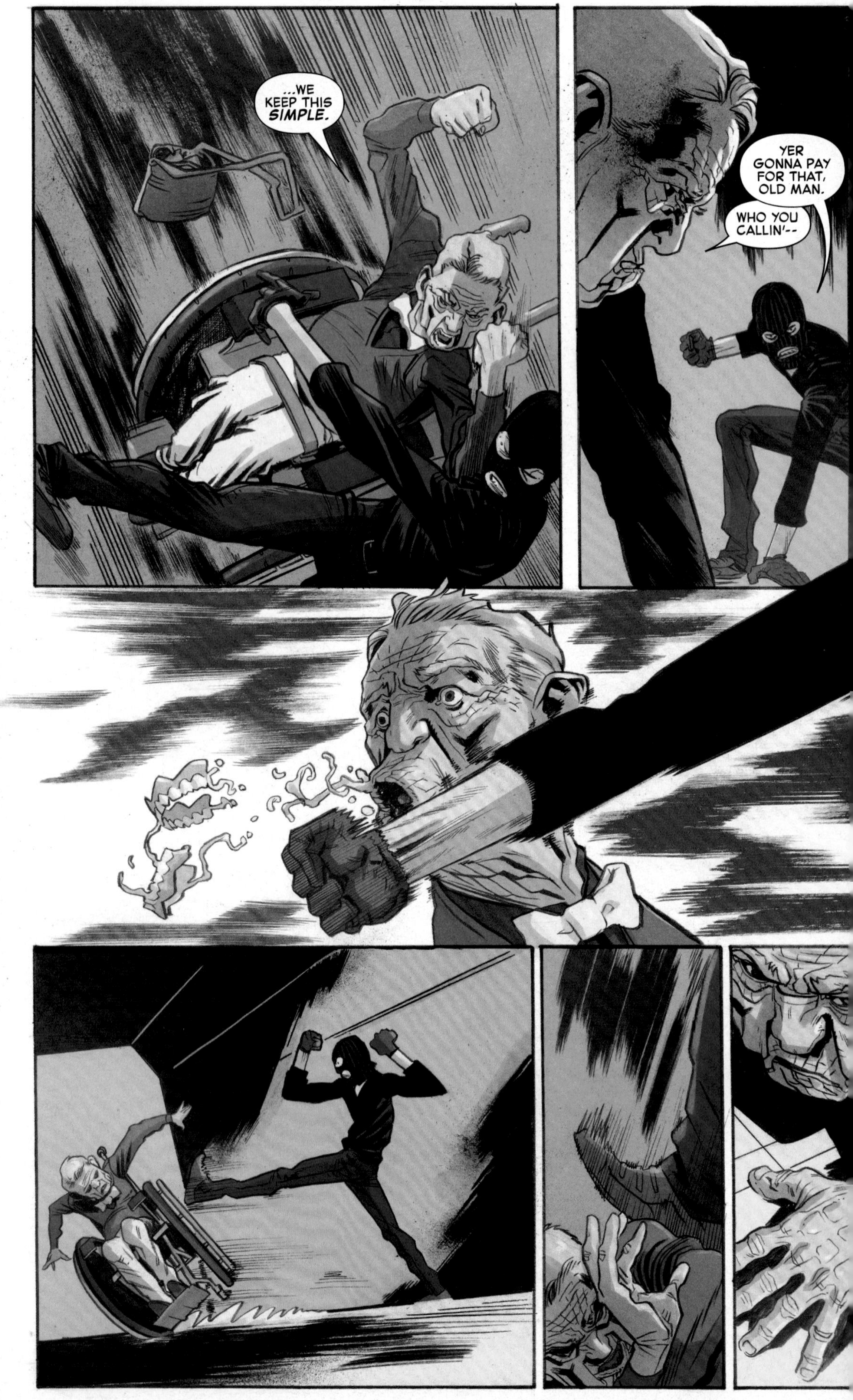

...WE KEEP THIS SIMPLE.
YER GONNA PAY FOR THAT, OLD MAN.
WHO YOU CALLIN'--

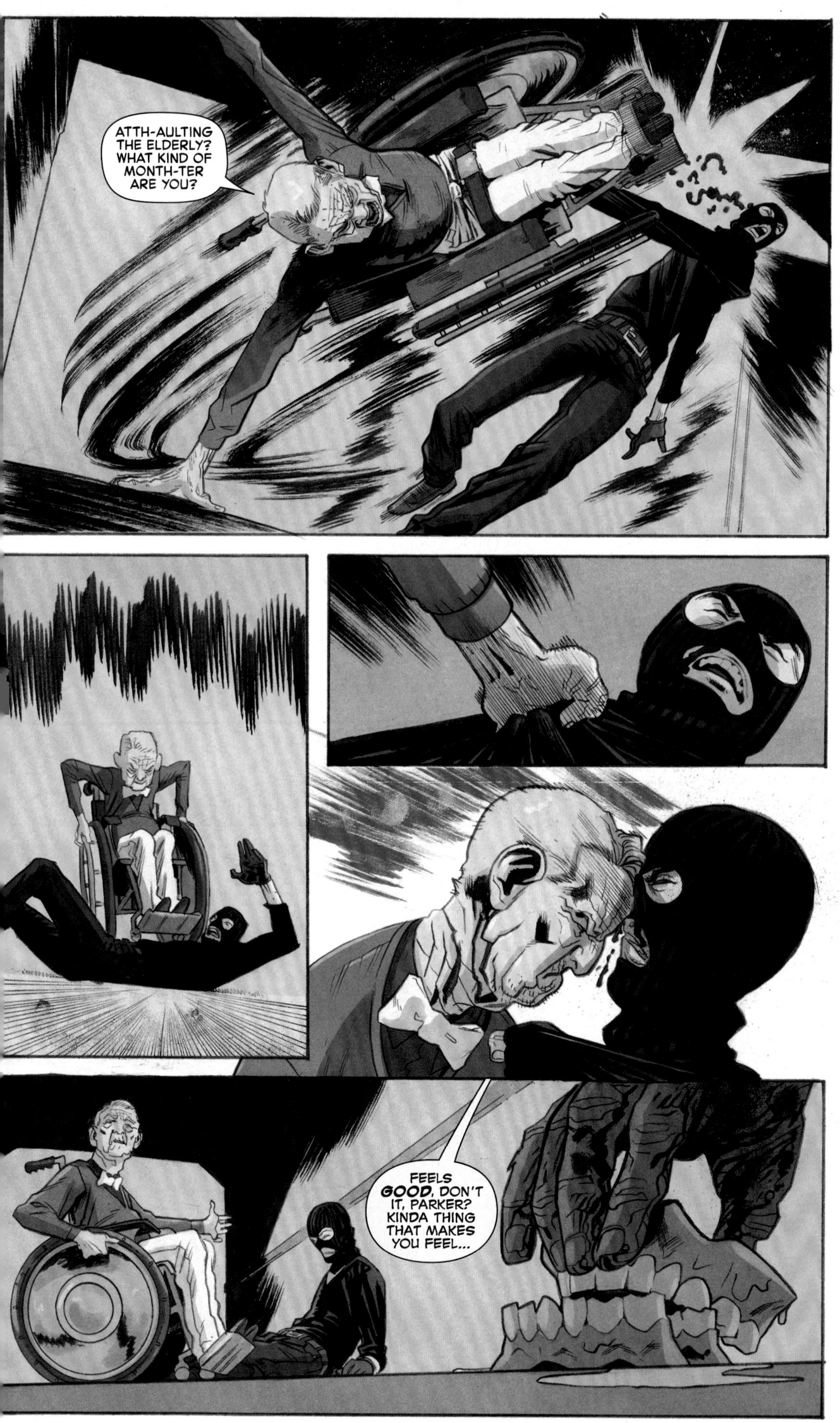
ATTH-AULTING THE ELDERLY? WHAT KIND OF MONTH-TER ARE YOU?
FEELS GOOD, DON'T IT, PARKER? KINDA THING THAT MAKES YOU FEEL...

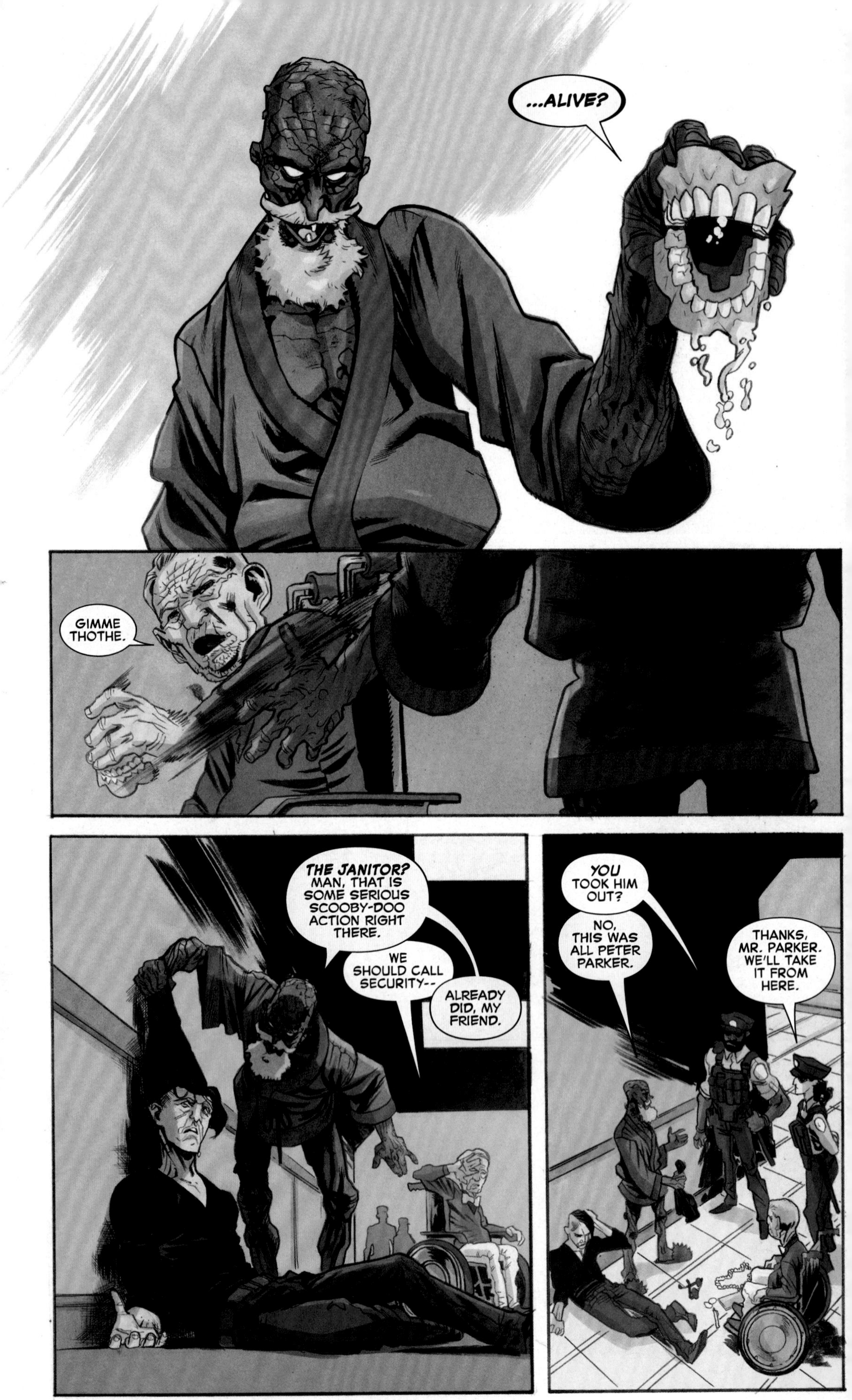

...ALIVE?
GIMME THOTHE.
THE JANITOR? MAN, THAT IS SOME SERIOUS SCOOBY-DOO ACTION RIGHT THERE.
WE SHOULD CALL SECURITY--
ALREADY DID, MY FRIEND.
YOU TOOK HIM OUT?
NO, THIS WAS ALL PETER PARKER.
THANKS, MR. PARKER. WE'LL TAKE IT FROM HERE.

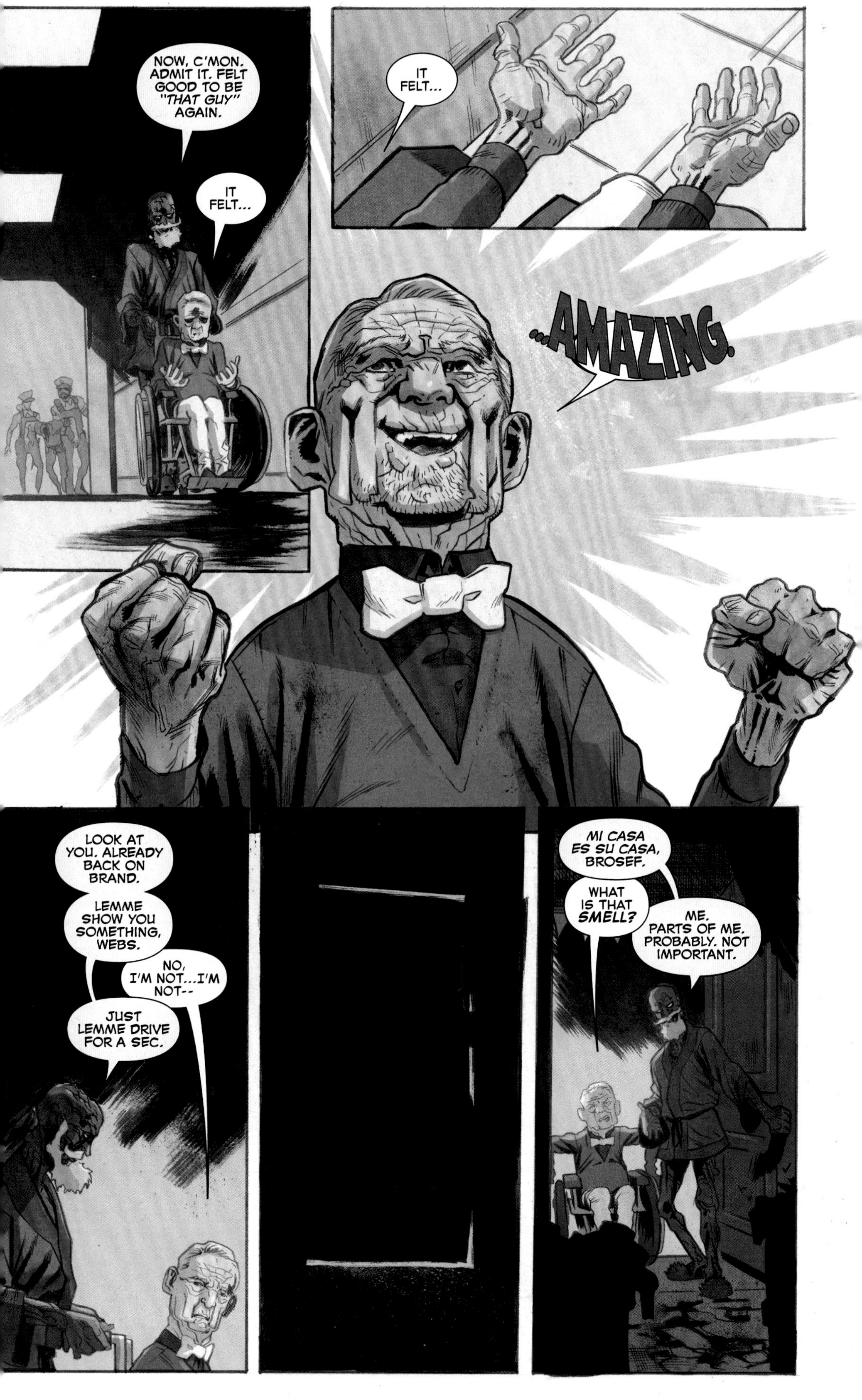
NOW, C'MON. ADMIT IT. FELT GOOD TO BE "THAT GUY" AGAIN.
IT FELT...
IT FELT...
...AMAZING.
LOOK AT YOU. ALREADY BACK ON BRAND.
LEMME SHOW YOU SOMETHING, WEBS.
NO, I'M NOT...I'M NOT--
JUST LEMME DRIVE FOR A SEC.
MI CASA ES SU CASA, BROSEF.
WHAT IS THAT SMELL?
ME. PARTS OF ME. PROBABLY. NOT IMPORTANT.

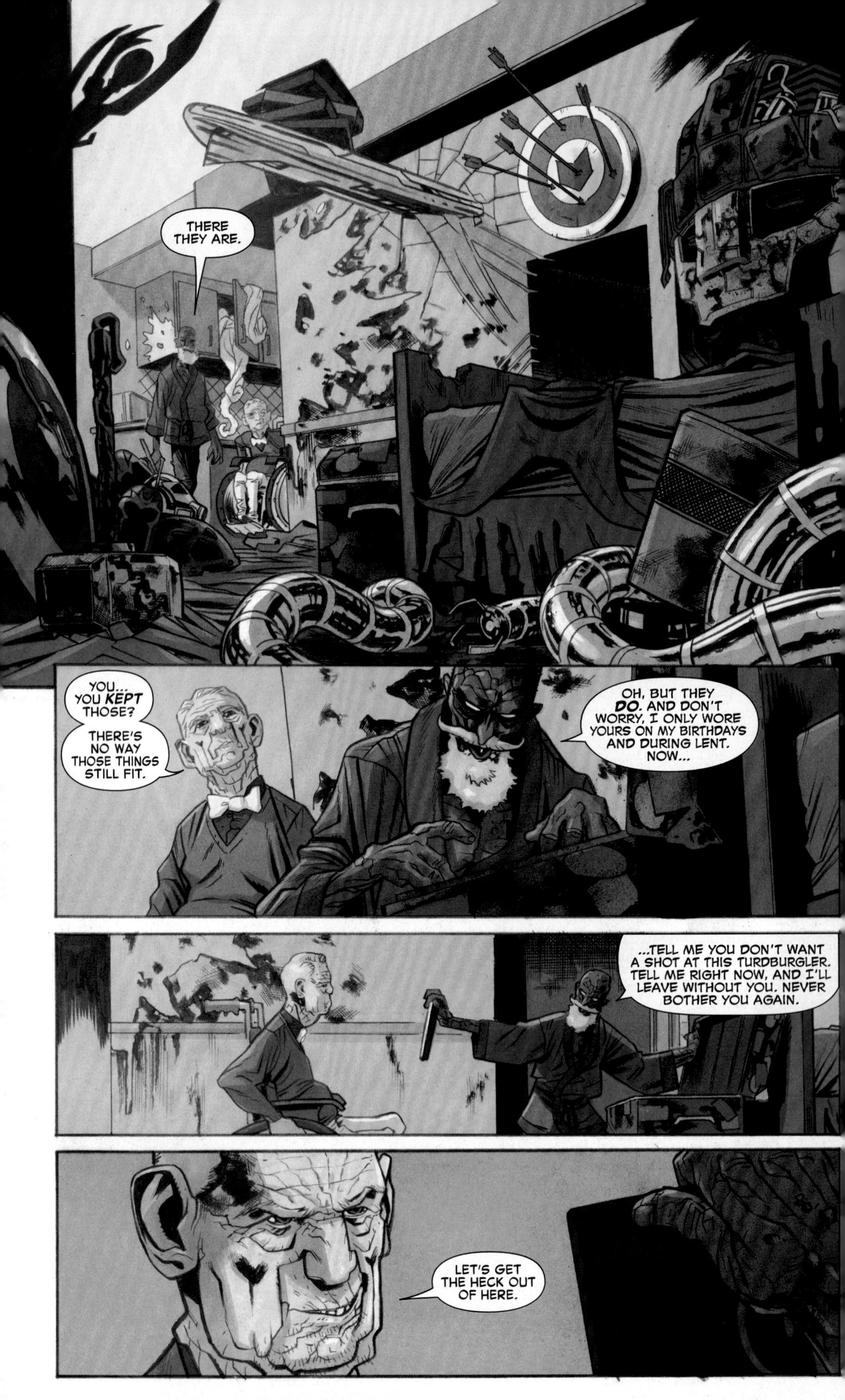
THERE THEY ARE.
YOU... YOU KEPT THOSE?
THERE'S NO WAY THOSE THINGS STILL FIT.
OH, BUT THEY DO. AND DON'T WORRY, I ONLY WORE YOURS ON MY BIRTHDAYS AND DURING LENT. NOW...
...TELL ME YOU DON'T WANT A SHOT AT THIS TURDBURGLER. TELL ME RIGHT NOW, AND I'LL LEAVE WITHOUT YOU. NEVER BOTHER YOU AGAIN.
LET'S GET THE HECK OUT OF HERE.

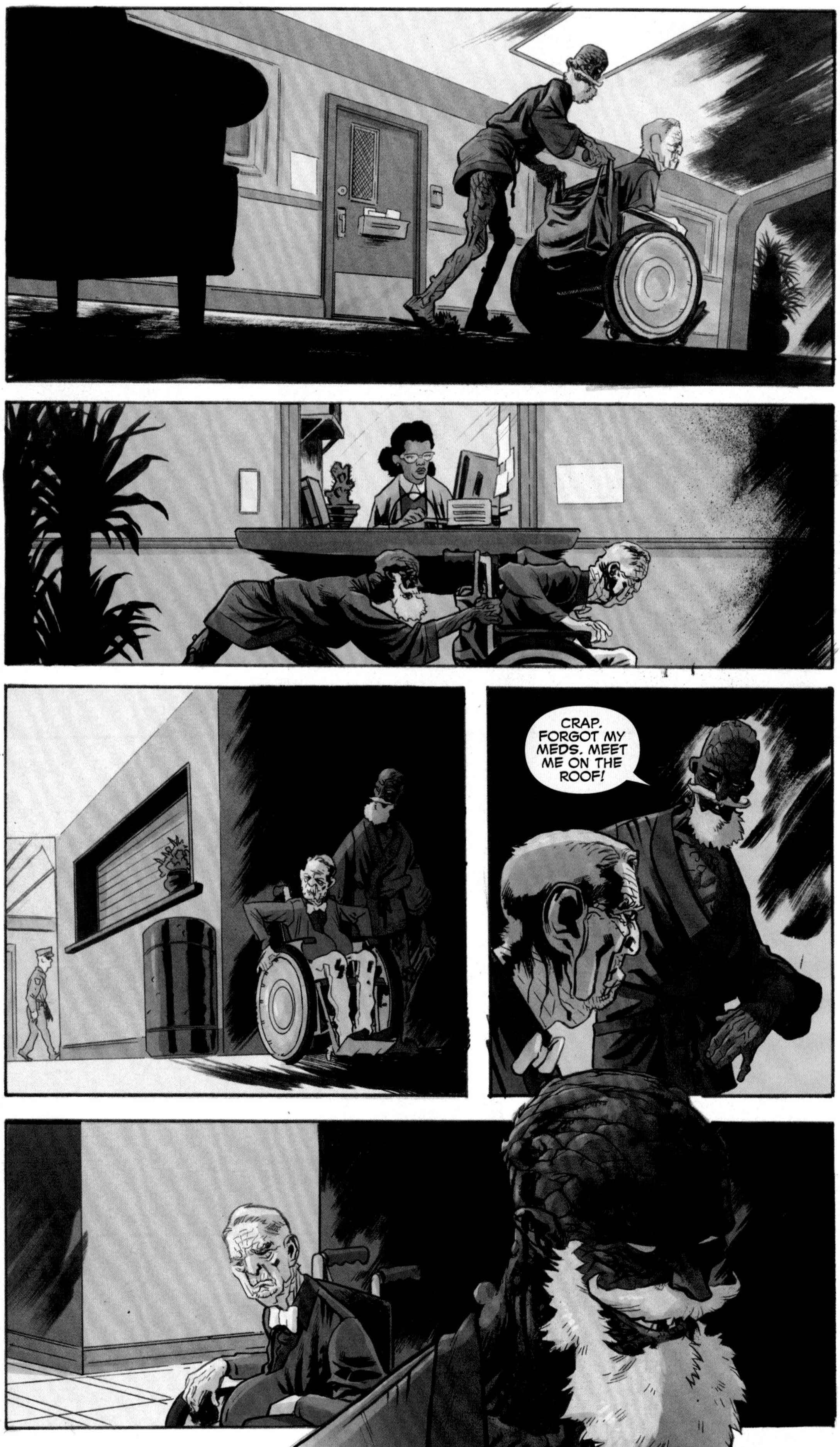
CRAP. FORGOT MY MEDS. MEET ME ON THE ROOF!

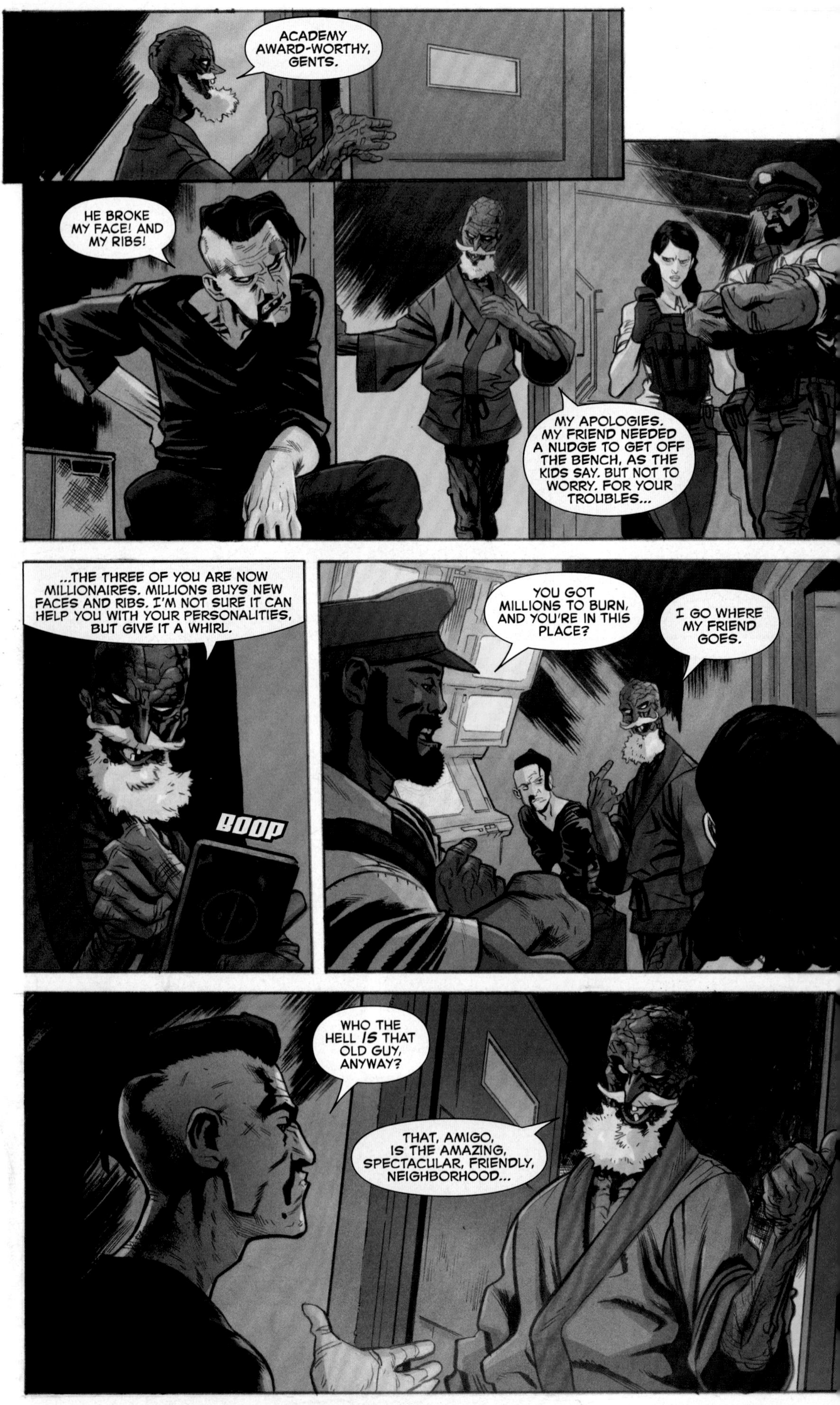
ACADEMY AWARD-WORTHY, GENTS.
HE BROKE MY FACE! AND MY RIBS!
MY APOLOGIES. MY FRIEND NEEDED A NUDGE TO GET OFF THE BENCH, AS THE KIDS SAY. BUT NOT TO WORRY. FOR YOUR TROUBLES...
...THE THREE OF YOU ARE NOW MILLIONAIRES. MILLIONS BUYS NEW FACES AND RIBS. I'M NOT SURE IT CAN HELP YOU WITH YOUR PERSONALITIES, BUT GIVE IT A WHIRL.
BOOP
YOU GOT MILLIONS TO BURN, AND YOU'RE IN THIS PLACE?
I GO WHERE MY FRIEND GOES.
WHO THE HELL *IS* THAT OLD GUY, ANYWAY?
THAT, AMIGO, IS THE AMAZING, SPECTACULAR, FRIENDLY, NEIGHBORHOOD...

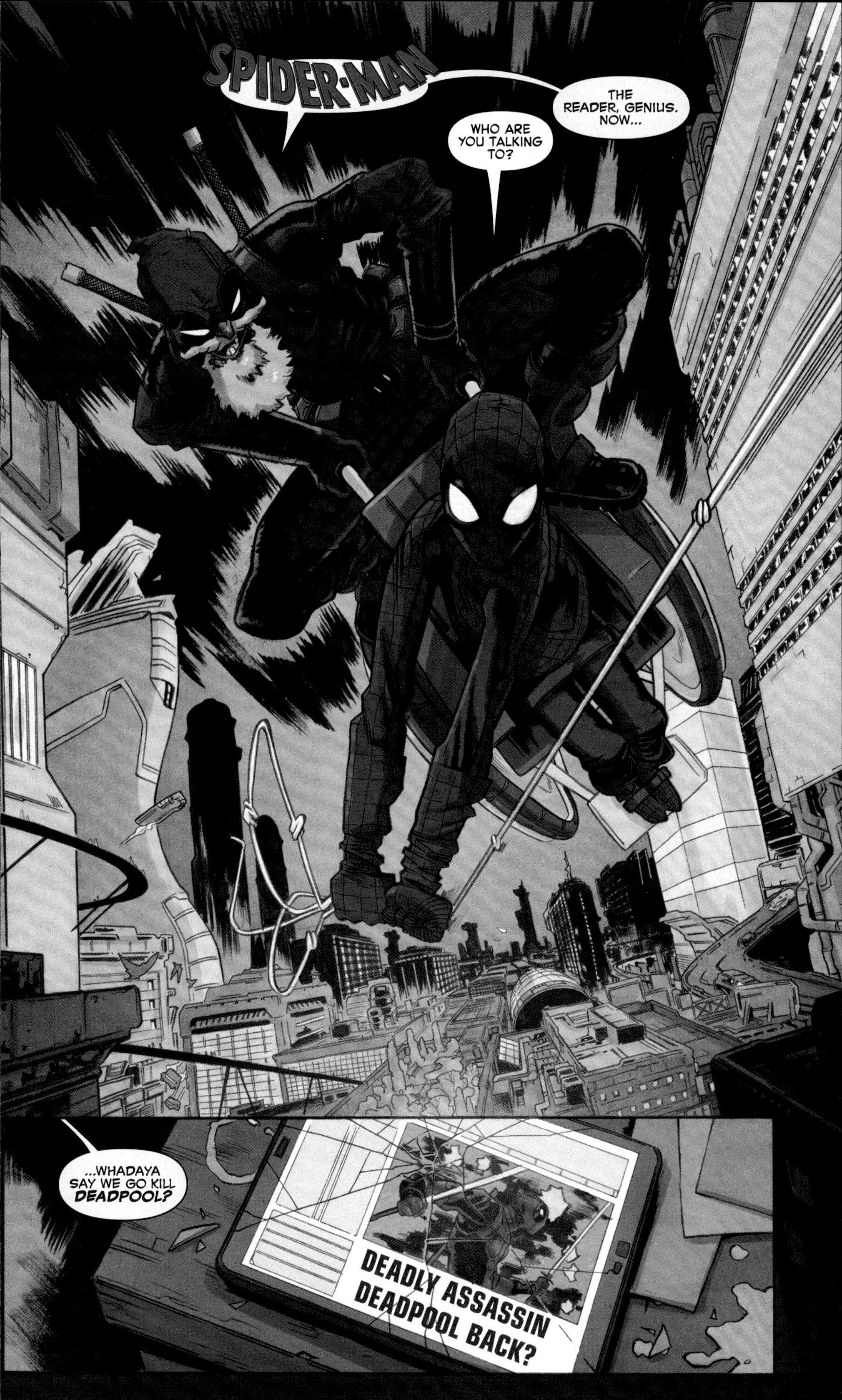
SPIDER-MAN
THE READER, GENIUS. NOW...
WHO ARE YOU TALKING TO?
...WHADAYA SAY WE GO KILL DEADPOOL?
DEADLY ASSASSIN DEADPOOL BACK?

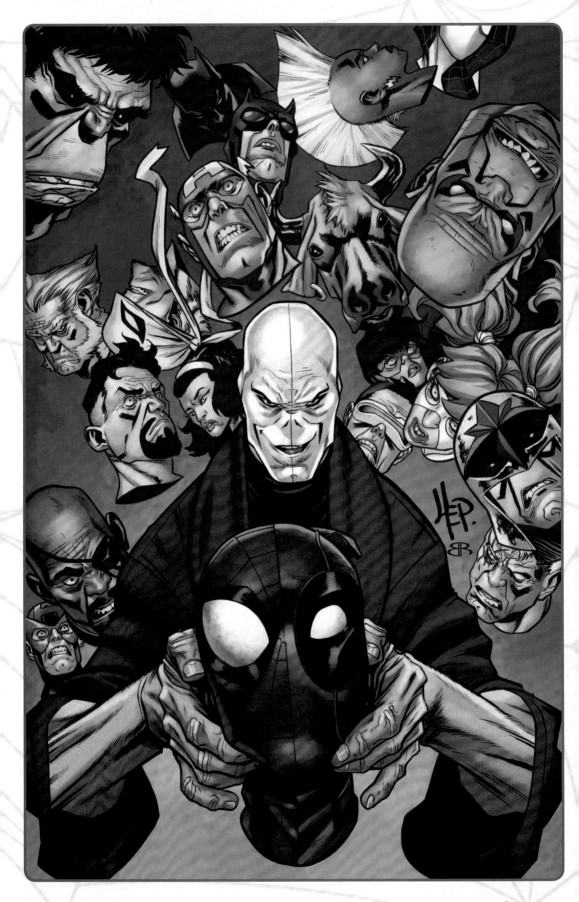

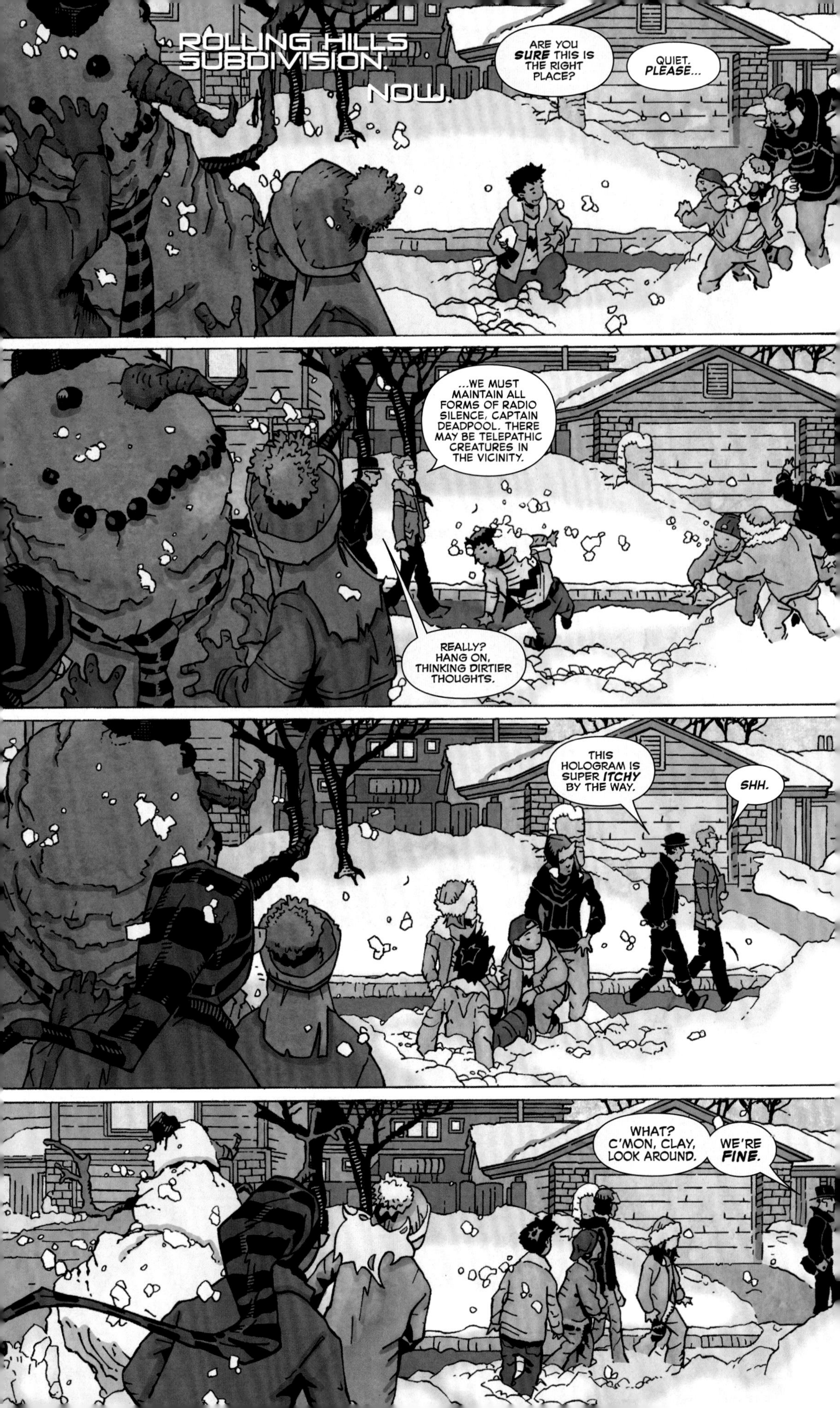
ROLLING HILLS SUBDIVISION.
NOW.
ARE YOU SURE THIS IS THE RIGHT PLACE?
QUIET. PLEASE...
...WE MUST MAINTAIN ALL FORMS OF RADIO SILENCE, CAPTAIN DEADPOOL. THERE MAY BE TELEPATHIC CREATURES IN THE VICINITY.
REALLY? HANG ON, THINKING DIRTIER THOUGHTS.
THIS HOLOGRAM IS SUPER ITCHY BY THE WAY.
SHH.
WHAT? C'MON, CLAY, LOOK AROUND.
WE'RE FINE.

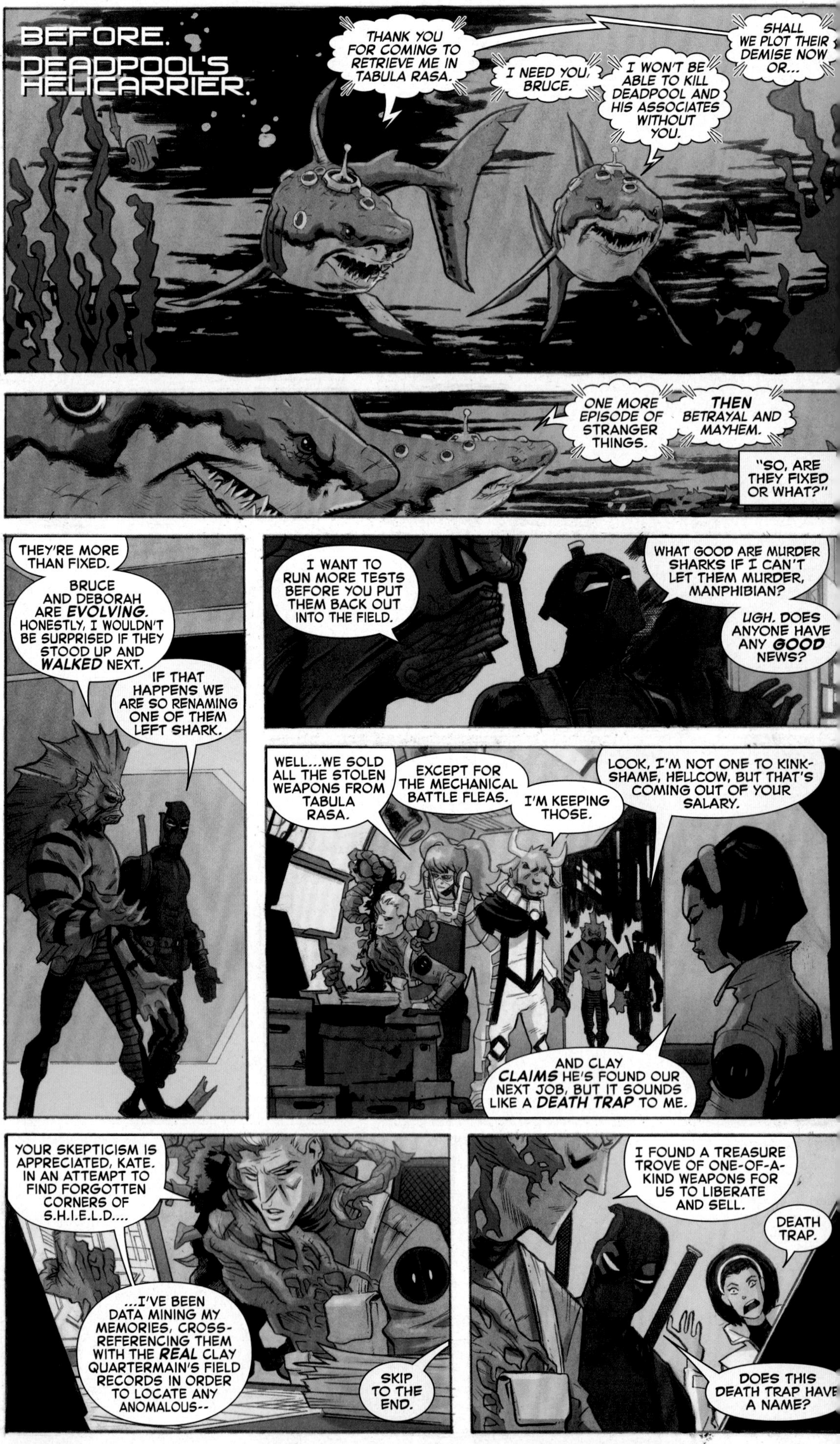

BEFORE. DEADPOOL'S HELICARRIER.
THANK YOU FOR COMING TO RETRIEVE ME IN TABULA RASA.
I NEED YOU, BRUCE.
I WON'T BE ABLE TO KILL DEADPOOL AND HIS ASSOCIATES WITHOUT YOU.
SHALL WE PLOT THEIR DEMISE NOW OR...
ONE MORE EPISODE OF STRANGER THINGS.
THEN BETRAYAL AND MAYHEM.
"SO, ARE THEY FIXED OR WHAT?"
THEY'RE MORE THAN FIXED.
BRUCE AND DEBORAH ARE EVOLVING. HONESTLY, I WOULDN'T BE SURPRISED IF THEY STOOD UP AND WALKED NEXT.
IF THAT HAPPENS WE ARE SO RENAMING ONE OF THEM LEFT SHARK.
I WANT TO RUN MORE TESTS BEFORE YOU PUT THEM BACK OUT INTO THE FIELD.
WHAT GOOD ARE MURDER SHARKS IF I CAN'T LET THEM MURDER, MANPHIBIAN?
UGH. DOES ANYONE HAVE ANY GOOD NEWS?
WELL...WE SOLD ALL THE STOLEN WEAPONS FROM TABULA RASA.
EXCEPT FOR THE MECHANICAL BATTLE FLEAS.
I'M KEEPING THOSE.
LOOK, I'M NOT ONE TO KINK-SHAME, HELLCOW, BUT THAT'S COMING OUT OF YOUR SALARY.
AND CLAY CLAIMS HE'S FOUND OUR NEXT JOB, BUT IT SOUNDS LIKE A DEATH TRAP TO ME.
YOUR SKEPTICISM IS APPRECIATED, KATE. IN AN ATTEMPT TO FIND FORGOTTEN CORNERS OF S.H.I.E.L.D....
...I'VE BEEN DATA MINING MY MEMORIES, CROSS-REFERENCING THEM WITH THE REAL CLAY QUARTERMAIN'S FIELD RECORDS IN ORDER TO LOCATE ANY ANOMALOUS--
SKIP TO THE END.
I FOUND A TREASURE TROVE OF ONE-OF-A-KIND WEAPONS FOR US TO LIBERATE AND SELL.
DEATH TRAP.
DOES THIS DEATH TRAP HAVE A NAME?

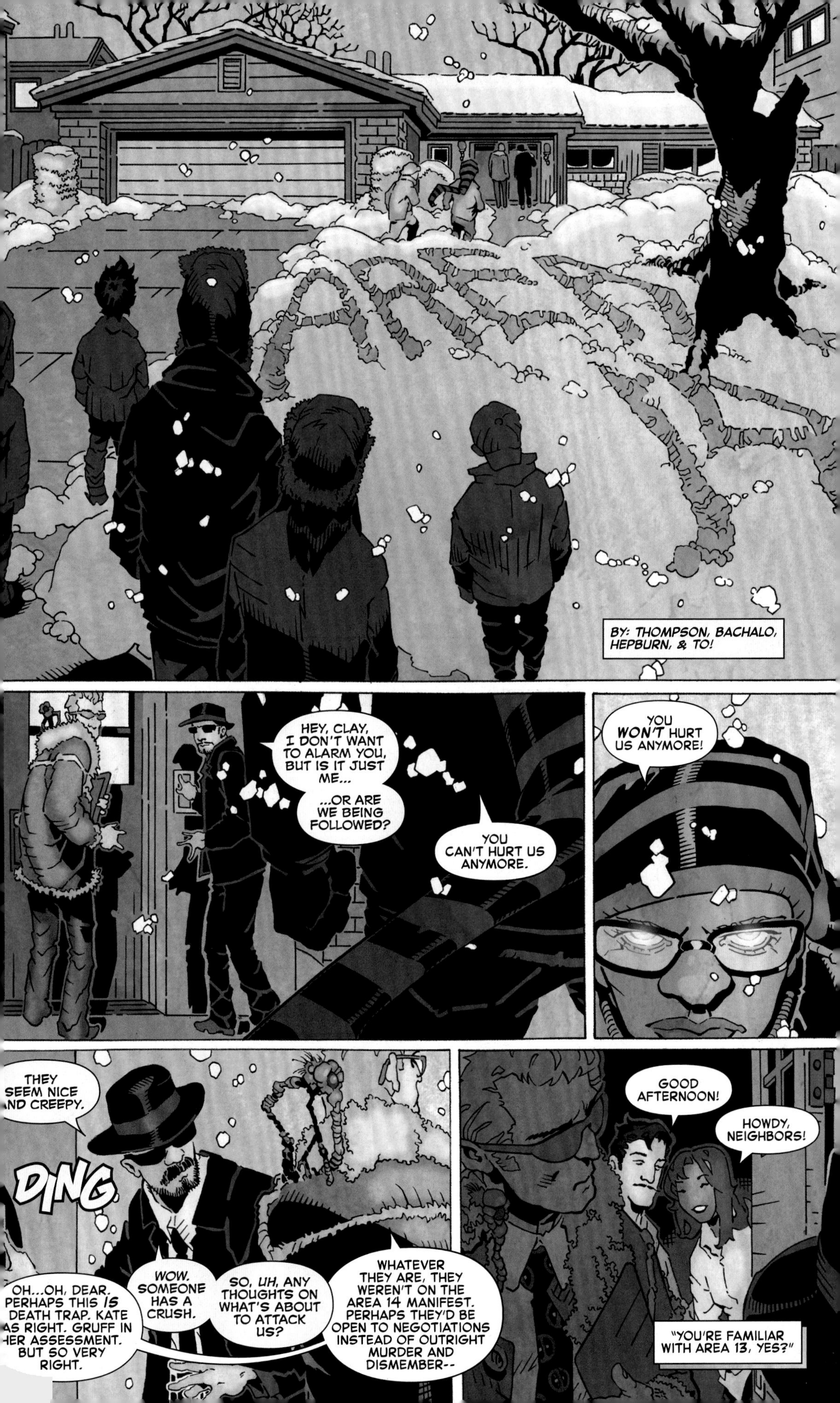

BY: THOMPSON, BACHALO, HEPBURN, & TO!
HEY, CLAY, I DON'T WANT TO ALARM YOU, BUT IS IT JUST ME...
...OR ARE WE BEING FOLLOWED?
YOU CAN'T HURT US ANYMORE.
YOU WON'T HURT US ANYMORE!
THEY SEEM NICE AND CREEPY.
DING
OH...OH, DEAR. PERHAPS THIS IS DEATH TRAP. KATE AS RIGHT. GRUFF IN HER ASSESSMENT. BUT SO VERY RIGHT.
WOW. SOMEONE HAS A CRUSH.
SO, UH, ANY THOUGHTS ON WHAT'S ABOUT TO ATTACK US?
WHATEVER THEY ARE, THEY WEREN'T ON THE AREA 14 MANIFEST. PERHAPS THEY'D BE OPEN TO NEGOTIATIONS INSTEAD OF OUTRIGHT MURDER AND DISMEMBER--
GOOD AFTERNOON!
HOWDY, NEIGHBORS!
"YOU'RE FAMILIAR WITH AREA 13, YES?"

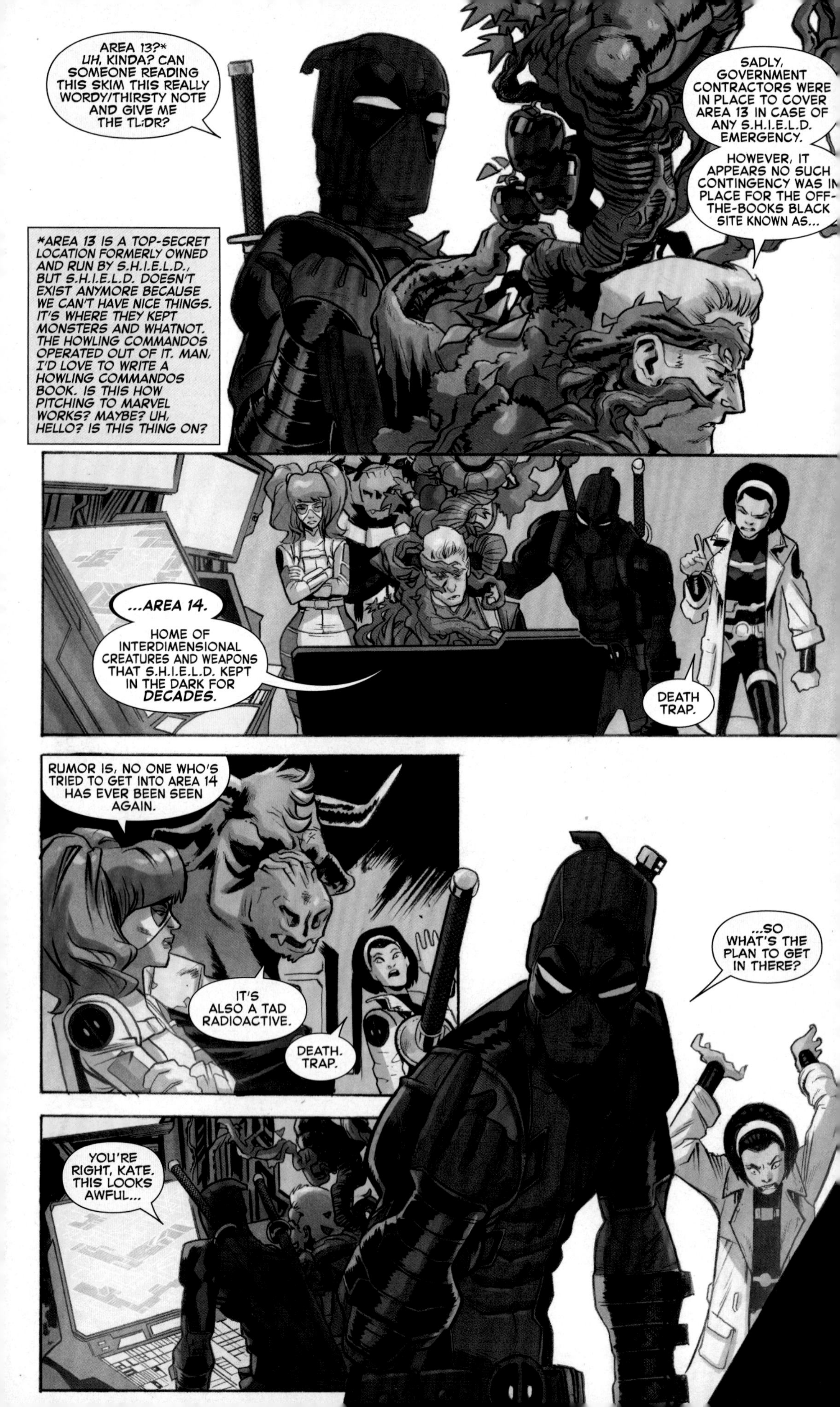

AREA 13?* UH, KINDA? CAN SOMEONE READING THIS SKIM THIS REALLY WORDY/THIRSTY NOTE AND GIVE ME THE TL;DR?
*AREA 13 IS A TOP-SECRET LOCATION FORMERLY OWNED AND RUN BY S.H.I.E.L.D., BUT S.H.I.E.L.D. DOESN'T EXIST ANYMORE BECAUSE WE CAN'T HAVE NICE THINGS. IT'S WHERE THEY KEPT MONSTERS AND WHATNOT. THE HOWLING COMMANDOS OPERATED OUT OF IT. MAN, I'D LOVE TO WRITE A HOWLING COMMANDOS BOOK. IS THIS HOW PITCHING TO MARVEL WORKS? MAYBE? UH, HELLO? IS THIS THING ON?
SADLY, GOVERNMENT CONTRACTORS WERE IN PLACE TO COVER AREA 13 IN CASE OF ANY S.H.I.E.L.D. EMERGENCY.
HOWEVER, IT APPEARS NO SUCH CONTINGENCY WAS IN PLACE FOR THE OFF-THE-BOOKS BLACK SITE KNOWN AS...
...AREA 14.
HOME OF INTERDIMENSIONAL CREATURES AND WEAPONS THAT S.H.I.E.L.D. KEPT IN THE DARK FOR DECADES.
DEATH TRAP.
RUMOR IS, NO ONE WHO'S TRIED TO GET INTO AREA 14 HAS EVER BEEN SEEN AGAIN.
IT'S ALSO A TAD RADIOACTIVE.
DEATH. TRAP.
...SO WHAT'S THE PLAN TO GET IN THERE?
YOU'RE RIGHT, KATE. THIS LOOKS AWFUL...

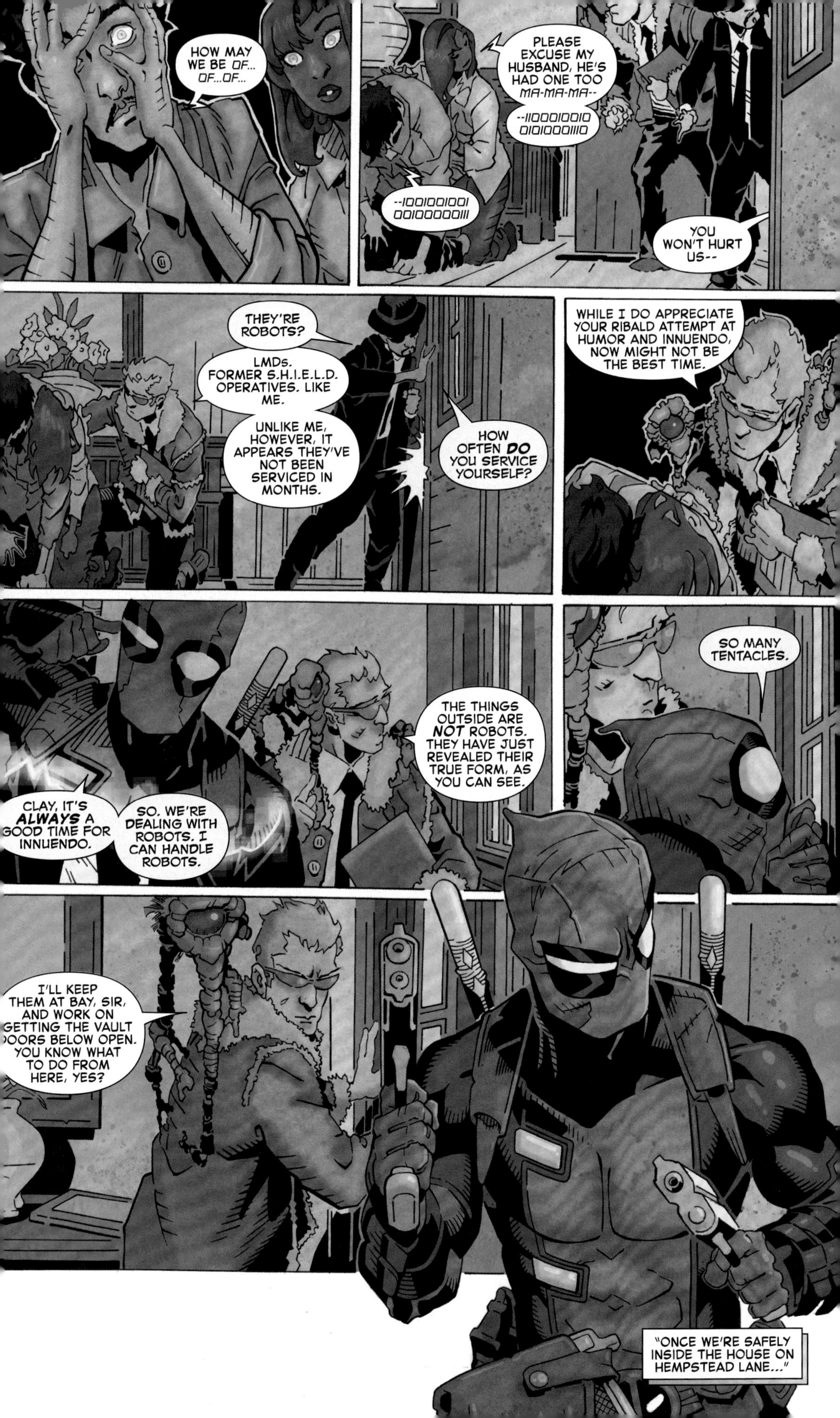
HOW MAY WE BE OF... OF...OF...
PLEASE EXCUSE MY HUSBAND, HE'S HAD ONE TOO MA-MA-MA--
--1100010010 0101000110
--100100100 1001000000111
YOU WON'T HURT US--
THEY'RE ROBOTS?
LMDs. FORMER S.H.I.E.L.D. OPERATIVES. LIKE ME.
UNLIKE ME, HOWEVER, IT APPEARS THEY'VE NOT BEEN SERVICED IN MONTHS.
HOW OFTEN DO YOU SERVICE YOURSELF?
WHILE I DO APPRECIATE YOUR RIBALD ATTEMPT AT HUMOR AND INNUENDO, NOW MIGHT NOT BE THE BEST TIME.
CLAY, IT'S ALWAYS A GOOD TIME FOR INNUENDO.
SO. WE'RE DEALING WITH ROBOTS. I CAN HANDLE ROBOTS.
THE THINGS OUTSIDE ARE NOT ROBOTS. THEY HAVE JUST REVEALED THEIR TRUE FORM, AS YOU CAN SEE.
SO MANY TENTACLES.
I'LL KEEP THEM AT BAY, SIR, AND WORK ON GETTING THE VAULT DOORS BELOW OPEN. YOU KNOW WHAT TO DO FROM HERE, YES?
"ONCE WE'RE SAFELY INSIDE THE HOUSE ON HEMPSTEAD LANE..."

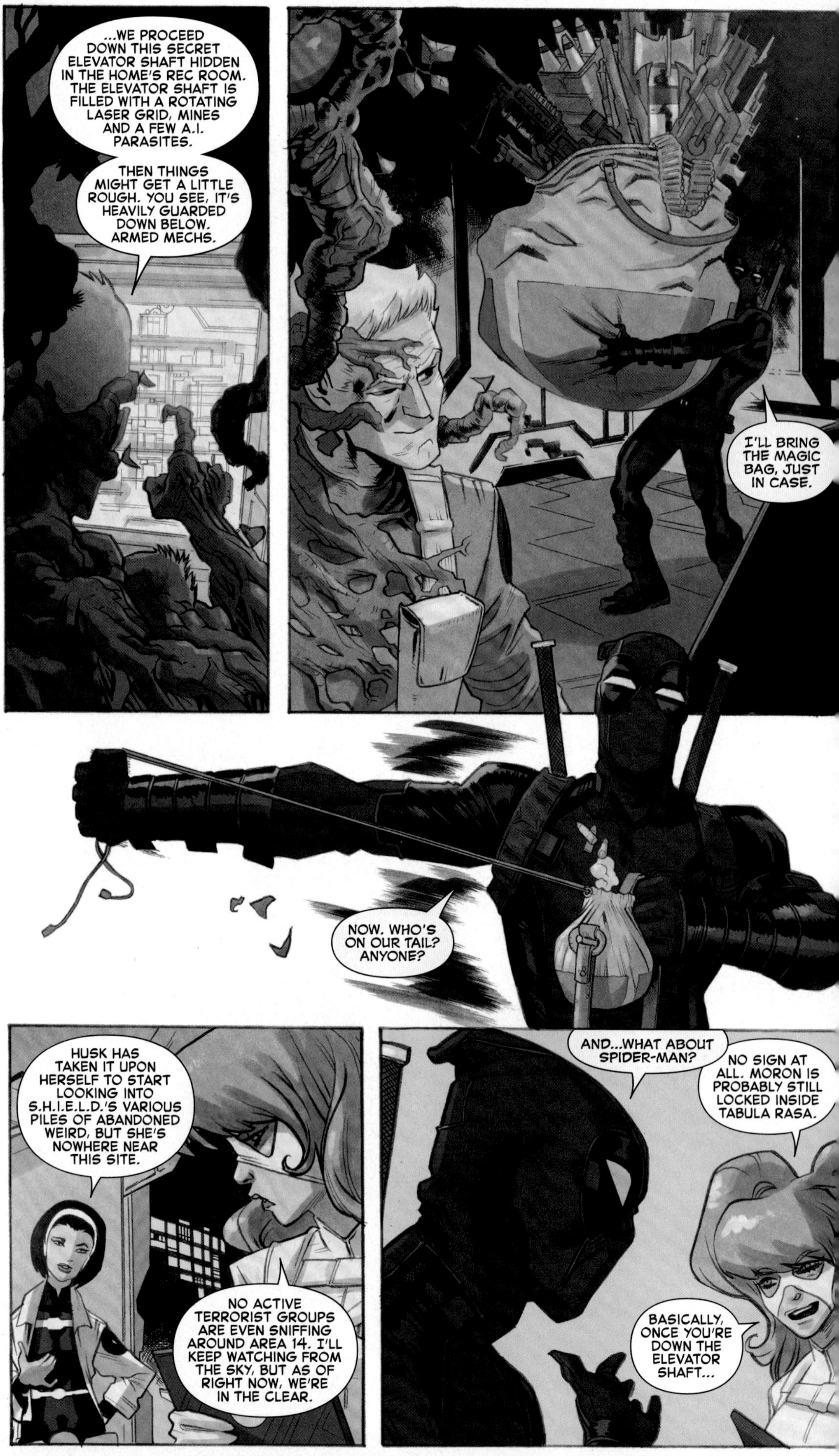
...WE PROCEED DOWN THIS SECRET ELEVATOR SHAFT HIDDEN IN THE HOME'S REC ROOM. THE ELEVATOR SHAFT IS FILLED WITH A ROTATING LASER GRID, MINES AND A FEW A.I. PARASITES.
THEN THINGS MIGHT GET A LITTLE ROUGH. YOU SEE, IT'S HEAVILY GUARDED DOWN BELOW. ARMED MECHS.
I'LL BRING THE MAGIC BAG, JUST IN CASE.
NOW. WHO'S ON OUR TAIL? ANYONE?
HUSK HAS TAKEN IT UPON HERSELF TO START LOOKING INTO S.H.I.E.L.D.'S VARIOUS PILES OF ABANDONED WEIRD, BUT SHE'S NOWHERE NEAR THIS SITE.
NO ACTIVE TERRORIST GROUPS ARE EVEN SNIFFING AROUND AREA 14. I'LL KEEP WATCHING FROM THE SKY, BUT AS OF RIGHT NOW, WE'RE IN THE CLEAR.
AND...WHAT ABOUT SPIDER-MAN?
NO SIGN AT ALL. MORON IS PROBABLY STILL LOCKED INSIDE TABULA RASA.
BASICALLY, ONCE YOU'RE DOWN THE ELEVATOR SHAFT...

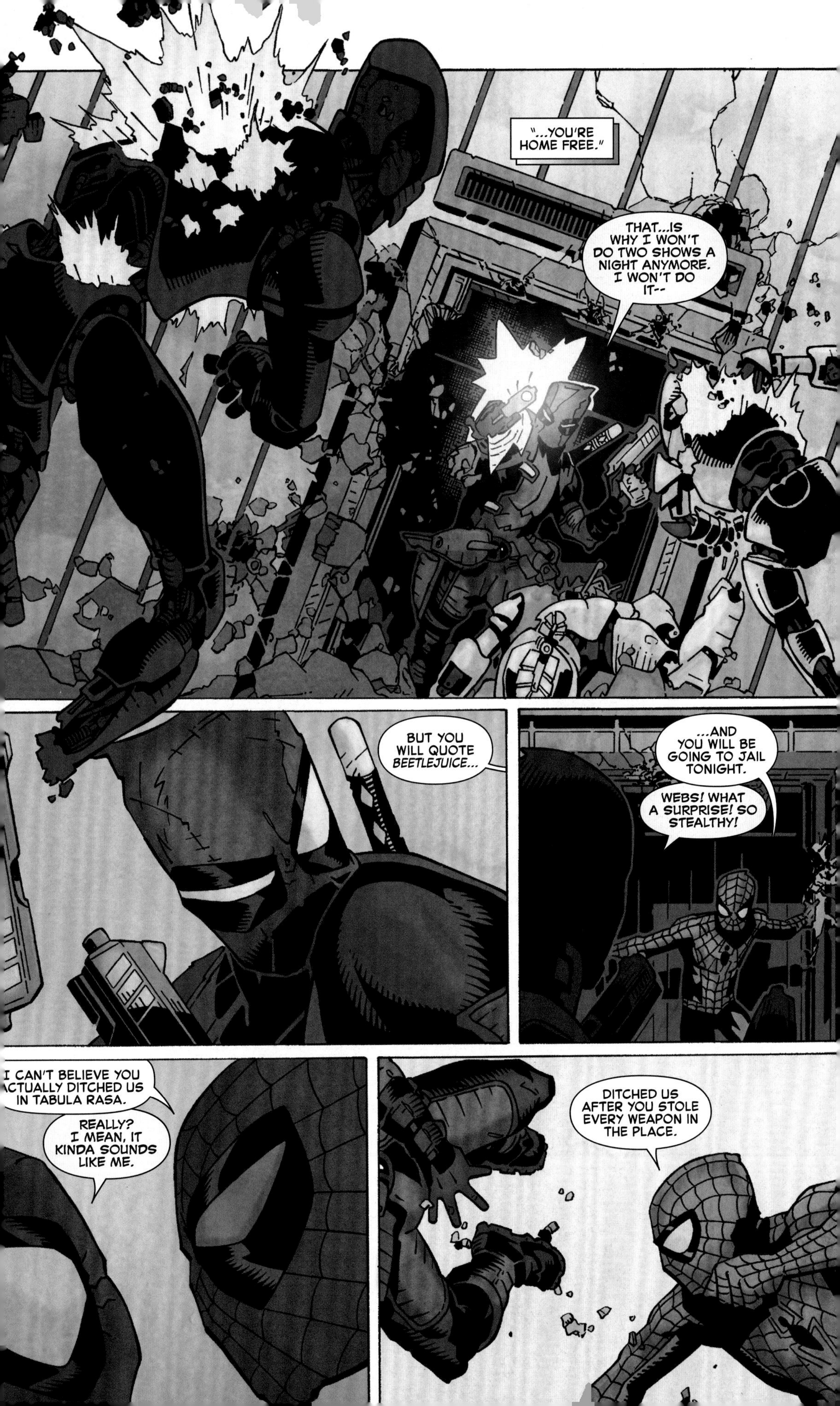
"...YOU'RE HOME FREE."
THAT...IS WHY I WON'T DO TWO SHOWS A NIGHT ANYMORE. I WON'T DO IT--
BUT YOU WILL QUOTE *BEETLEJUICE*...
...AND YOU WILL BE GOING TO JAIL TONIGHT.
WEBS! WHAT A SURPRISE! SO STEALTHY!
I CAN'T BELIEVE YOU ACTUALLY DITCHED US IN TABULA RASA.
REALLY? I MEAN, IT KINDA SOUNDS LIKE ME.
DITCHED US AFTER YOU STOLE EVERY WEAPON IN THE PLACE.

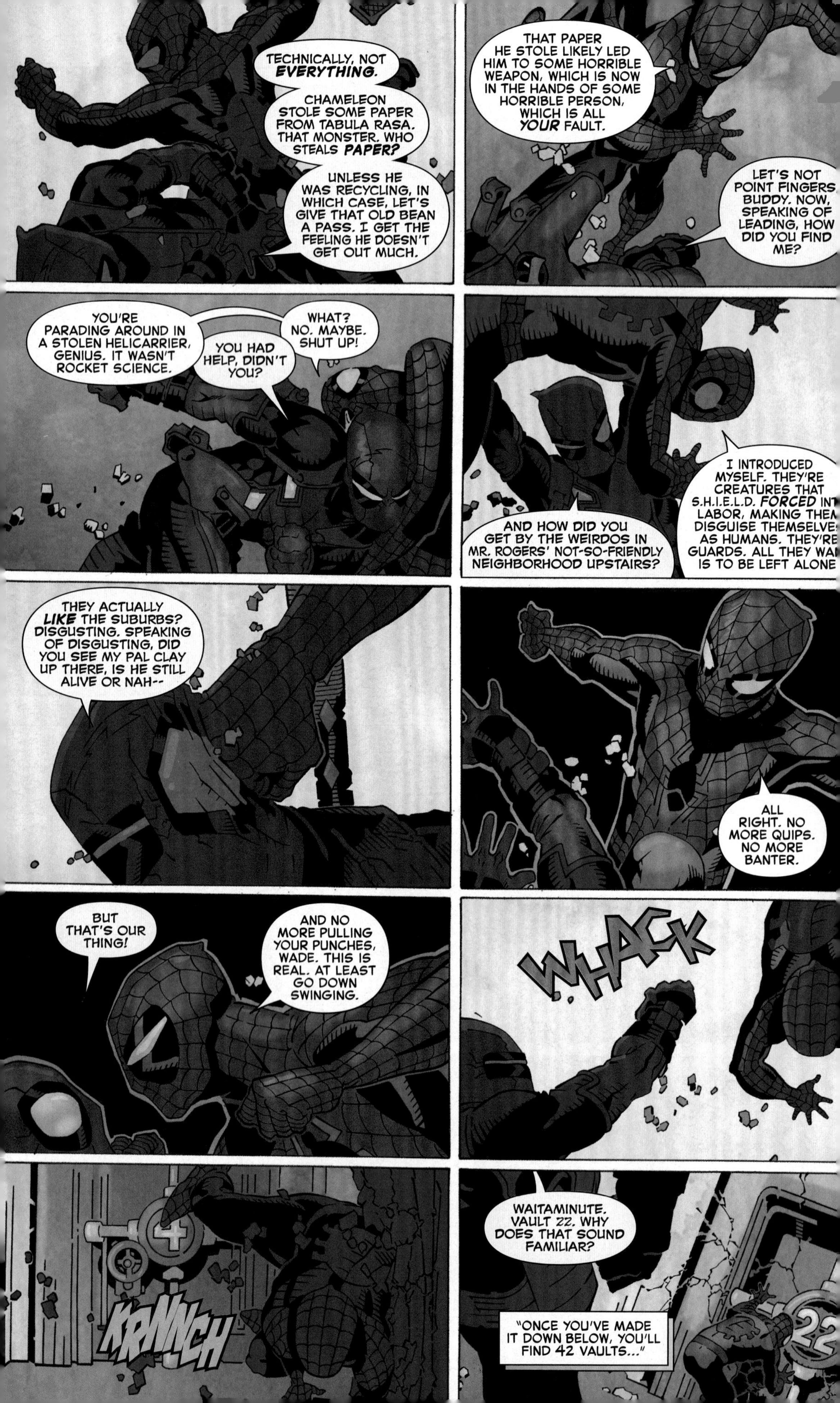
TECHNICALLY, NOT EVERYTHING.
CHAMELEON STOLE SOME PAPER FROM TABULA RASA. THAT MONSTER. WHO STEALS PAPER?
UNLESS HE WAS RECYCLING, IN WHICH CASE, LET'S GIVE THAT OLD BEAN A PASS. I GET THE FEELING HE DOESN'T GET OUT MUCH.
THAT PAPER HE STOLE LIKELY LED HIM TO SOME HORRIBLE WEAPON, WHICH IS NOW IN THE HANDS OF SOME HORRIBLE PERSON, WHICH IS ALL YOUR FAULT.
LET'S NOT POINT FINGERS, BUDDY. NOW, SPEAKING OF LEADING, HOW DID YOU FIND ME?
YOU'RE PARADING AROUND IN A STOLEN HELICARRIER, GENIUS. IT WASN'T ROCKET SCIENCE.
YOU HAD HELP, DIDN'T YOU?
WHAT? NO. MAYBE. SHUT UP!
AND HOW DID YOU GET BY THE WEIRDOS IN MR. ROGERS' NOT-SO-FRIENDLY NEIGHBORHOOD UPSTAIRS?
I INTRODUCED MYSELF. THEY'RE CREATURES THAT S.H.I.E.L.D. FORCED INT LABOR, MAKING THEM DISGUISE THEMSELVES AS HUMANS. THEY'RE GUARDS. ALL THEY WA IS TO BE LEFT ALONE
THEY ACTUALLY LIKE THE SUBURBS? DISGUSTING. SPEAKING OF DISGUSTING, DID YOU SEE MY PAL CLAY UP THERE, IS HE STILL ALIVE OR NAH--
ALL RIGHT. NO MORE QUIPS. NO MORE BANTER.
BUT THAT'S OUR THING!
AND NO MORE PULLING YOUR PUNCHES, WADE. THIS IS REAL. AT LEAST GO DOWN SWINGING.
WHACK
KRNNCH
WAITAMINUTE. VAULT 22. WHY DOES THAT SOUND FAMILIAR?
"ONCE YOU'VE MADE IT DOWN BELOW, YOU'LL FIND 42 VAULTS..."
22

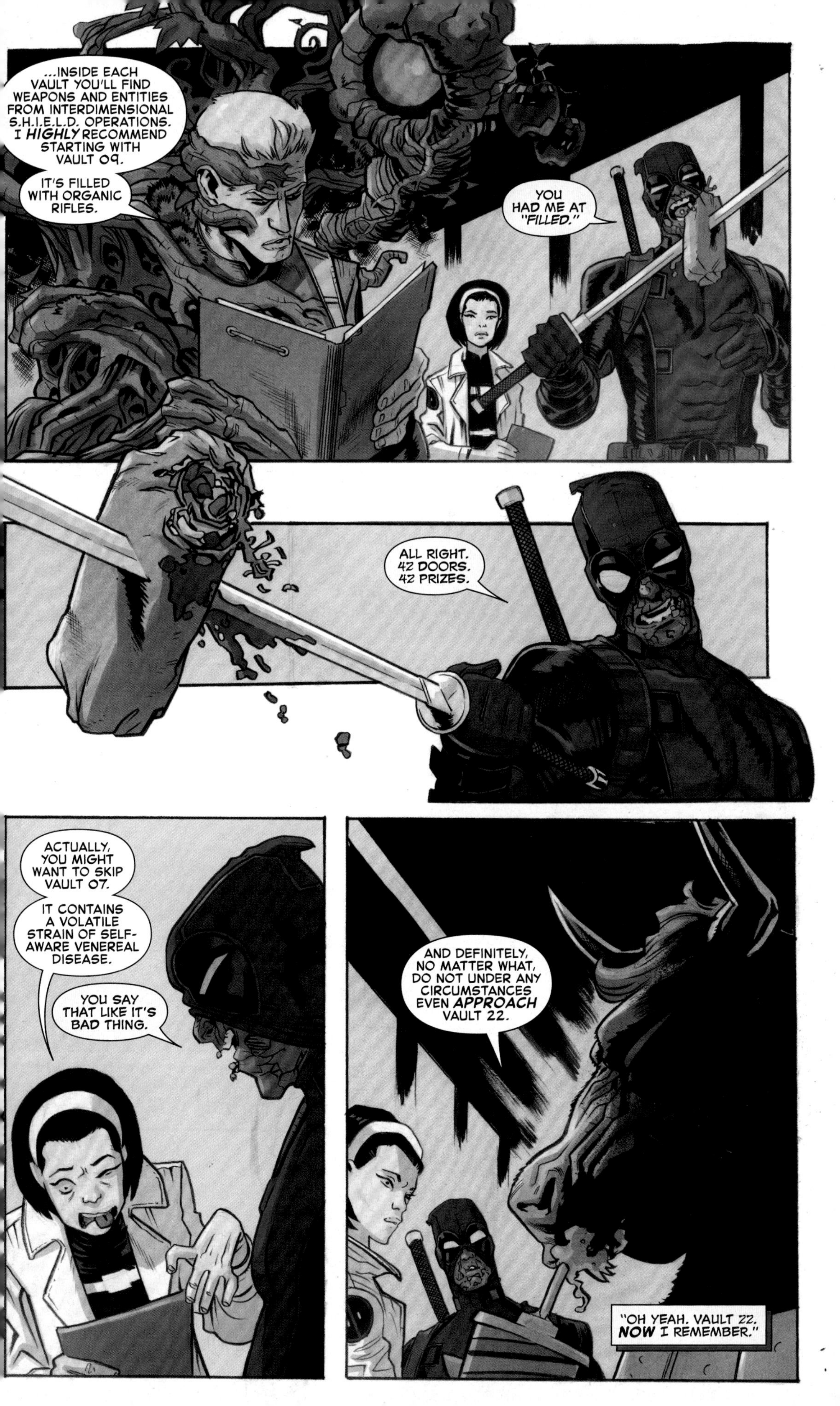

...INSIDE EACH VAULT YOU'LL FIND WEAPONS AND ENTITIES FROM INTERDIMENSIONAL S.H.I.E.L.D. OPERATIONS. I *HIGHLY* RECOMMEND STARTING WITH VAULT 09.
IT'S FILLED WITH ORGANIC RIFLES.
YOU HAD ME AT *"FILLED."*
ALL RIGHT. 42 **DOORS.** 42 PRIZES.
ACTUALLY, YOU MIGHT WANT TO SKIP VAULT 07.
IT CONTAINS A VOLATILE STRAIN OF SELF-AWARE VENEREAL DISEASE.
YOU SAY THAT LIKE IT'S BAD THING.
AND DEFINITELY, NO MATTER WHAT, DO NOT UNDER ANY CIRCUMSTANCES EVEN *APPROACH* VAULT 22.
"OH YEAH. VAULT 22. ***NOW*** I REMEMBER."

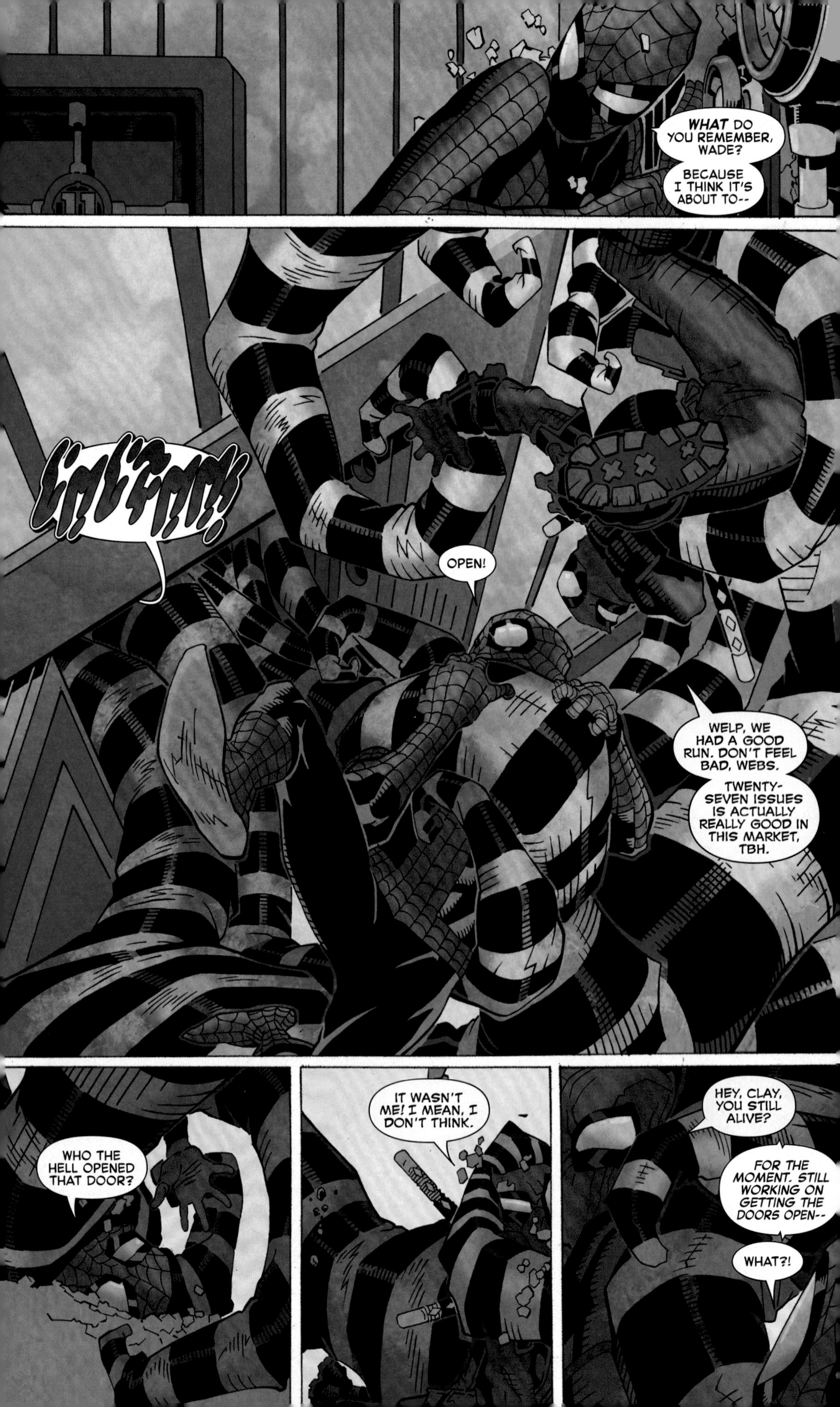
WHAT DO YOU REMEMBER, WADE?
BECAUSE I THINK IT'S ABOUT TO--
OPEN!
WELP, WE HAD A GOOD RUN. DON'T FEEL BAD, WEBS.
TWENTY-SEVEN ISSUES IS ACTUALLY REALLY GOOD IN THIS MARKET, TBH.
WHO THE HELL OPENED THAT DOOR?
IT WASN'T ME! I MEAN, I DON'T THINK.
HEY, CLAY, YOU STILL ALIVE?
FOR THE MOMENT. STILL WORKING ON GETTING THE DOORS OPEN--
WHAT?!

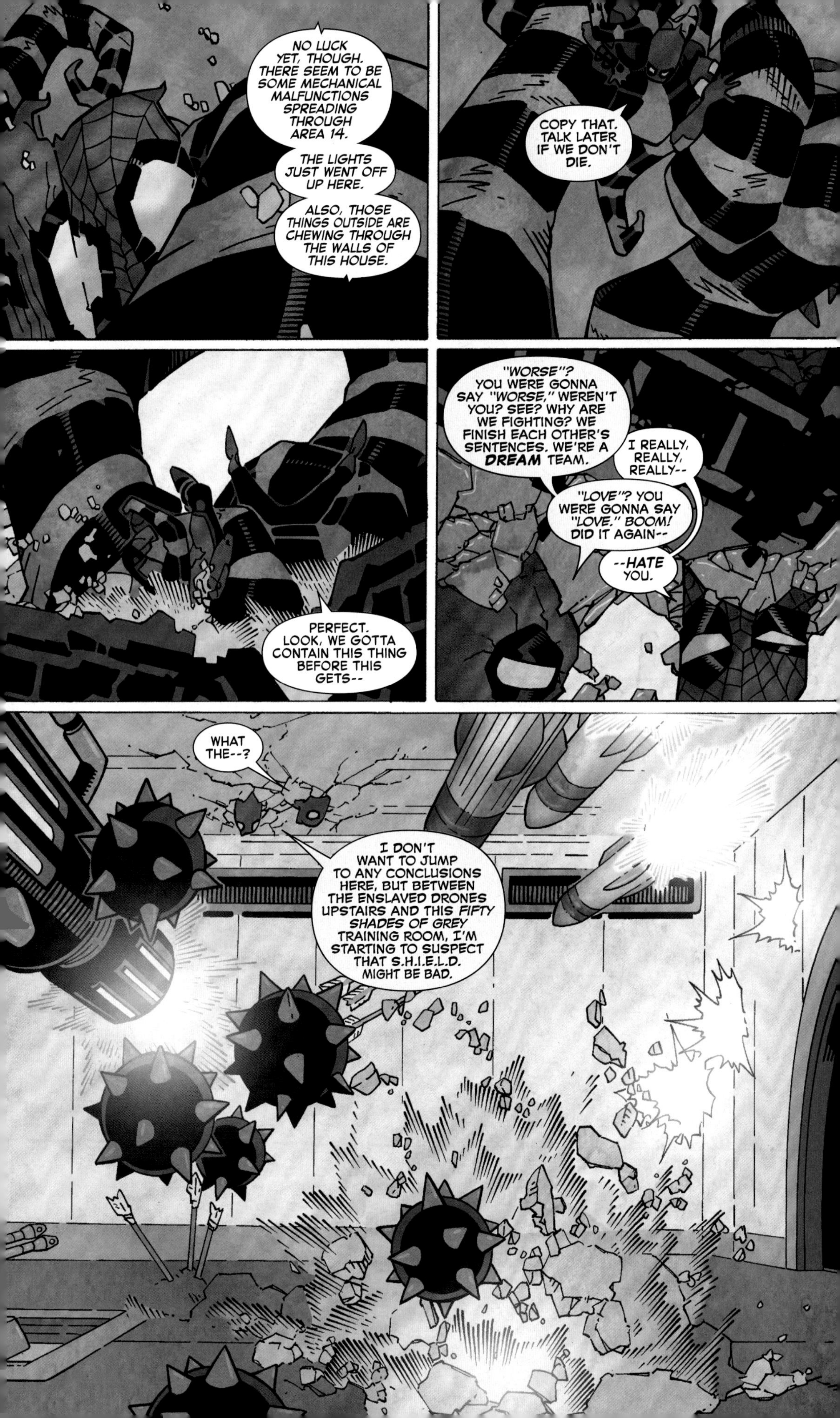
NO LUCK YET, THOUGH. THERE SEEM TO BE SOME MECHANICAL MALFUNCTIONS SPREADING THROUGH AREA 14.
THE LIGHTS JUST WENT OFF UP HERE.
ALSO, THOSE THINGS OUTSIDE ARE CHEWING THROUGH THE WALLS OF THIS HOUSE.
COPY THAT. TALK LATER IF WE DON'T DIE.
PERFECT. LOOK, WE GOTTA CONTAIN THIS THING BEFORE THIS GETS--
"WORSE"? YOU WERE GONNA SAY "WORSE," WEREN'T YOU? SEE? WHY ARE WE FIGHTING? WE FINISH EACH OTHER'S SENTENCES. WE'RE A DREAM TEAM.
I REALLY, REALLY, REALLY--
"LOVE"? YOU WERE GONNA SAY "LOVE." BOOM! DID IT AGAIN--
--HATE YOU.
WHAT THE--?
I DON'T WANT TO JUMP TO ANY CONCLUSIONS HERE, BUT BETWEEN THE ENSLAVED DRONES UPSTAIRS AND THIS FIFTY SHADES OF GREY TRAINING ROOM, I'M STARTING TO SUSPECT THAT S.H.I.E.L.D. MIGHT BE BAD.

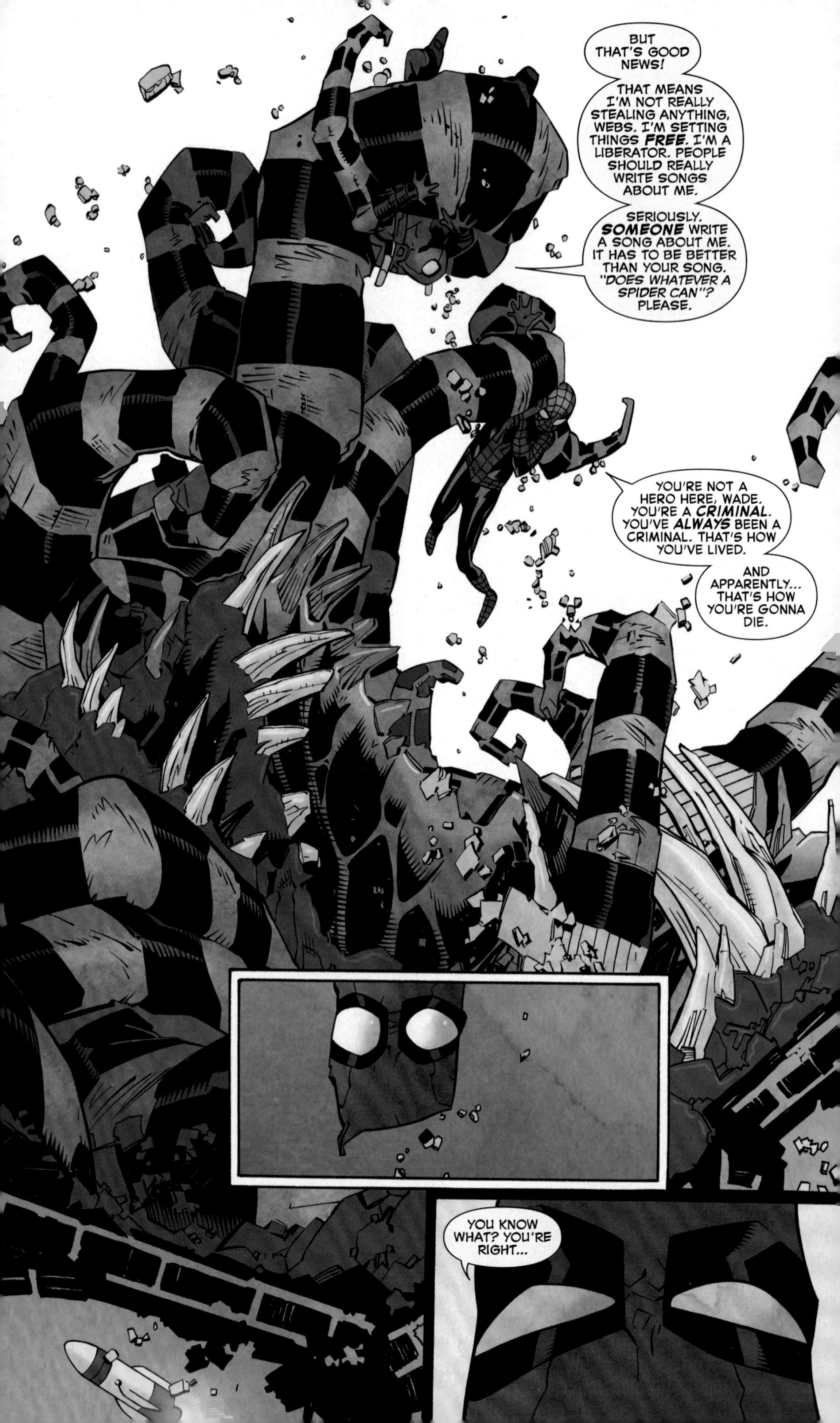
BUT THAT'S GOOD NEWS!
THAT MEANS I'M NOT REALLY STEALING ANYTHING, WEBS. I'M SETTING THINGS FREE. I'M A LIBERATOR. PEOPLE SHOULD REALLY WRITE SONGS ABOUT ME.
SERIOUSLY. SOMEONE WRITE A SONG ABOUT ME. IT HAS TO BE BETTER THAN YOUR SONG. "DOES WHATEVER A SPIDER CAN"? PLEASE.
YOU'RE NOT A HERO HERE, WADE. YOU'RE A CRIMINAL. YOU'VE ALWAYS BEEN A CRIMINAL. THAT'S HOW YOU'VE LIVED.
AND APPARENTLY... THAT'S HOW YOU'RE GONNA DIE.
YOU KNOW WHAT? YOU'RE RIGHT...

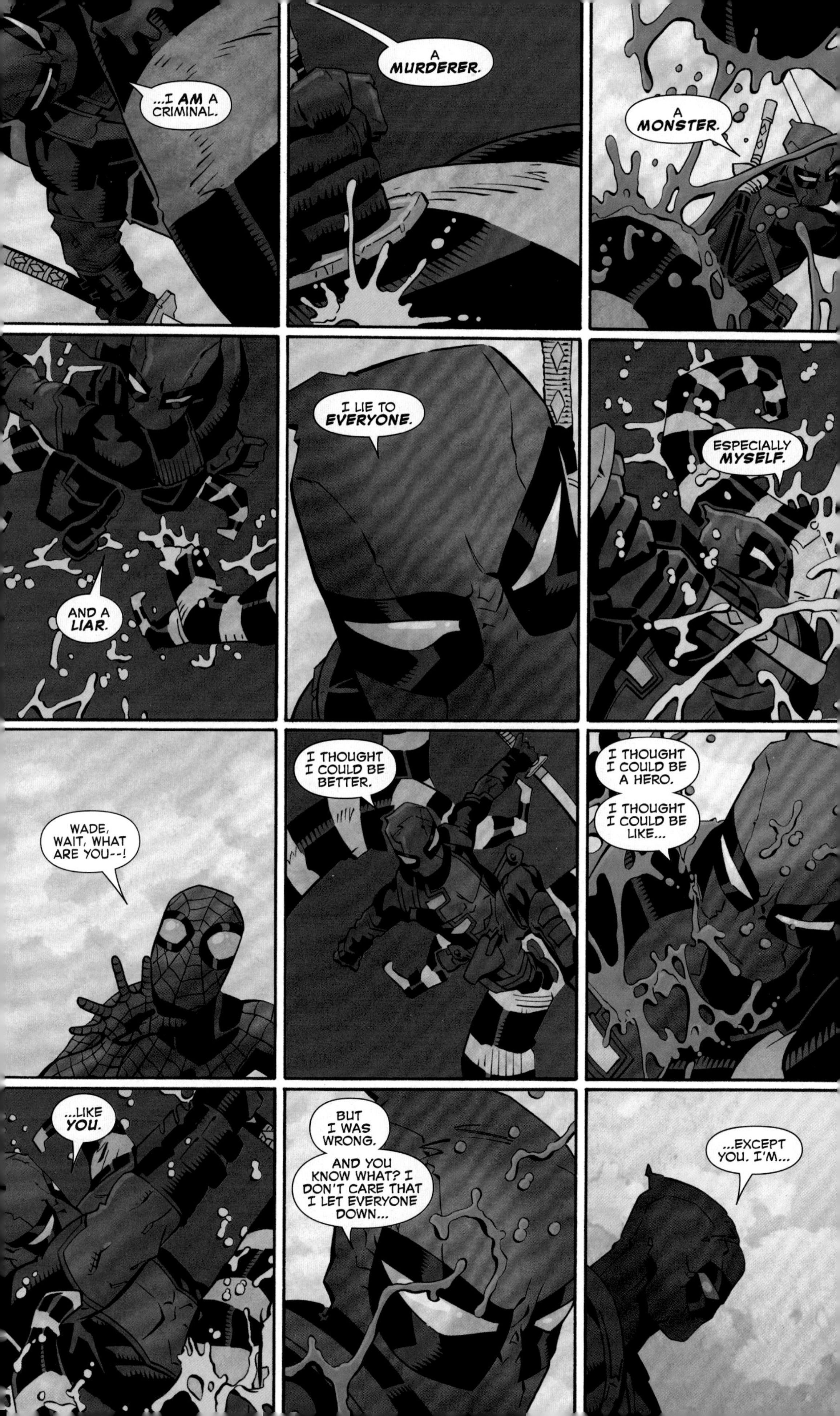
...I AM A CRIMINAL.
A MURDERER.
A MONSTER.
AND A LIAR.
I LIE TO EVERYONE.
ESPECIALLY MYSELF.
WADE, WAIT, WHAT ARE YOU--!
I THOUGHT I COULD BE BETTER.
I THOUGHT I COULD BE A HERO.
I THOUGHT I COULD BE LIKE...
...LIKE YOU.
BUT I WAS WRONG.
AND YOU KNOW WHAT? I DON'T CARE THAT I LET EVERYONE DOWN...
...EXCEPT YOU. I'M...

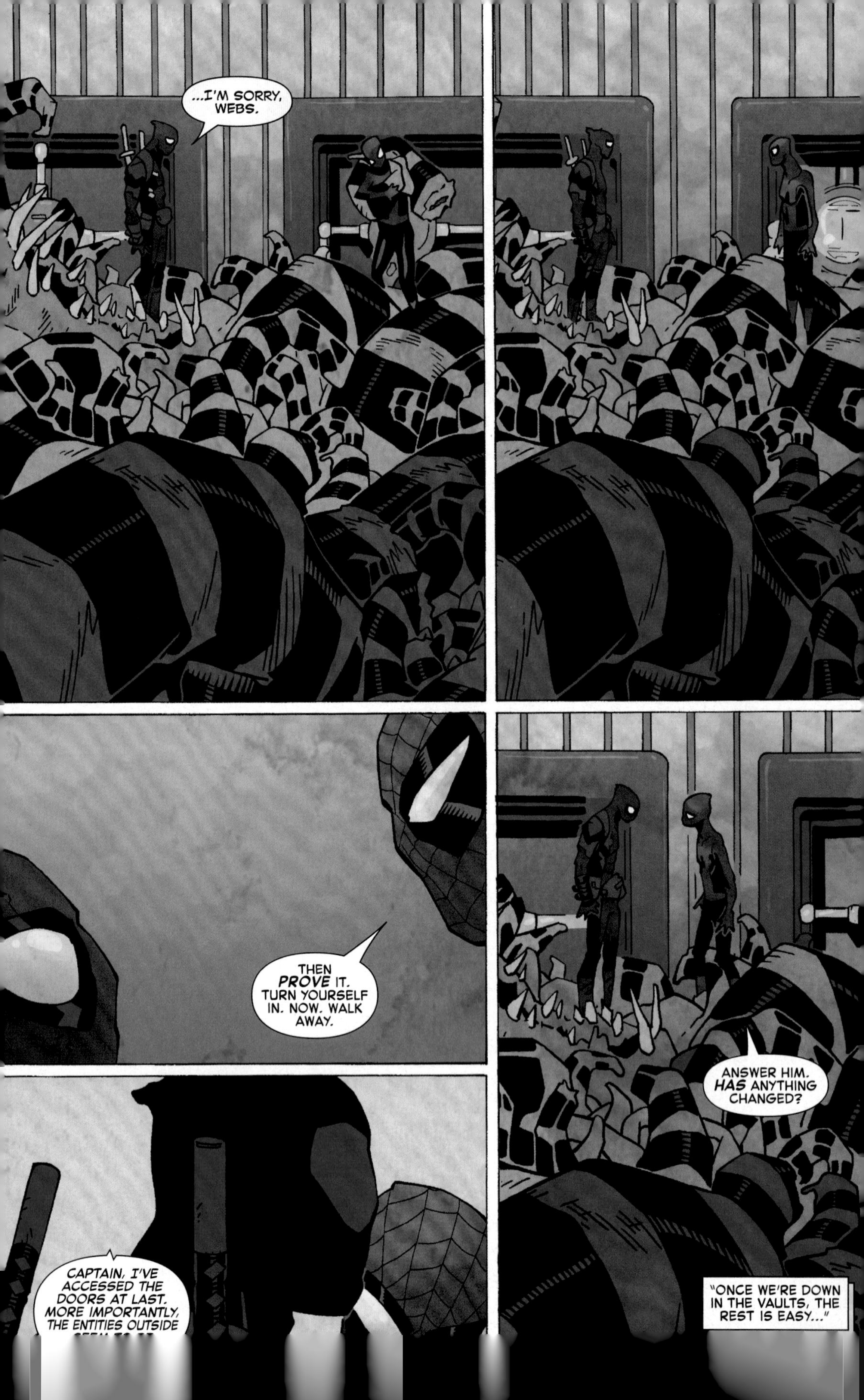
...I'M SORRY, WEBS.
THEN PROVE IT. TURN YOURSELF IN. NOW. WALK AWAY.
ANSWER HIM. HAS ANYTHING CHANGED?
CAPTAIN, I'VE ACCESSED THE DOORS AT LAST. MORE IMPORTANTLY, THE ENTITIES OUTSIDE
"ONCE WE'RE DOWN IN THE VAULTS, THE REST IS EASY..."

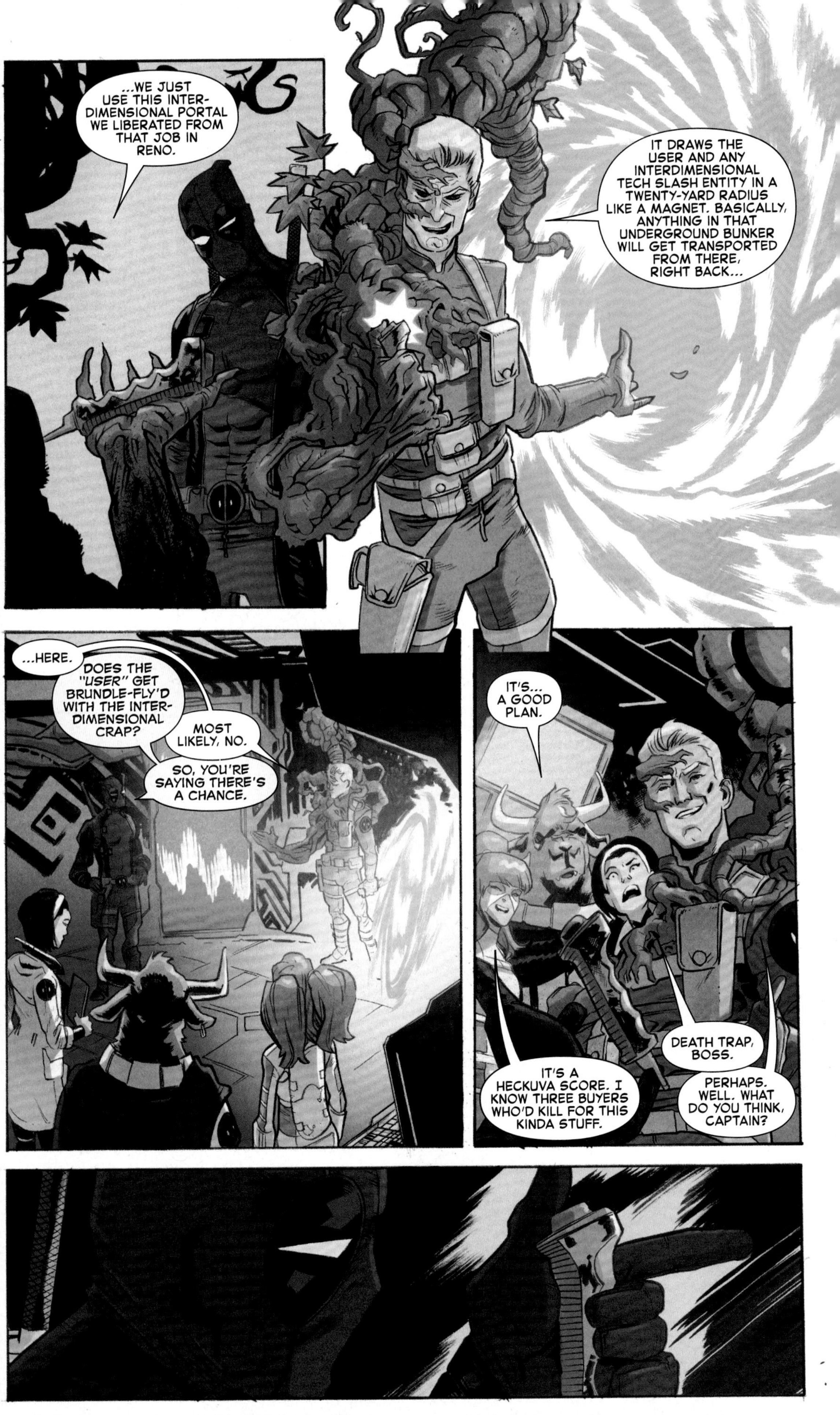
...WE JUST USE THIS INTER-DIMENSIONAL PORTAL WE LIBERATED FROM THAT JOB IN RENO.
IT DRAWS THE USER AND ANY INTERDIMENSIONAL TECH SLASH ENTITY IN A TWENTY-YARD RADIUS LIKE A MAGNET. BASICALLY, ANYTHING IN THAT UNDERGROUND BUNKER WILL GET TRANSPORTED FROM THERE, RIGHT BACK...
...HERE.
DOES THE "USER" GET BRUNDLE-FLY'D WITH THE INTER-DIMENSIONAL CRAP?
MOST LIKELY, NO.
SO, YOU'RE SAYING THERE'S A CHANCE.
IT'S... A GOOD PLAN.
DEATH TRAP, BOSS.
IT'S A HECKUVA SCORE. I KNOW THREE BUYERS WHO'D KILL FOR THIS KINDA STUFF.
PERHAPS. WELL. WHAT DO YOU THINK, CAPTAIN?

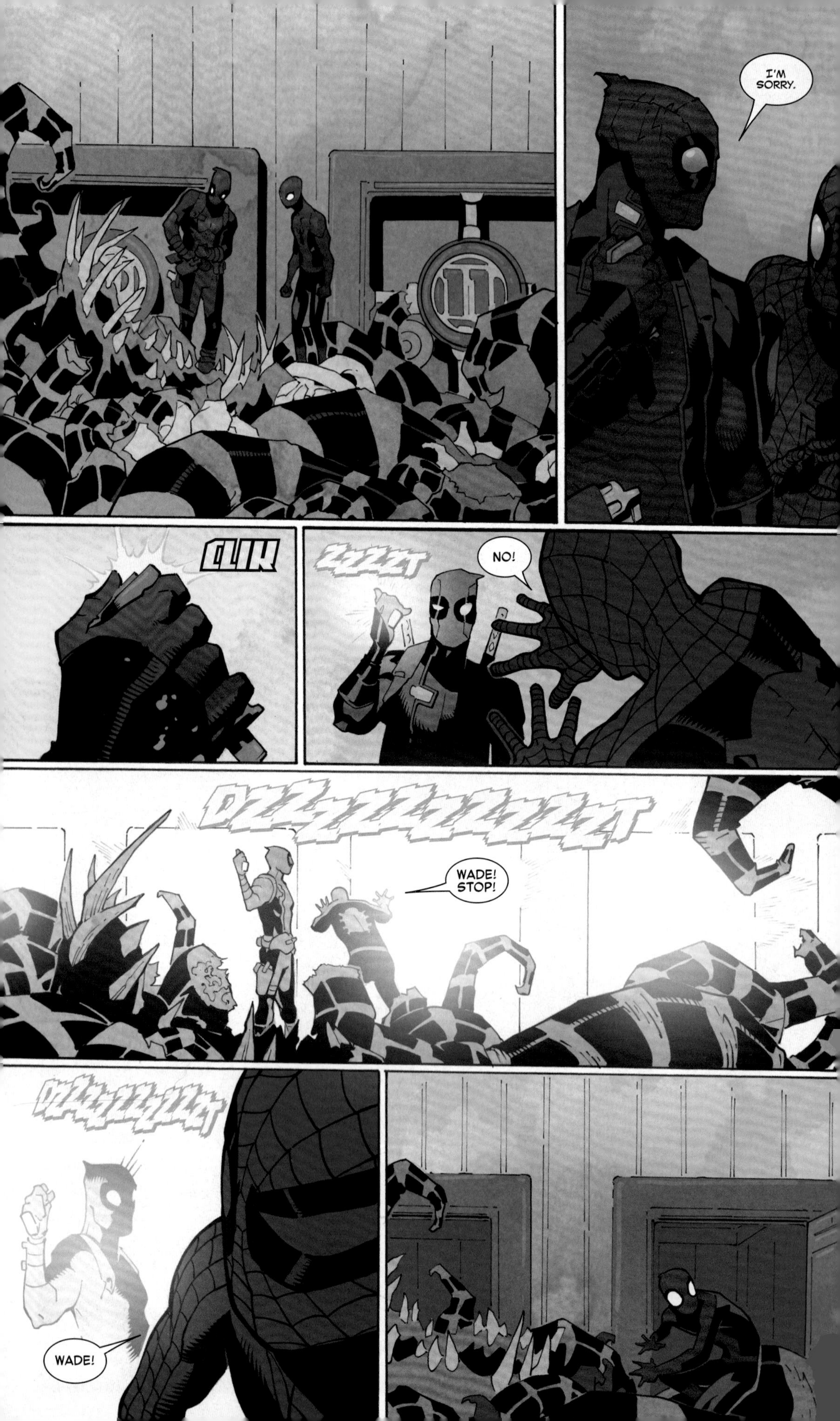
I'M SORRY.
CLIK
ZZZZT
NO!
DZZZZZZZZZZZT
WADE! STOP!
DZZZZZZZZZT
WADE!

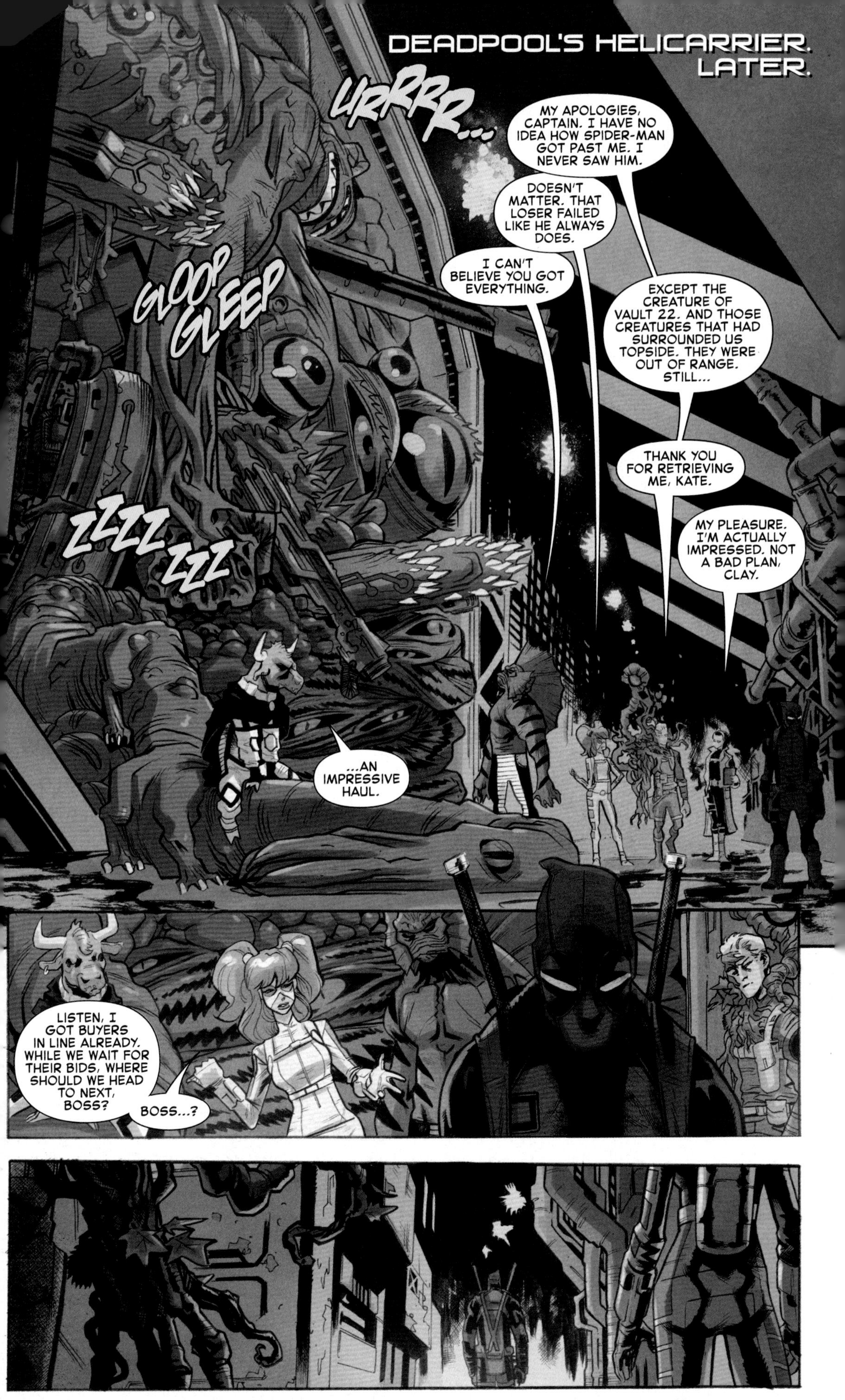
DEADPOOL'S HELICARRIER. LATER.
URRRR...
GLOOP GLEEP
ZZZZ ZZZ
MY APOLOGIES, CAPTAIN. I HAVE NO IDEA HOW SPIDER-MAN GOT PAST ME. I NEVER SAW HIM.
DOESN'T MATTER. THAT LOSER FAILED LIKE HE ALWAYS DOES.
I CAN'T BELIEVE YOU GOT EVERYTHING.
EXCEPT THE CREATURE OF VAULT 22. AND THOSE CREATURES THAT HAD SURROUNDED US TOPSIDE. THEY WERE OUT OF RANGE. STILL...
THANK YOU FOR RETRIEVING ME, KATE.
MY PLEASURE. I'M ACTUALLY IMPRESSED. NOT A BAD PLAN, CLAY.
...AN IMPRESSIVE HAUL.
LISTEN, I GOT BUYERS IN LINE ALREADY. WHILE WE WAIT FOR THEIR BIDS, WHERE SHOULD WE HEAD TO NEXT, BOSS?
BOSS...?

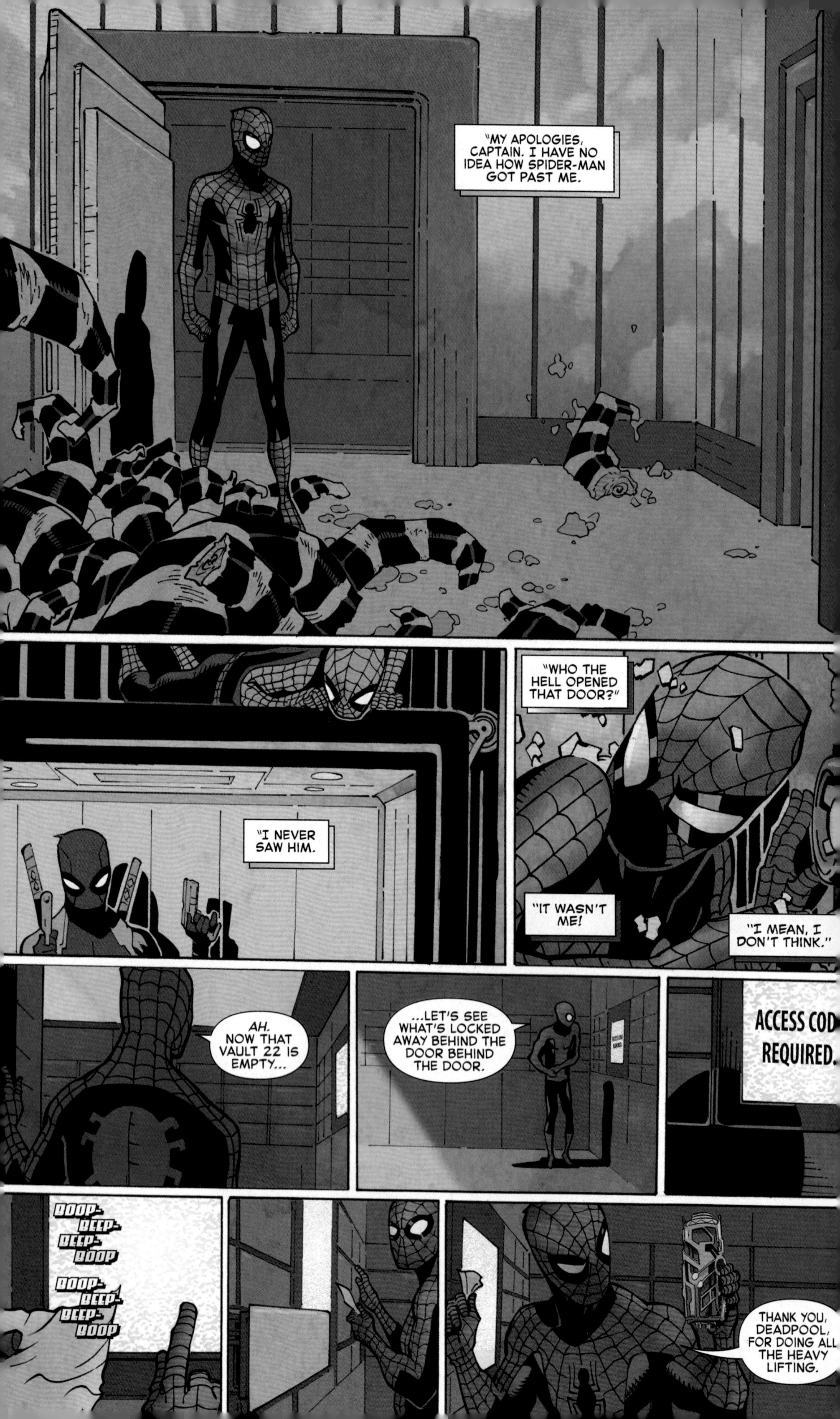

"MY APOLOGIES, CAPTAIN. I HAVE NO IDEA HOW SPIDER-MAN GOT PAST ME.
"WHO THE HELL OPENED THAT DOOR?"
"I NEVER SAW HIM.
"IT WASN'T ME!
"I MEAN, I DON'T THINK."
AH. NOW THAT VAULT 22 IS EMPTY...
...LET'S SEE WHAT'S LOCKED AWAY BEHIND THE DOOR BEHIND THE DOOR.
ACCESS COD REQUIRED.
BOOP- BEEP- BEEP- BOOP
BOOP- BEEP- BEEP- BOOP
THANK YOU, DEADPOOL, FOR DOING ALL THE HEAVY LIFTING.

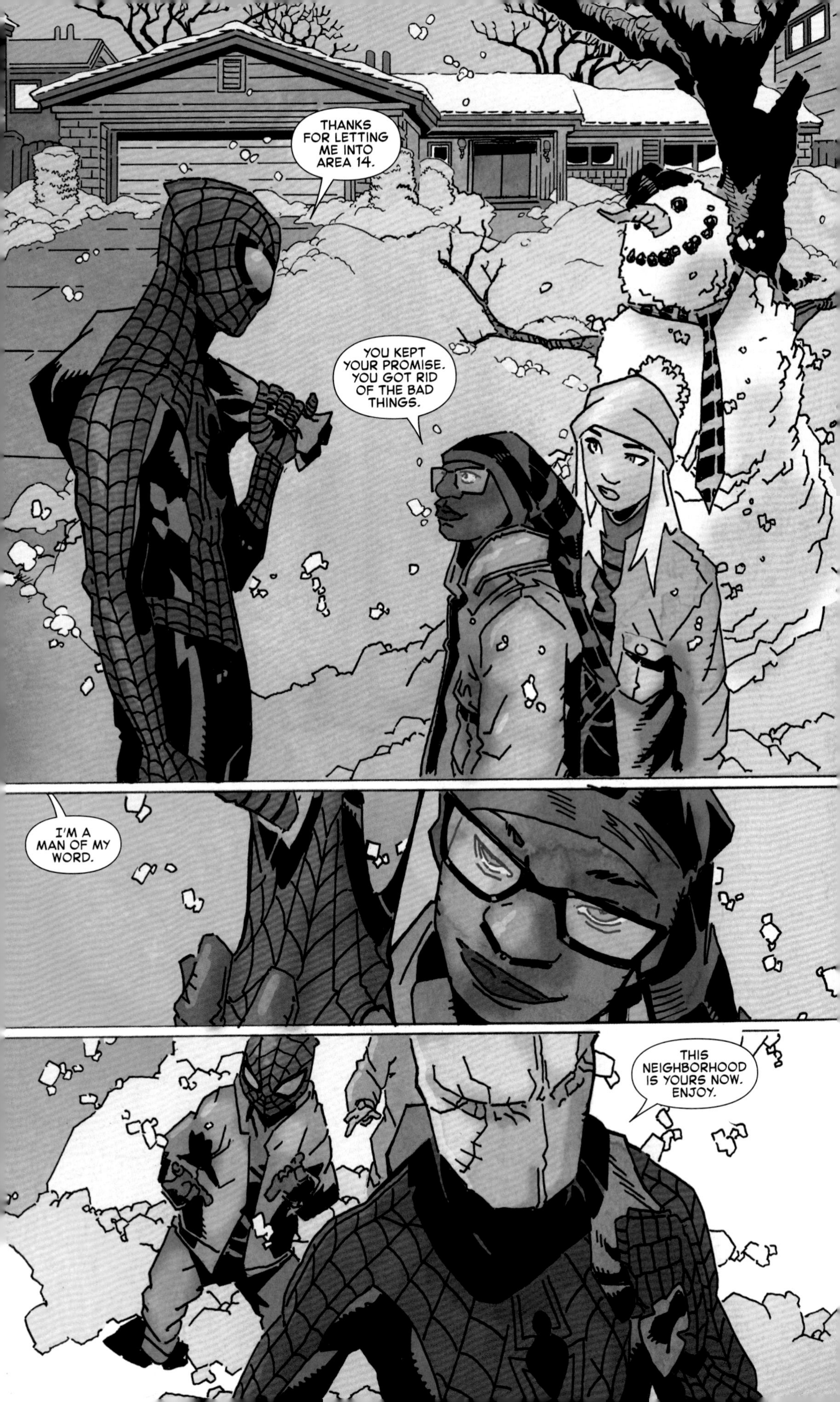
THANKS FOR LETTING ME INTO AREA 14.
YOU KEPT YOUR PROMISE. YOU GOT RID OF THE BAD THINGS.
I'M A MAN OF MY WORD.
THIS NEIGHBORHOOD IS YOURS NOW. ENJOY.

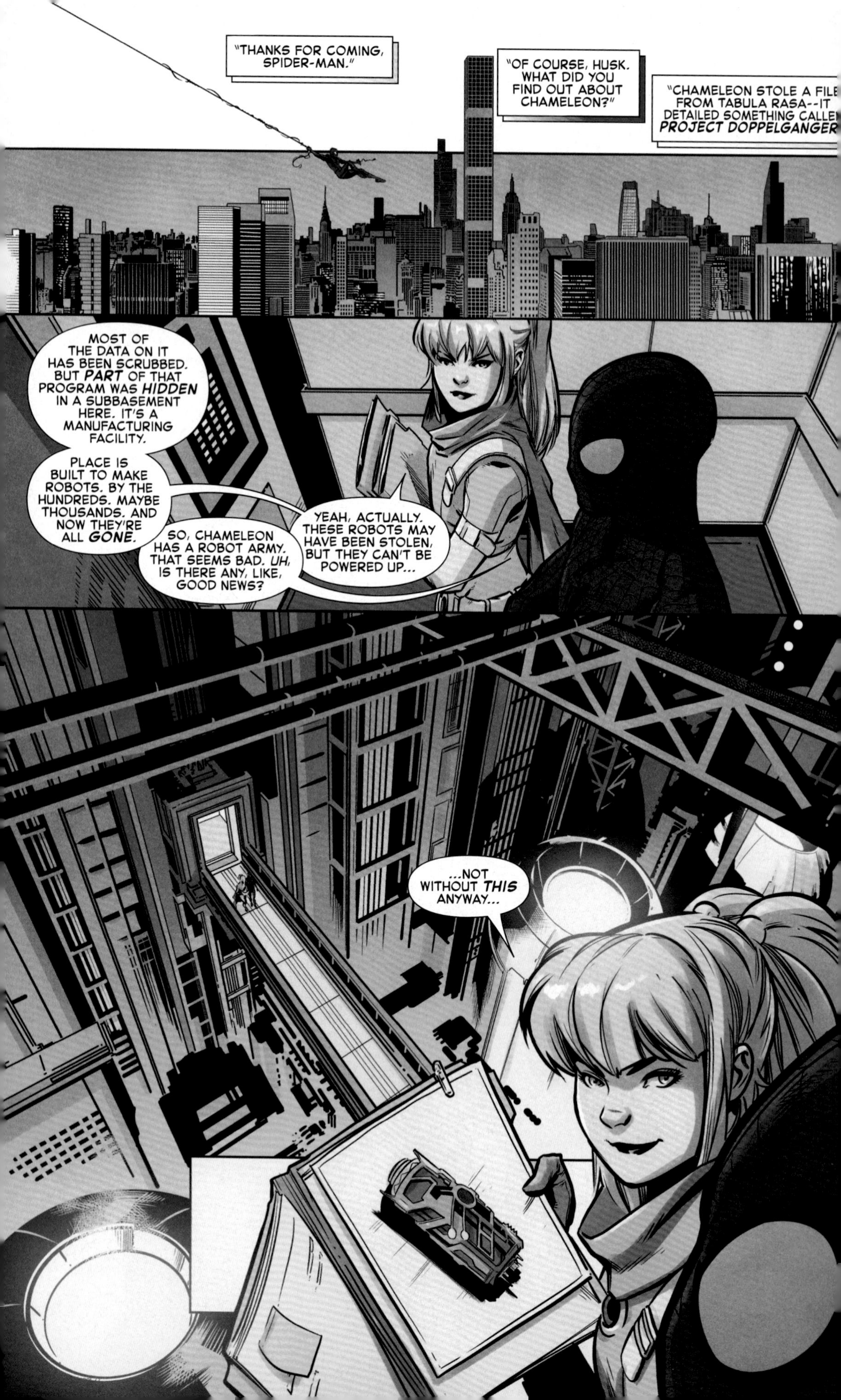
"THANKS FOR COMING, SPIDER-MAN."
"OF COURSE, HUSK. WHAT DID YOU FIND OUT ABOUT CHAMELEON?"
"CHAMELEON STOLE A FILE FROM TABULA RASA--IT DETAILED SOMETHING CALLED *PROJECT DOPPELGANGER*
MOST OF THE DATA ON IT HAS BEEN SCRUBBED. BUT *PART* OF THAT PROGRAM WAS *HIDDEN* IN A SUBBASEMENT HERE. IT'S A MANUFACTURING FACILITY.
PLACE IS BUILT TO MAKE ROBOTS. BY THE HUNDREDS. MAYBE THOUSANDS. AND NOW THEY'RE ALL *GONE*.
SO, CHAMELEON HAS A ROBOT ARMY. THAT SEEMS BAD. *UH*, IS THERE ANY, LIKE, GOOD NEWS?
YEAH, ACTUALLY. THESE ROBOTS MAY HAVE BEEN STOLEN, BUT THEY CAN'T BE POWERED UP...
...NOT WITHOUT *THIS* ANYWAY...

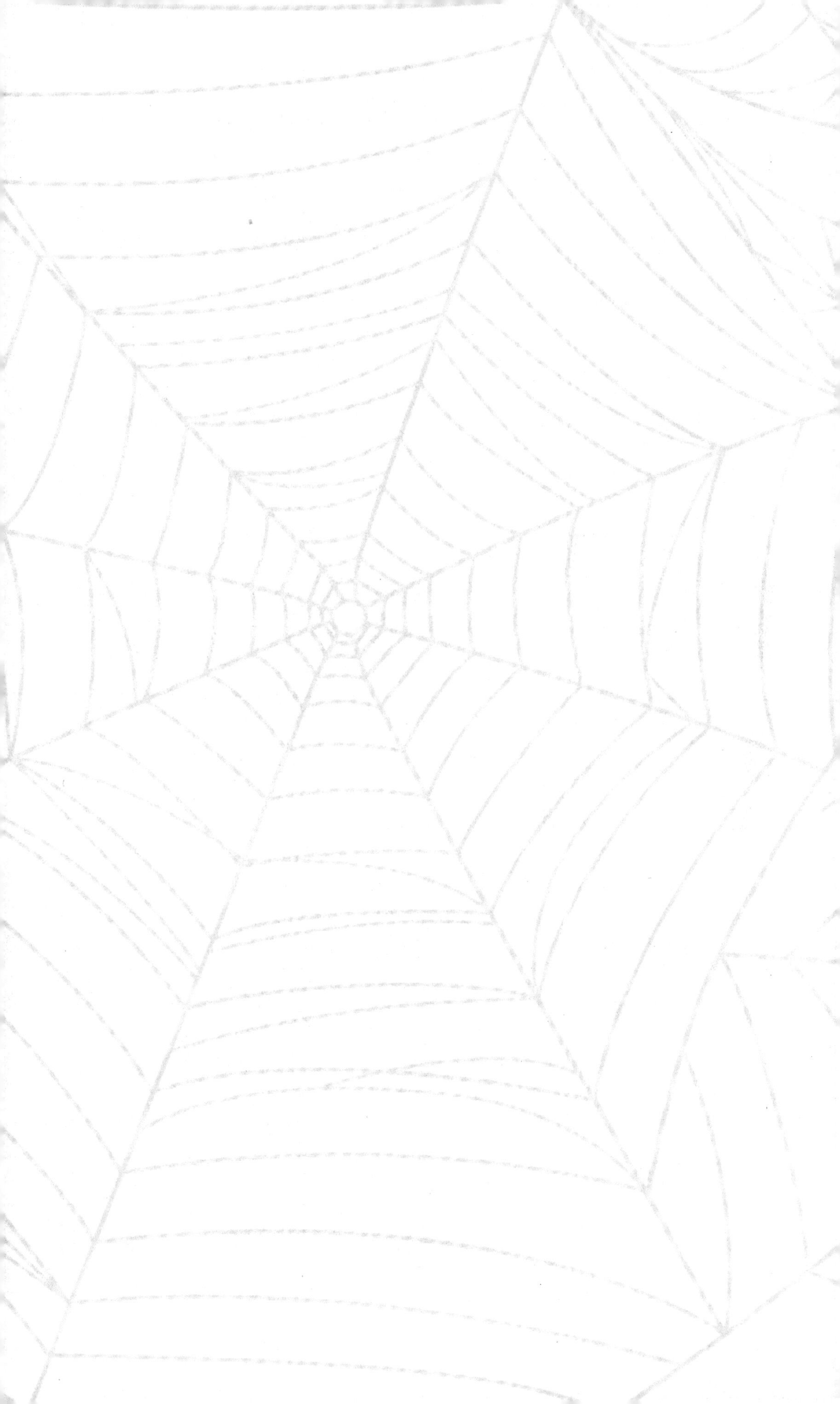

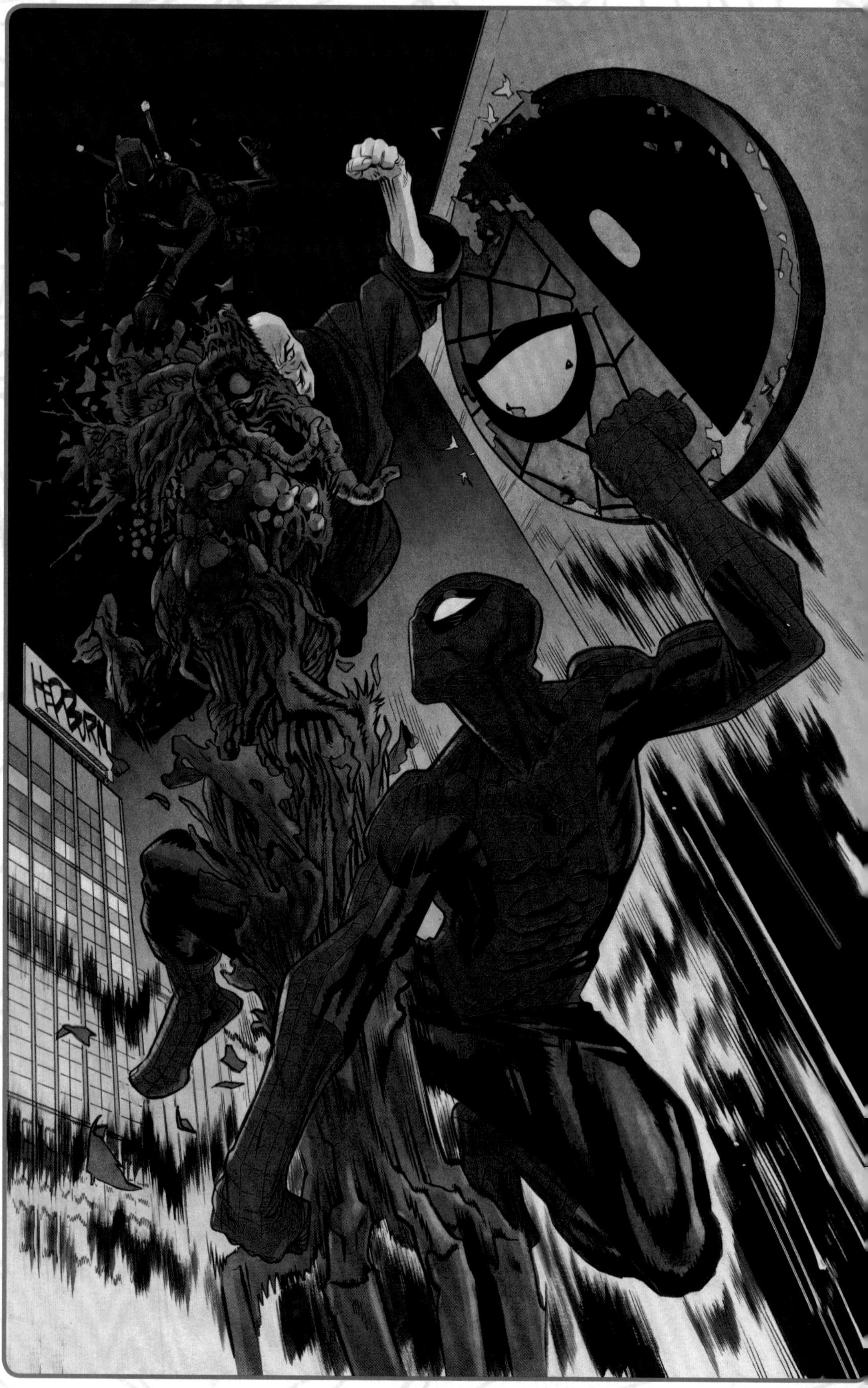

HEPBURN

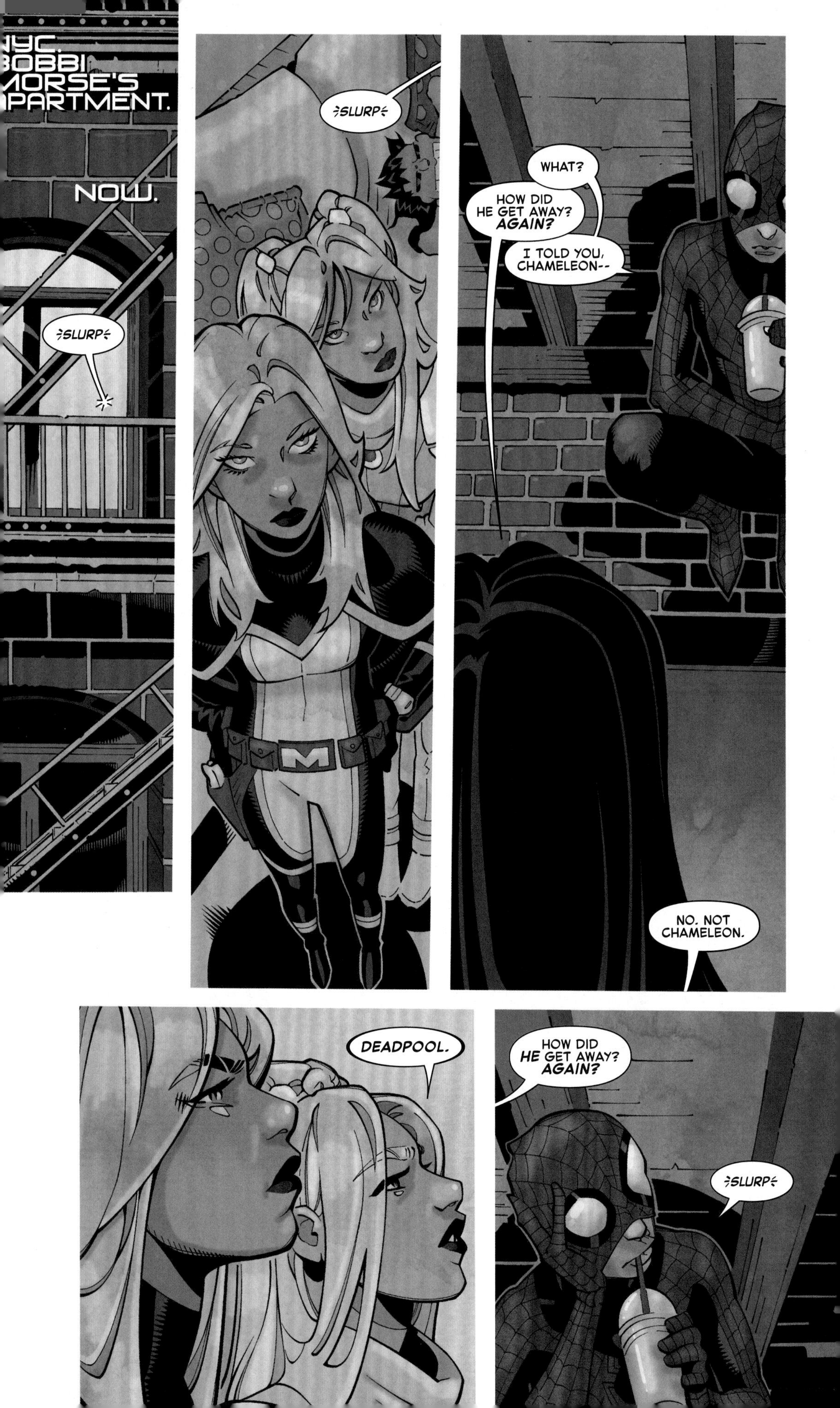

NYC. BOBBI MORSE'S APARTMENT.
NOW.
SLURP
SLURP
WHAT?
HOW DID HE GET AWAY? AGAIN?
I TOLD YOU, CHAMELEON--
NO. NOT CHAMELEON.
DEADPOOL.
HOW DID HE GET AWAY? AGAIN?
SLURP

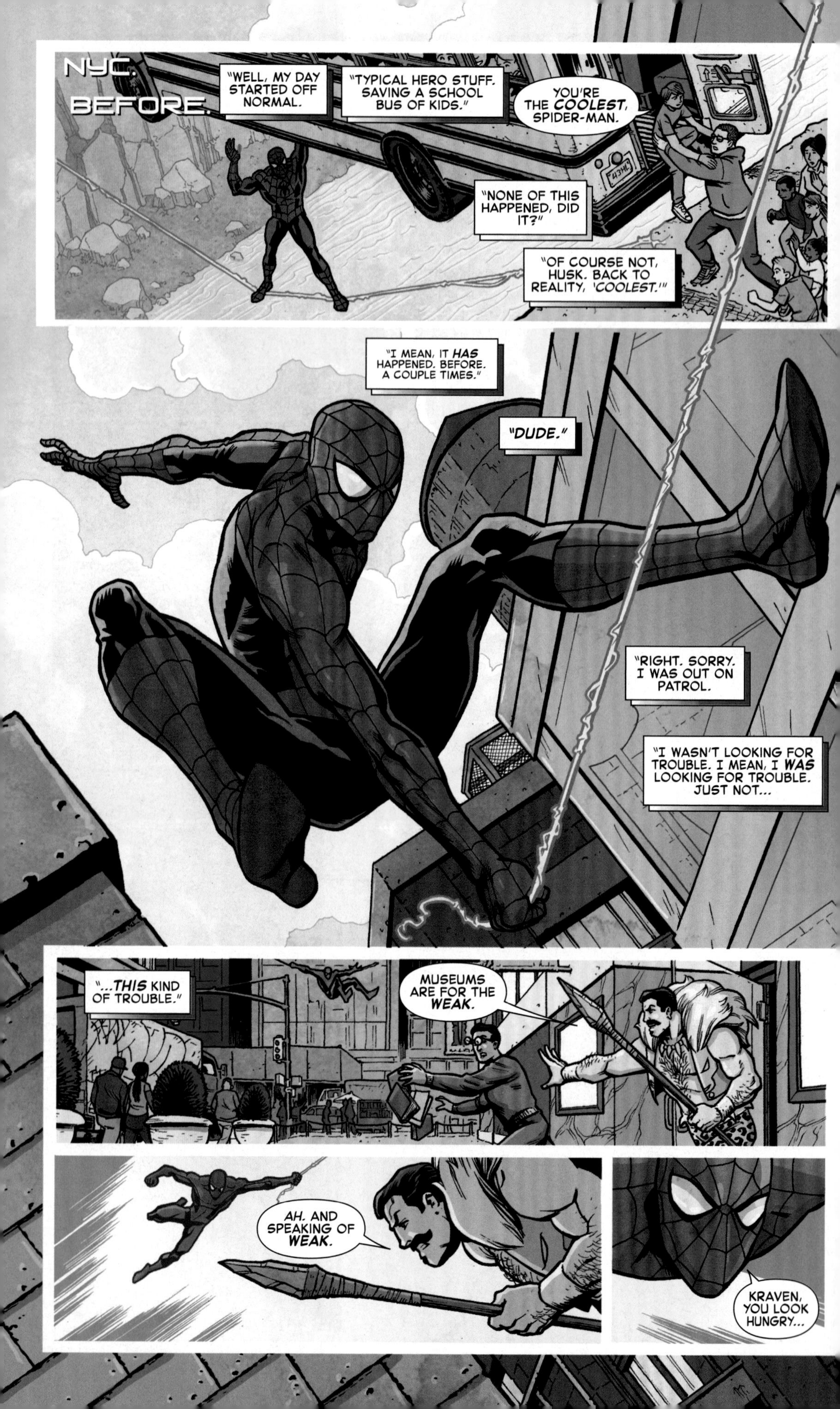
NYC. BEFORE.
"WELL, MY DAY STARTED OFF NORMAL.
"TYPICAL HERO STUFF. SAVING A SCHOOL BUS OF KIDS."
YOU'RE THE COOLEST, SPIDER-MAN.
"NONE OF THIS HAPPENED, DID IT?"
"OF COURSE NOT, HUSK. BACK TO REALITY, 'COOLEST.'"
"I MEAN, IT HAS HAPPENED. BEFORE. A COUPLE TIMES."
"DUDE."
"RIGHT. SORRY. I WAS OUT ON PATROL.
"I WASN'T LOOKING FOR TROUBLE. I MEAN, I WAS LOOKING FOR TROUBLE. JUST NOT...
"...THIS KIND OF TROUBLE."
MUSEUMS ARE FOR THE WEAK.
AH. AND SPEAKING OF WEAK.
KRAVEN, YOU LOOK HUNGRY...

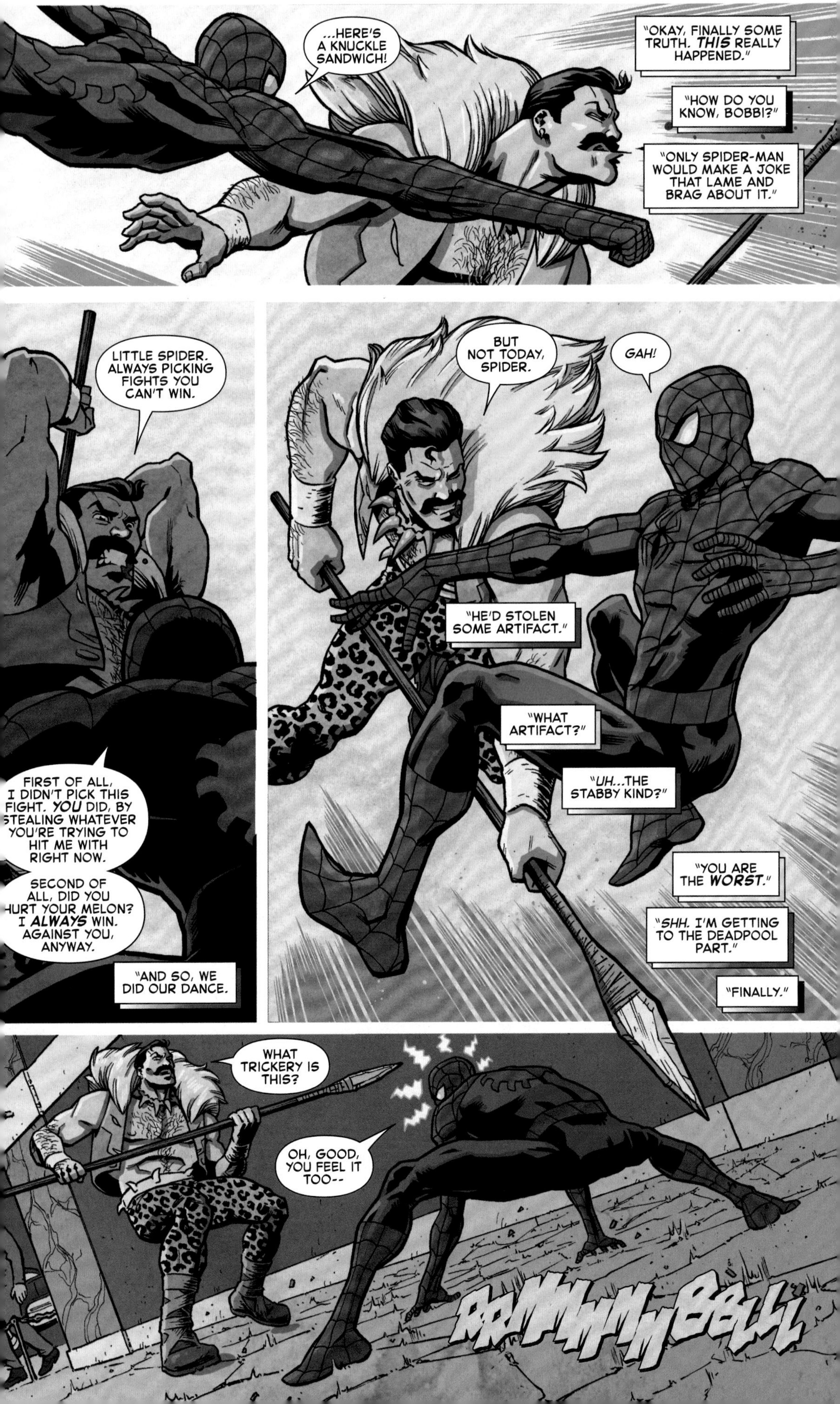

...HERE'S A KNUCKLE SANDWICH!
"OKAY, FINALLY SOME TRUTH. THIS REALLY HAPPENED."
"HOW DO YOU KNOW, BOBBI?"
"ONLY SPIDER-MAN WOULD MAKE A JOKE THAT LAME AND BRAG ABOUT IT."
LITTLE SPIDER. ALWAYS PICKING FIGHTS YOU CAN'T WIN.
FIRST OF ALL, I DIDN'T PICK THIS FIGHT. YOU DID, BY STEALING WHATEVER YOU'RE TRYING TO HIT ME WITH RIGHT NOW.
SECOND OF ALL, DID YOU HURT YOUR MELON? I ALWAYS WIN. AGAINST YOU, ANYWAY.
"AND SO, WE DID OUR DANCE.
BUT NOT TODAY, SPIDER.
GAH!
"HE'D STOLEN SOME ARTIFACT."
"WHAT ARTIFACT?"
"UH...THE STABBY KIND?"
"YOU ARE THE WORST."
"SHH. I'M GETTING TO THE DEADPOOL PART."
"FINALLY."
WHAT TRICKERY IS THIS?
OH, GOOD, YOU FEEL IT TOO--
RRMMMMBBLL

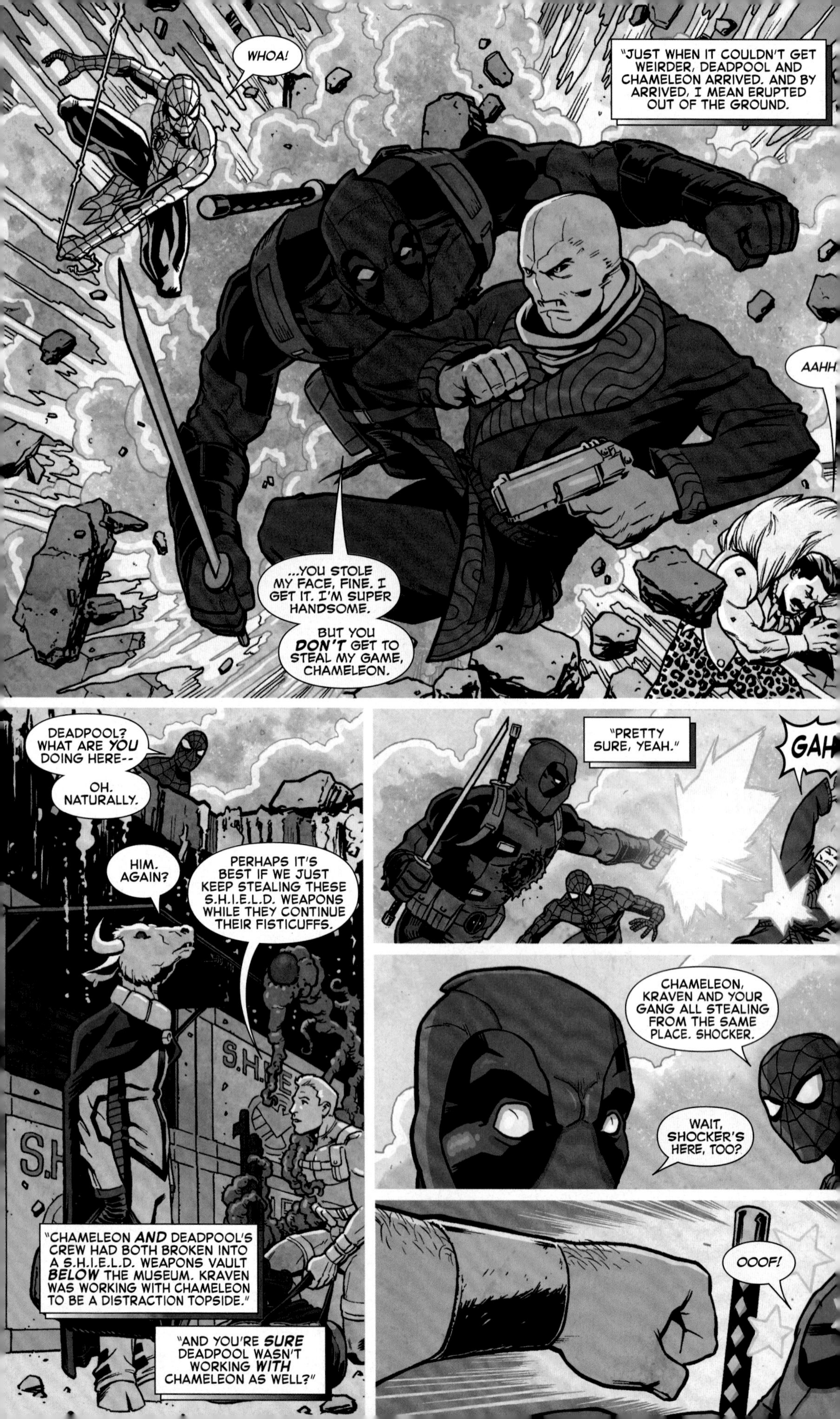
WHOA!
"JUST WHEN IT COULDN'T GET WEIRDER, DEADPOOL AND CHAMELEON ARRIVED. AND BY ARRIVED, I MEAN ERUPTED OUT OF THE GROUND.
AAHH
...YOU STOLE MY FACE, FINE. I GET IT. I'M SUPER HANDSOME.
BUT YOU DON'T GET TO STEAL MY GAME, CHAMELEON.
DEADPOOL? WHAT ARE YOU DOING HERE--
OH. NATURALLY.
HIM. AGAIN?
PERHAPS IT'S BEST IF WE JUST KEEP STEALING THESE S.H.I.E.L.D. WEAPONS WHILE THEY CONTINUE THEIR FISTICUFFS.
"CHAMELEON AND DEADPOOL'S CREW HAD BOTH BROKEN INTO A S.H.I.E.L.D. WEAPONS VAULT BELOW THE MUSEUM. KRAVEN WAS WORKING WITH CHAMELEON TO BE A DISTRACTION TOPSIDE."
"AND YOU'RE SURE DEADPOOL WASN'T WORKING WITH CHAMELEON AS WELL?"
"PRETTY SURE, YEAH."
GAH
CHAMELEON, KRAVEN AND YOUR GANG ALL STEALING FROM THE SAME PLACE. SHOCKER.
WAIT, SHOCKER'S HERE, TOO?
OOOF!

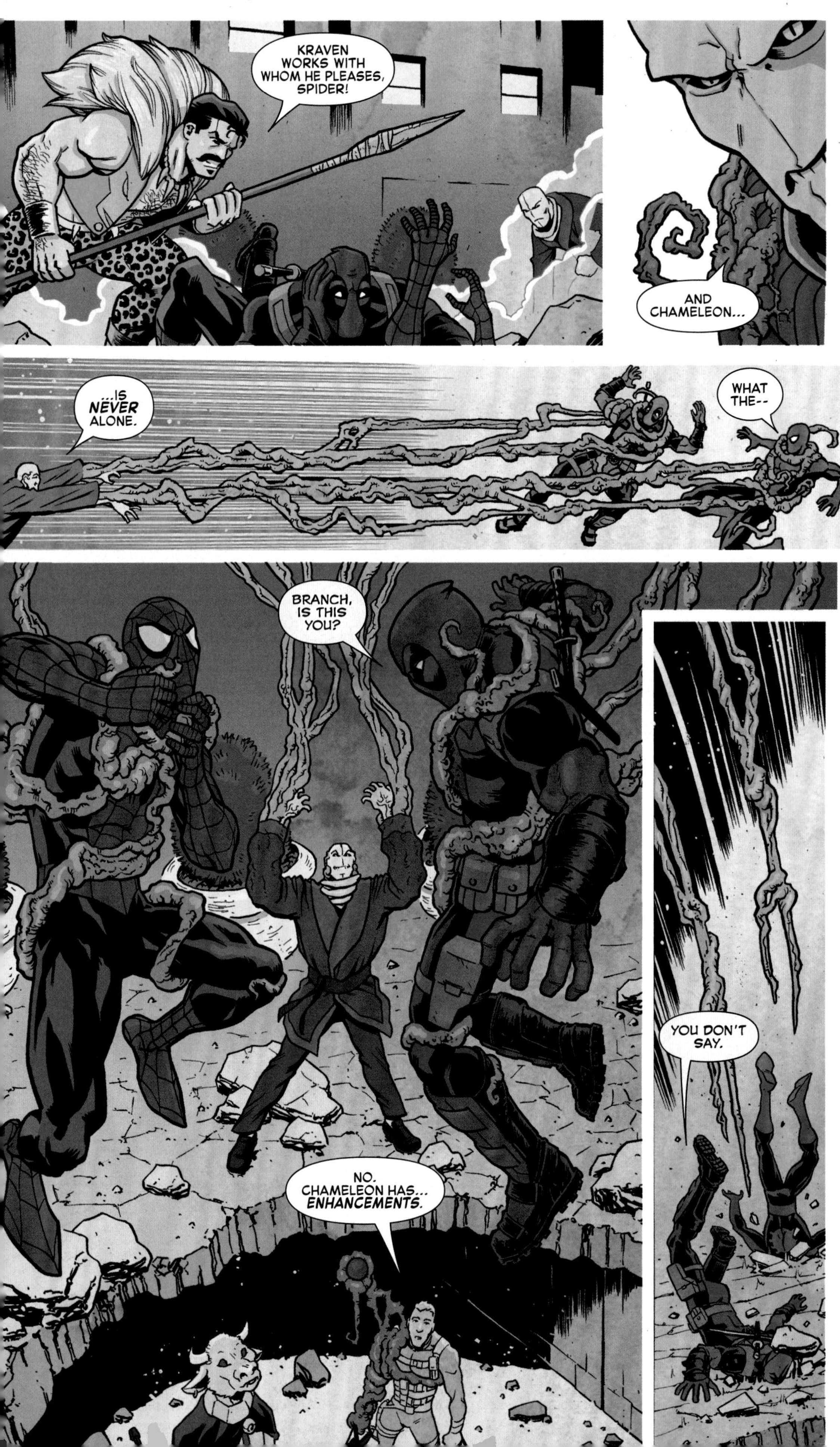
KRAVEN WORKS WITH WHOM HE PLEASES, SPIDER!
AND CHAMELEON...
...IS NEVER ALONE.
WHAT THE--
BRANCH, IS THIS YOU?
NO. CHAMELEON HAS... ENHANCEMENTS.
YOU DON'T SAY.

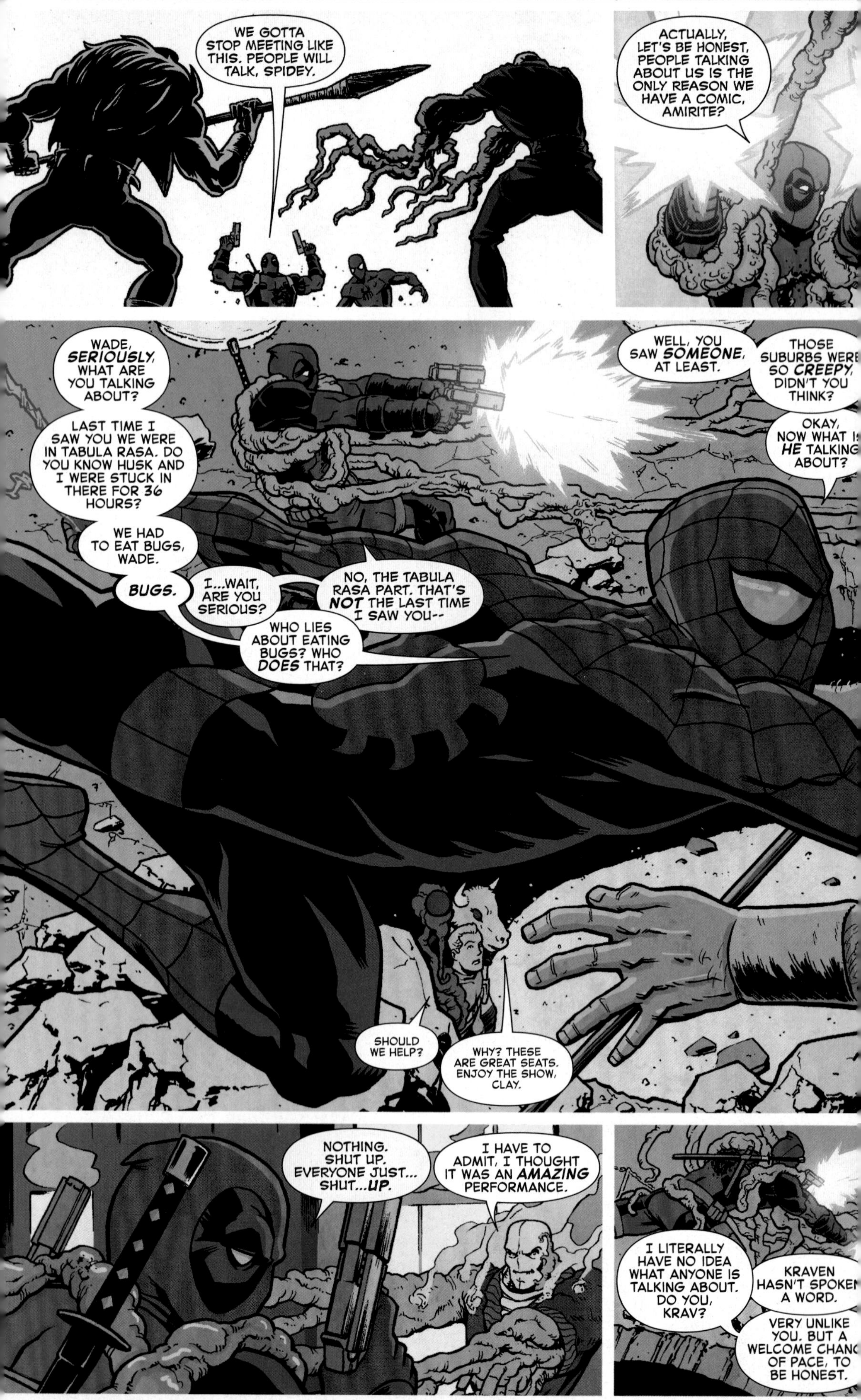
WE GOTTA STOP MEETING LIKE THIS. PEOPLE WILL TALK, SPIDEY.
ACTUALLY, LET'S BE HONEST, PEOPLE TALKING ABOUT US IS THE ONLY REASON WE HAVE A COMIC, AMIRITE?
WADE, SERIOUSLY, WHAT ARE YOU TALKING ABOUT?
LAST TIME I SAW YOU WE WERE IN TABULA RASA. DO YOU KNOW HUSK AND I WERE STUCK IN THERE FOR 36 HOURS?
WE HAD TO EAT BUGS, WADE.
BUGS.
I...WAIT, ARE YOU SERIOUS?
NO, THE TABULA RASA PART. THAT'S NOT THE LAST TIME I SAW YOU--
WHO LIES ABOUT EATING BUGS? WHO DOES THAT?
WELL, YOU SAW SOMEONE, AT LEAST.
THOSE SUBURBS WERE SO CREEPY, DIDN'T YOU THINK?
OKAY, NOW WHAT IS HE TALKING ABOUT?
SHOULD WE HELP?
WHY? THESE ARE GREAT SEATS. ENJOY THE SHOW, CLAY.
NOTHING. SHUT UP. EVERYONE JUST... SHUT...UP.
I HAVE TO ADMIT, I THOUGHT IT WAS AN AMAZING PERFORMANCE.
I LITERALLY HAVE NO IDEA WHAT ANYONE IS TALKING ABOUT. DO YOU, KRAV?
KRAVEN HASN'T SPOKEN A WORD.
VERY UNLIKE YOU. BUT A WELCOME CHANGE OF PACE, TO BE HONEST.

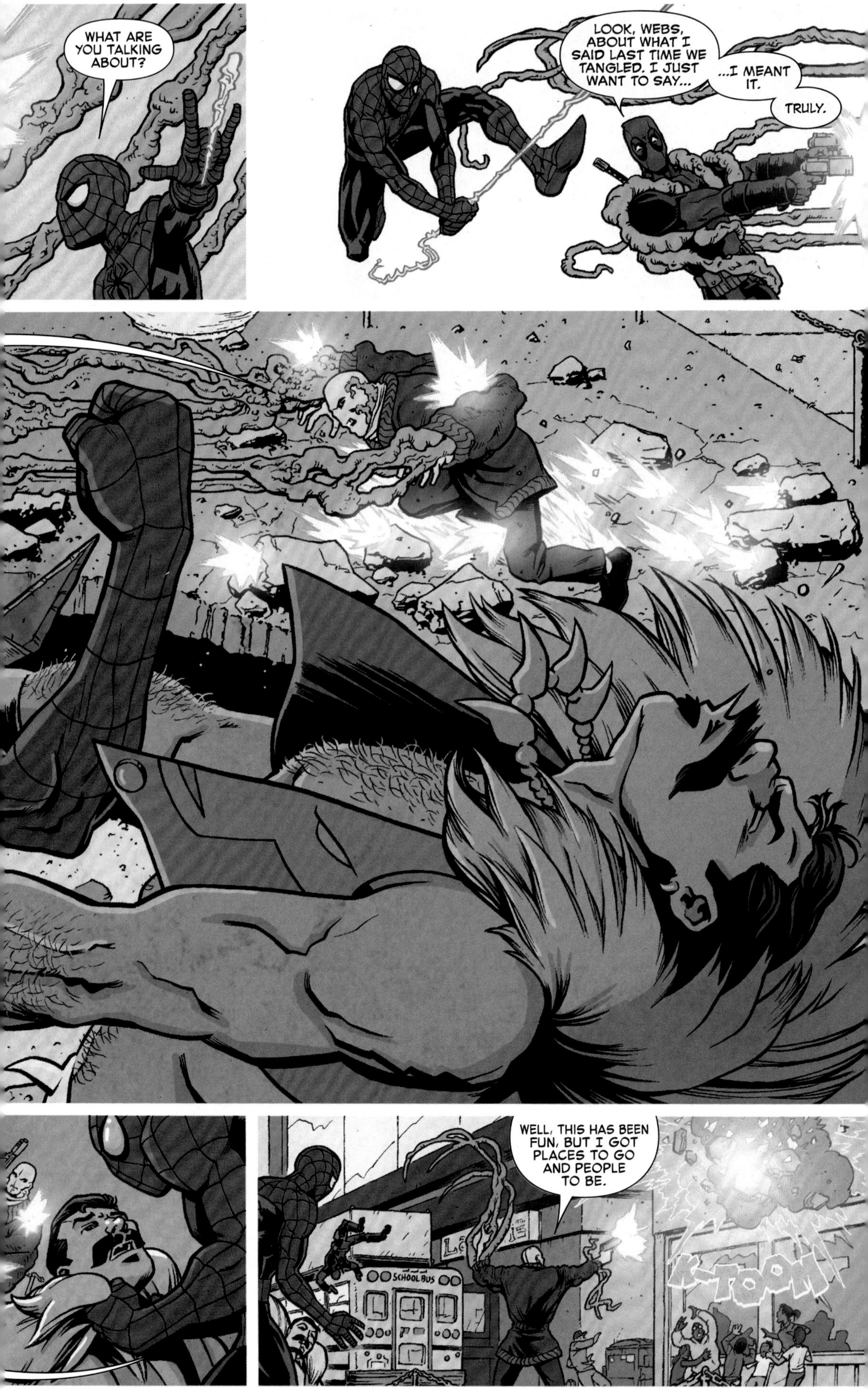
WHAT ARE YOU TALKING ABOUT?
LOOK, WEBS, ABOUT WHAT I SAID LAST TIME WE TANGLED. I JUST WANT TO SAY...
...I MEANT IT.
TRULY.
WELL, THIS HAS BEEN FUN, BUT I GOT PLACES TO GO AND PEOPLE TO BE.
SCHOOL BUS
K-TOOM!

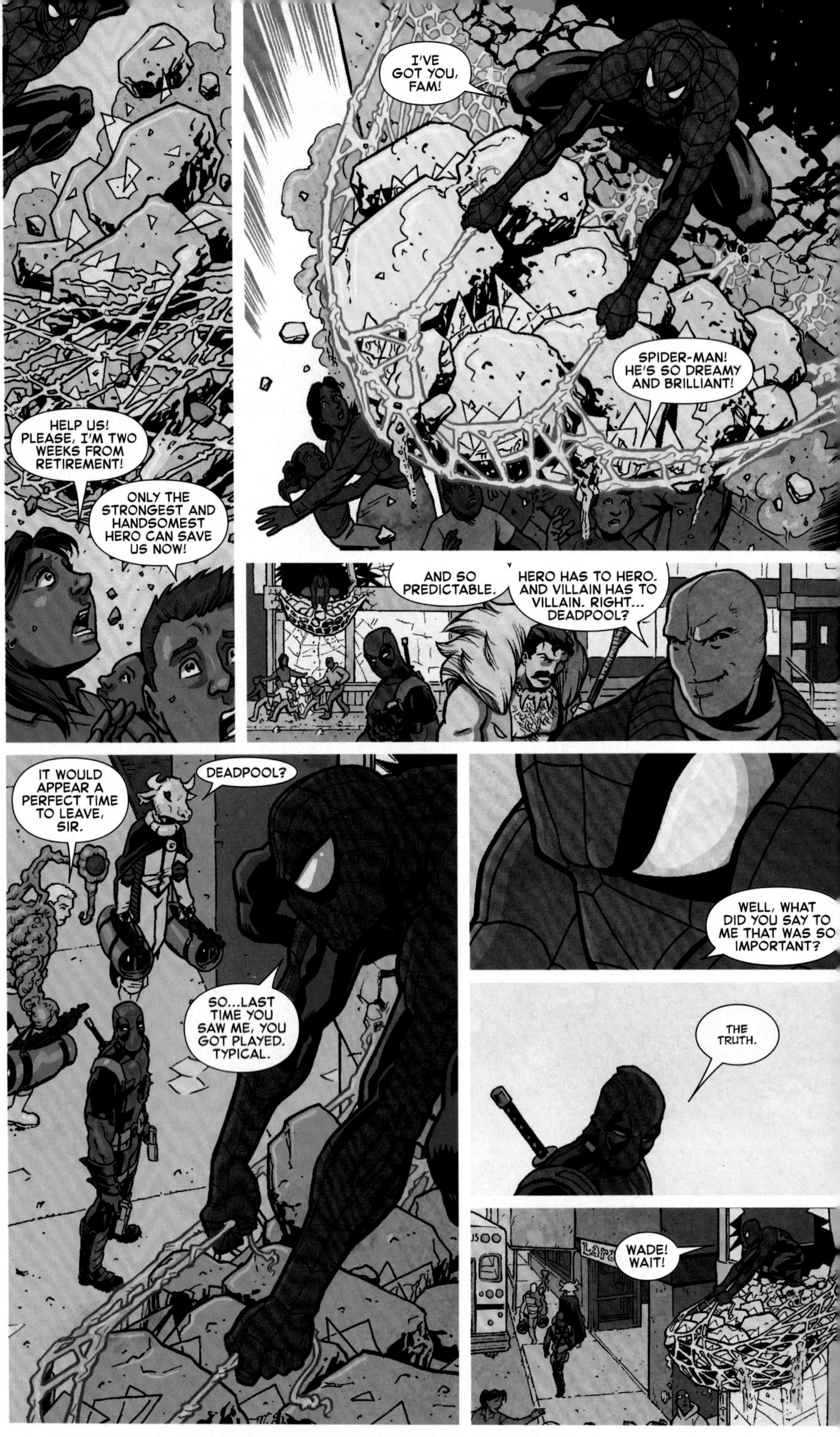
I'VE GOT YOU, FAM!
HELP US! PLEASE, I'M TWO WEEKS FROM RETIREMENT!
ONLY THE STRONGEST AND HANDSOMEST HERO CAN SAVE US NOW!
SPIDER-MAN! HE'S SO DREAMY AND BRILLIANT!
AND SO PREDICTABLE.
HERO HAS TO HERO. AND VILLAIN HAS TO VILLAIN. RIGHT... DEADPOOL?
IT WOULD APPEAR A PERFECT TIME TO LEAVE, SIR.
DEADPOOL?
SO...LAST TIME YOU SAW ME, YOU GOT PLAYED. TYPICAL.
WELL, WHAT DID YOU SAY TO ME THAT WAS SO IMPORTANT?
THE TRUTH.
WADE! WAIT!

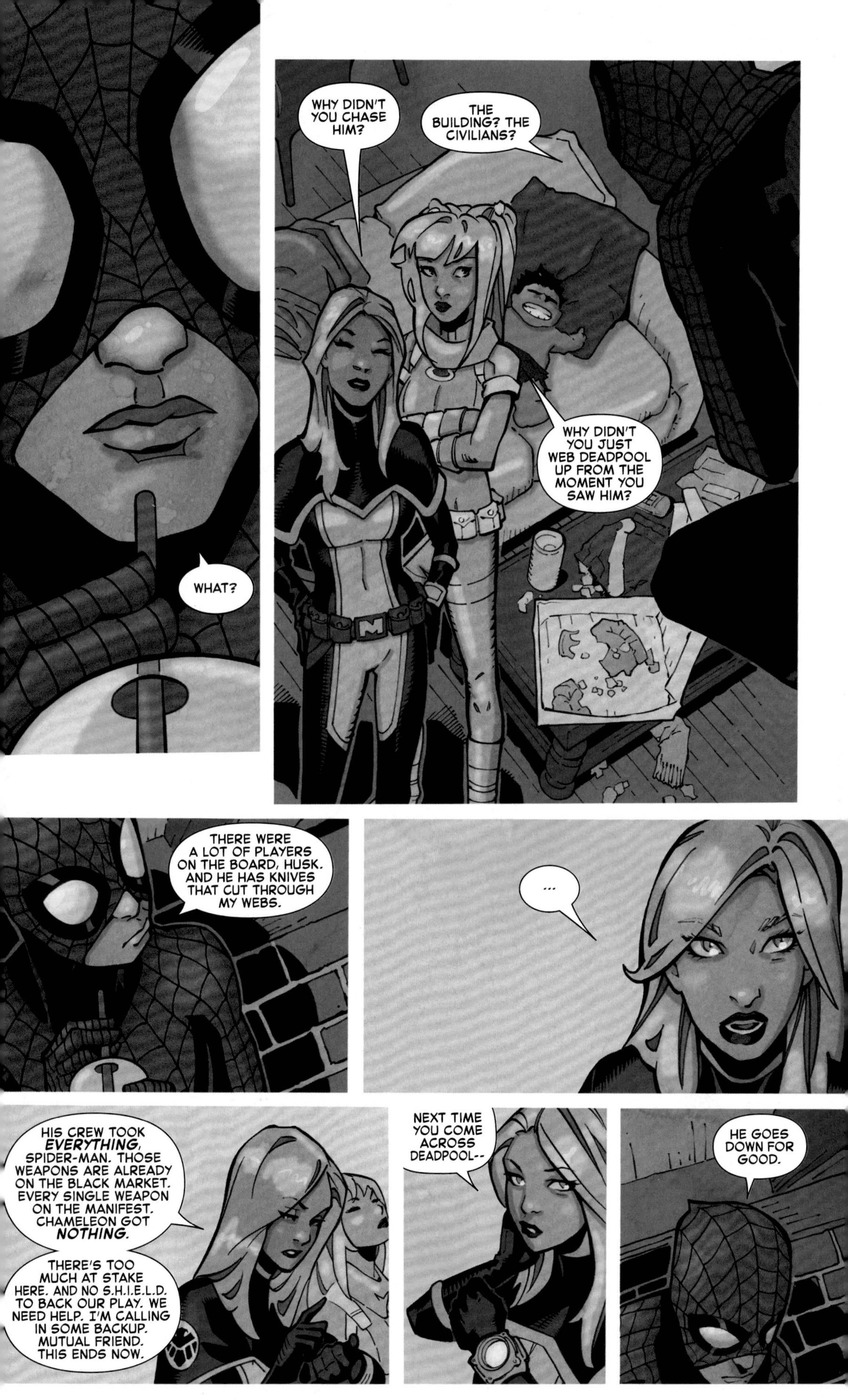
WHAT?
WHY DIDN'T YOU CHASE HIM?
THE BUILDING? THE CIVILIANS?
WHY DIDN'T YOU JUST WEB DEADPOOL UP FROM THE MOMENT YOU SAW HIM?
THERE WERE A LOT OF PLAYERS ON THE BOARD, HUSK. AND HE HAS KNIVES THAT CUT THROUGH MY WEBS.
...
HIS CREW TOOK *EVERYTHING*, SPIDER-MAN. THOSE WEAPONS ARE ALREADY ON THE BLACK MARKET. EVERY SINGLE WEAPON ON THE MANIFEST. CHAMELEON GOT *NOTHING*.
THERE'S TOO MUCH AT STAKE HERE. AND NO S.H.I.E.L.D. TO BACK OUR PLAY. WE NEED HELP. I'M CALLING IN SOME BACKUP. MUTUAL FRIEND. THIS ENDS NOW.
NEXT TIME YOU COME ACROSS DEADPOOL--
HE GOES DOWN FOR GOOD.

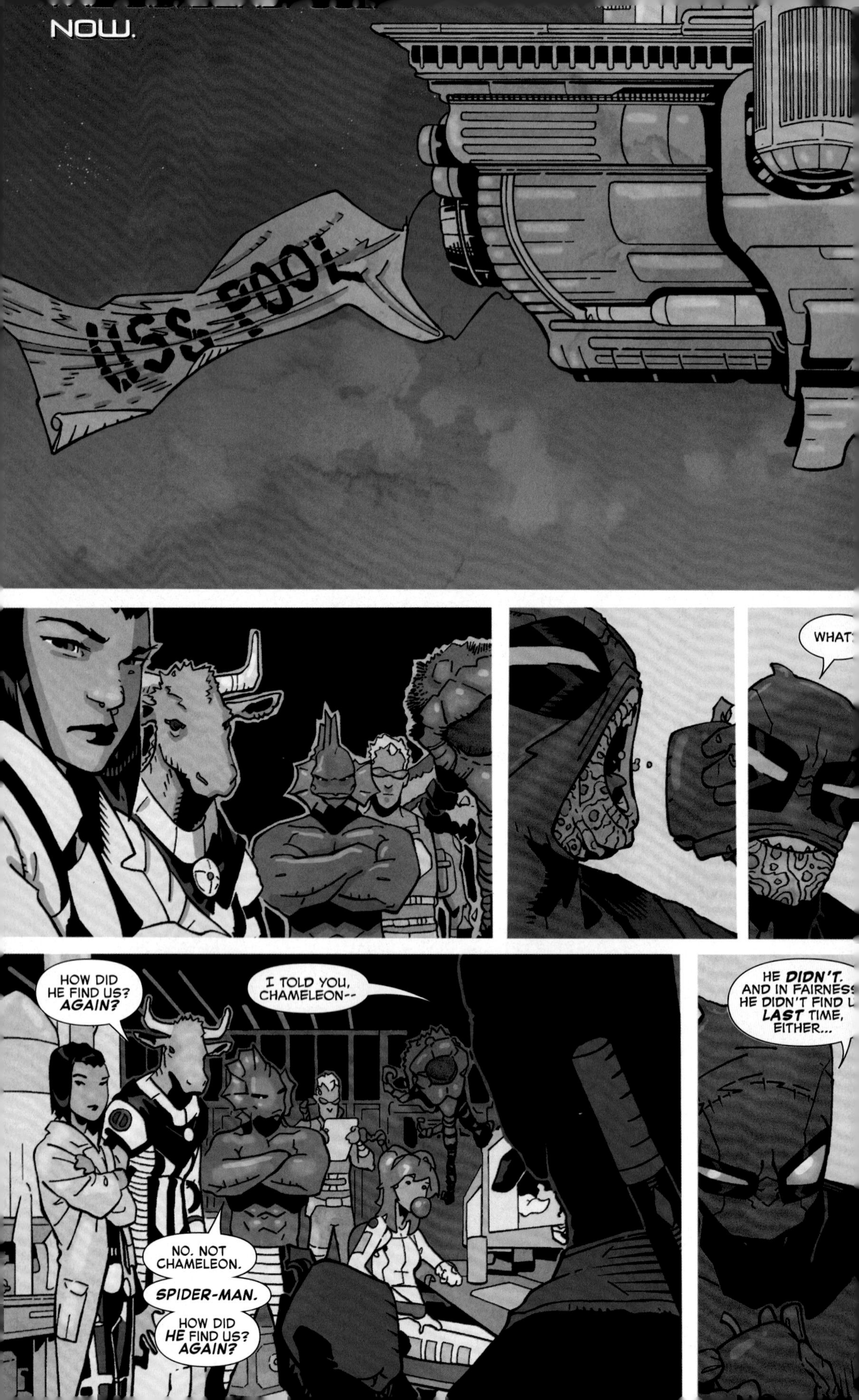
NOW.
USS FOOL
WHAT?
HOW DID HE FIND US? AGAIN?
I TOLD YOU, CHAMELEON--
NO. NOT CHAMELEON.
SPIDER-MAN.
HOW DID HE FIND US? AGAIN?
HE DIDN'T. AND IN FAIRNESS HE DIDN'T FIND US LAST TIME, EITHER...

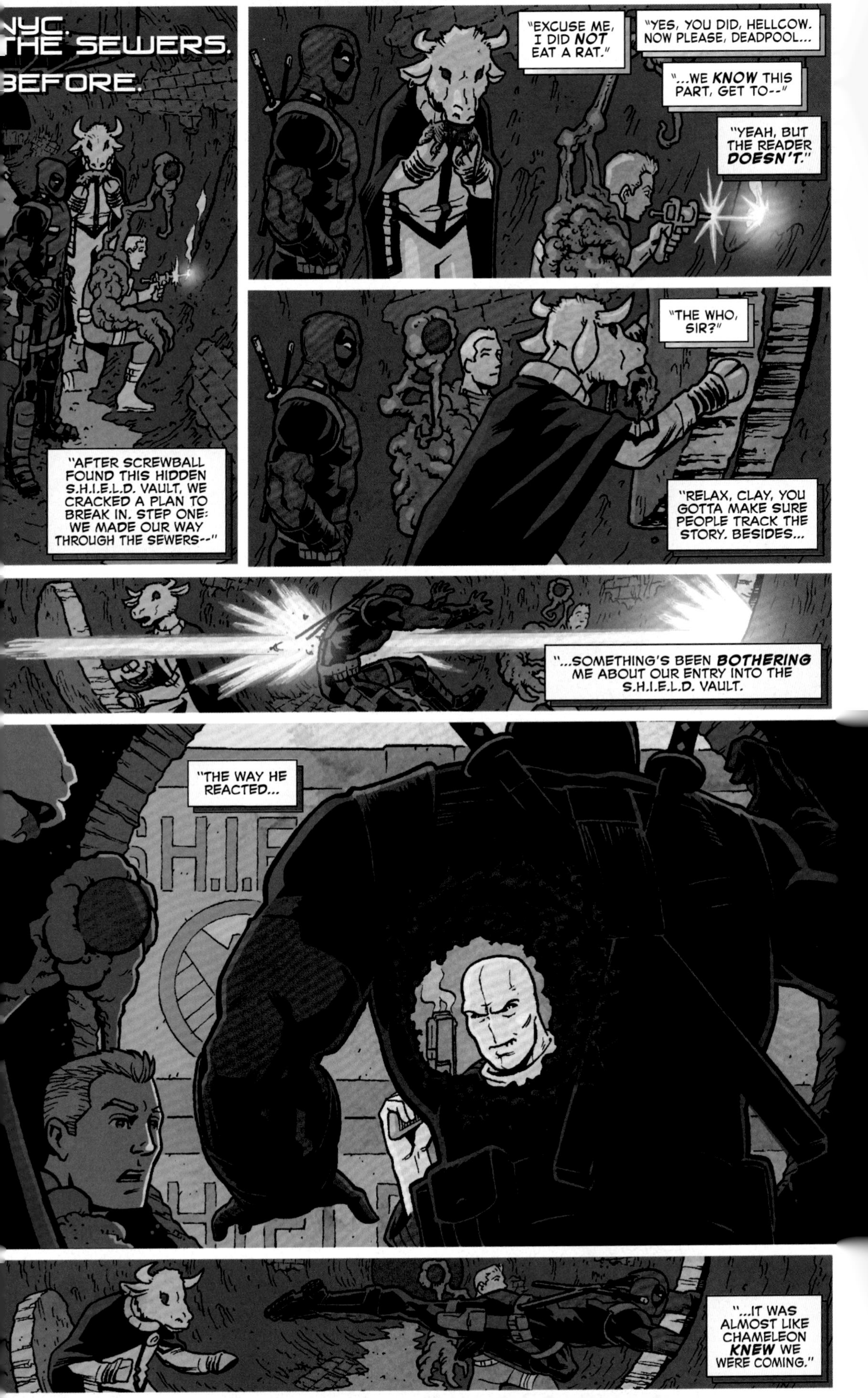
NYC.
THE SEWERS.
BEFORE.
"AFTER SCREWBALL FOUND THIS HIDDEN S.H.I.E.L.D. VAULT, WE CRACKED A PLAN TO BREAK IN. STEP ONE: WE MADE OUR WAY THROUGH THE SEWERS--"
"EXCUSE ME, I DID NOT EAT A RAT."
"YES, YOU DID, HELLCOW. NOW PLEASE, DEADPOOL...
"...WE KNOW THIS PART, GET TO--"
"YEAH, BUT THE READER DOESN'T."
"THE WHO, SIR?"
"RELAX, CLAY, YOU GOTTA MAKE SURE PEOPLE TRACK THE STORY. BESIDES...
"...SOMETHING'S BEEN BOTHERING ME ABOUT OUR ENTRY INTO THE S.H.I.E.L.D. VAULT.
"THE WAY HE REACTED...
"...IT WAS ALMOST LIKE CHAMELEON KNEW WE WERE COMING."

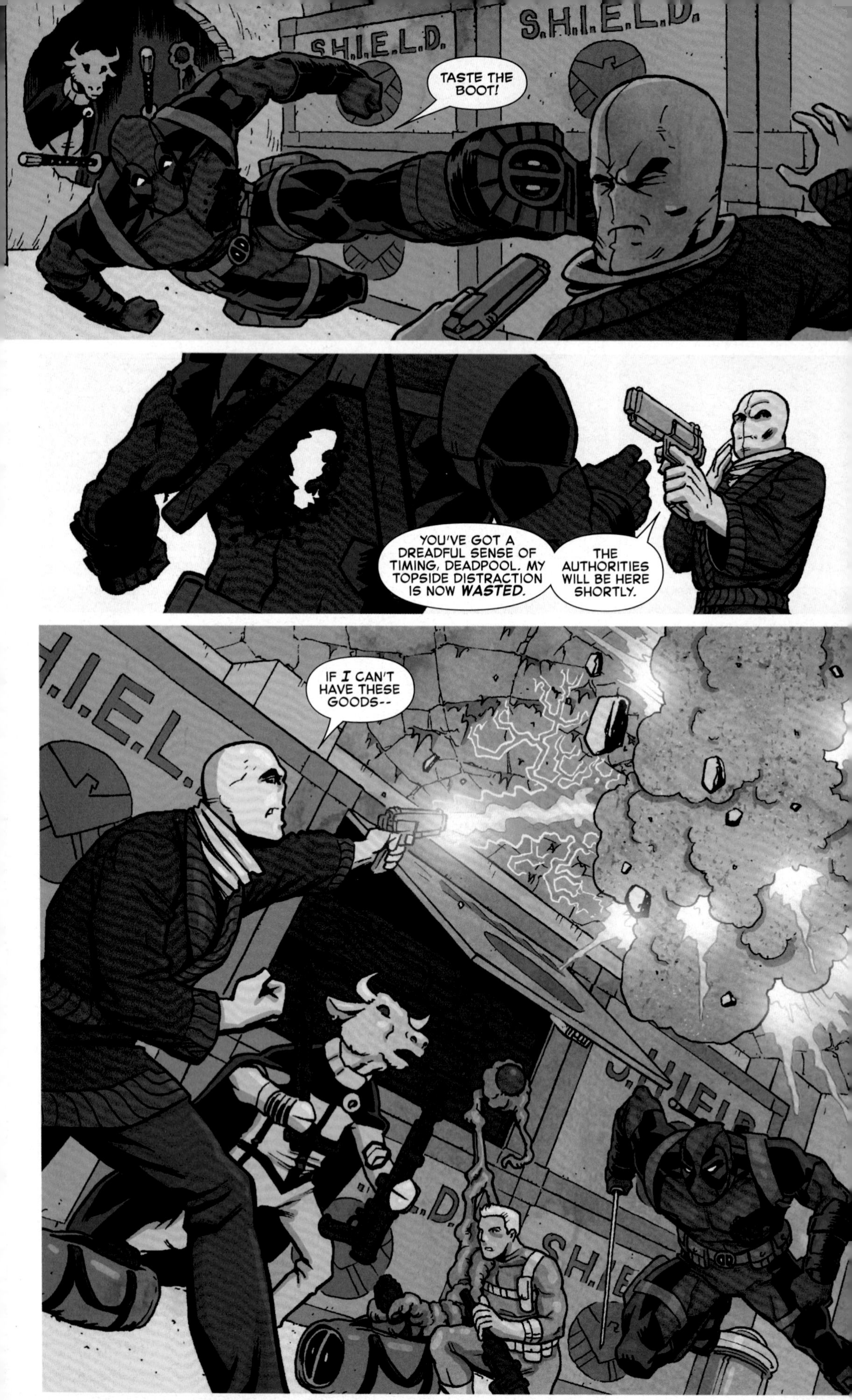

S.H.I.E.L.D.
S.H.I.E.L.D.
TASTE THE BOOT!
YOU'VE GOT A DREADFUL SENSE OF TIMING, DEADPOOL. MY TOPSIDE DISTRACTION IS NOW *WASTED.*
THE AUTHORITIES WILL BE HERE SHORTLY.
IF *I* CAN'T HAVE THESE GOODS--

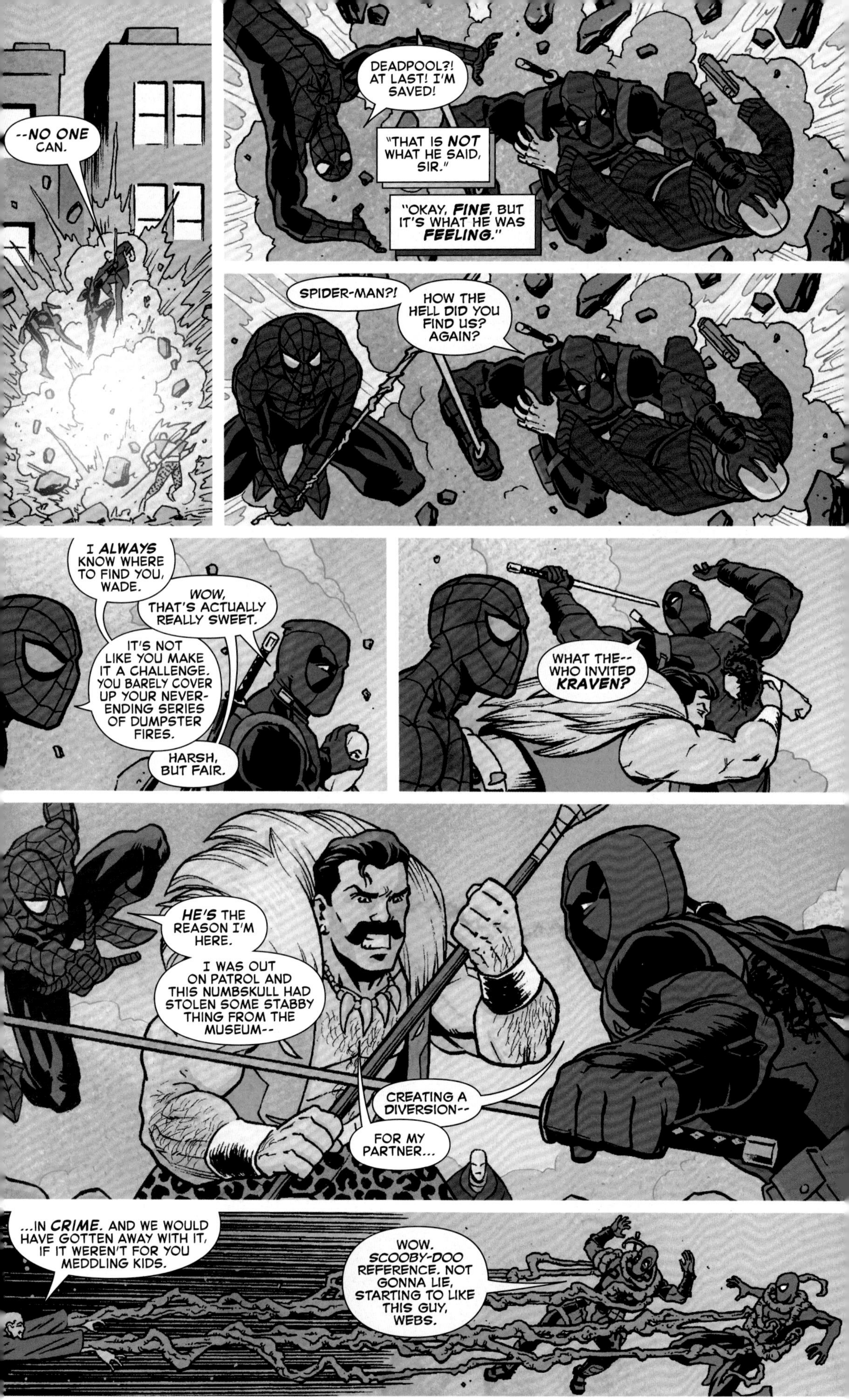
--NO ONE CAN.
DEADPOOL?! AT LAST! I'M SAVED!
"THAT IS NOT WHAT HE SAID, SIR."
"OKAY, FINE, BUT IT'S WHAT HE WAS FEELING."
SPIDER-MAN?!
HOW THE HELL DID YOU FIND US? AGAIN?
I ALWAYS KNOW WHERE TO FIND YOU, WADE.
WOW, THAT'S ACTUALLY REALLY SWEET.
IT'S NOT LIKE YOU MAKE IT A CHALLENGE. YOU BARELY COVER UP YOUR NEVER-ENDING SERIES OF DUMPSTER FIRES.
HARSH, BUT FAIR.
WHAT THE-- WHO INVITED KRAVEN?
HE'S THE REASON I'M HERE.
I WAS OUT ON PATROL AND THIS NUMBSKULL HAD STOLEN SOME STABBY THING FROM THE MUSEUM--
CREATING A DIVERSION--
FOR MY PARTNER...
...IN CRIME. AND WE WOULD HAVE GOTTEN AWAY WITH IT, IF IT WEREN'T FOR YOU MEDDLING KIDS.
WOW. SCOOBY-DOO REFERENCE. NOT GONNA LIE, STARTING TO LIKE THIS GUY, WEBS.

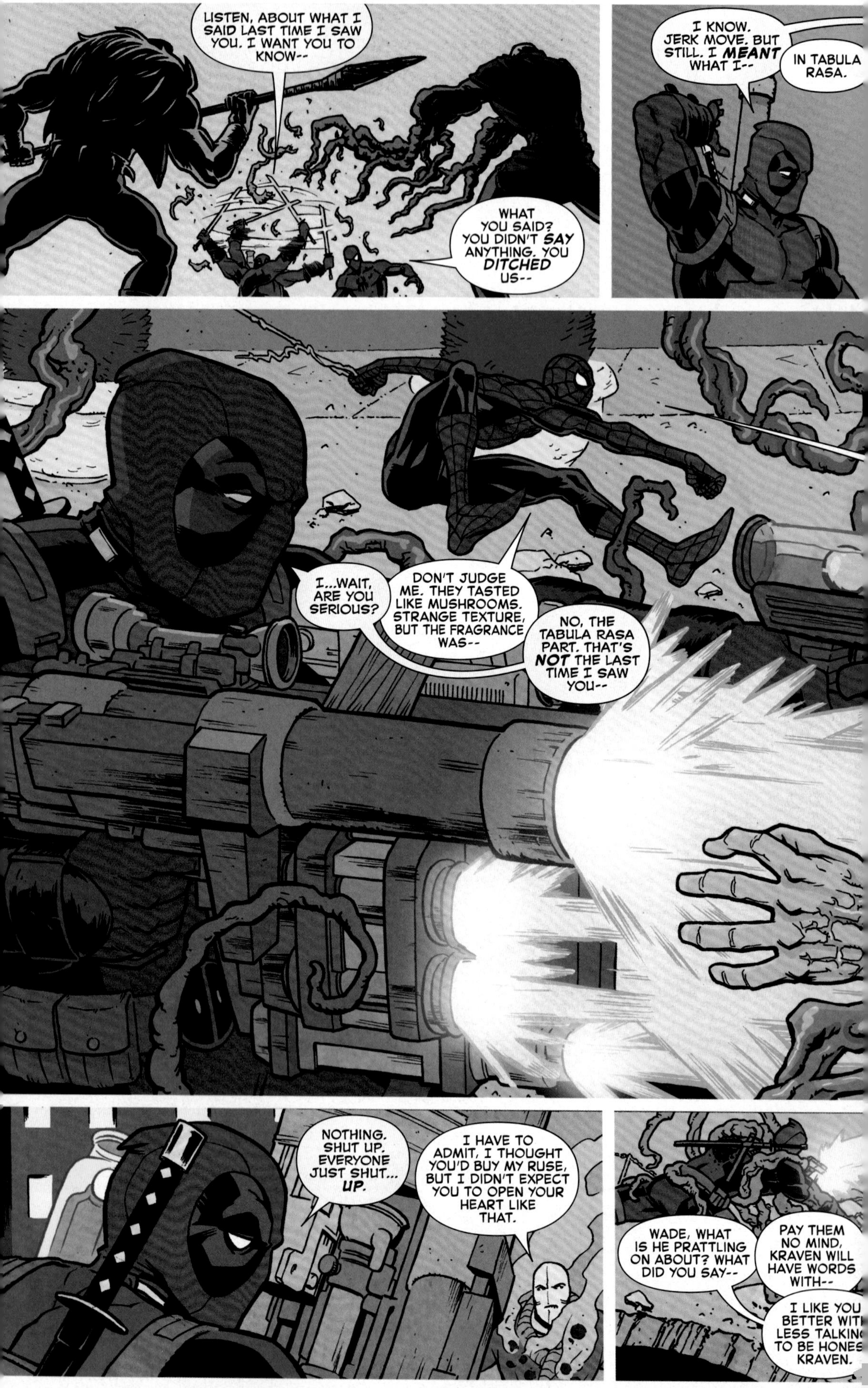
LISTEN, ABOUT WHAT I SAID LAST TIME I SAW YOU. I WANT YOU TO KNOW--
WHAT YOU SAID? YOU DIDN'T SAY ANYTHING. YOU DITCHED US--
I KNOW. JERK MOVE. BUT STILL. I MEANT WHAT I--
IN TABULA RASA.
I...WAIT, ARE YOU SERIOUS?
DON'T JUDGE ME. THEY TASTED LIKE MUSHROOMS. STRANGE TEXTURE, BUT THE FRAGRANCE WAS--
NO, THE TABULA RASA PART. THAT'S NOT THE LAST TIME I SAW YOU--
NOTHING. SHUT UP. EVERYONE JUST SHUT... UP.
I HAVE TO ADMIT, I THOUGHT YOU'D BUY MY RUSE, BUT I DIDN'T EXPECT YOU TO OPEN YOUR HEART LIKE THAT.
WADE, WHAT IS HE PRATTLING ON ABOUT? WHAT DID YOU SAY--
PAY THEM NO MIND, KRAVEN WILL HAVE WORDS WITH--
I LIKE YOU BETTER WIT LESS TALKIN TO BE HONES KRAVEN.

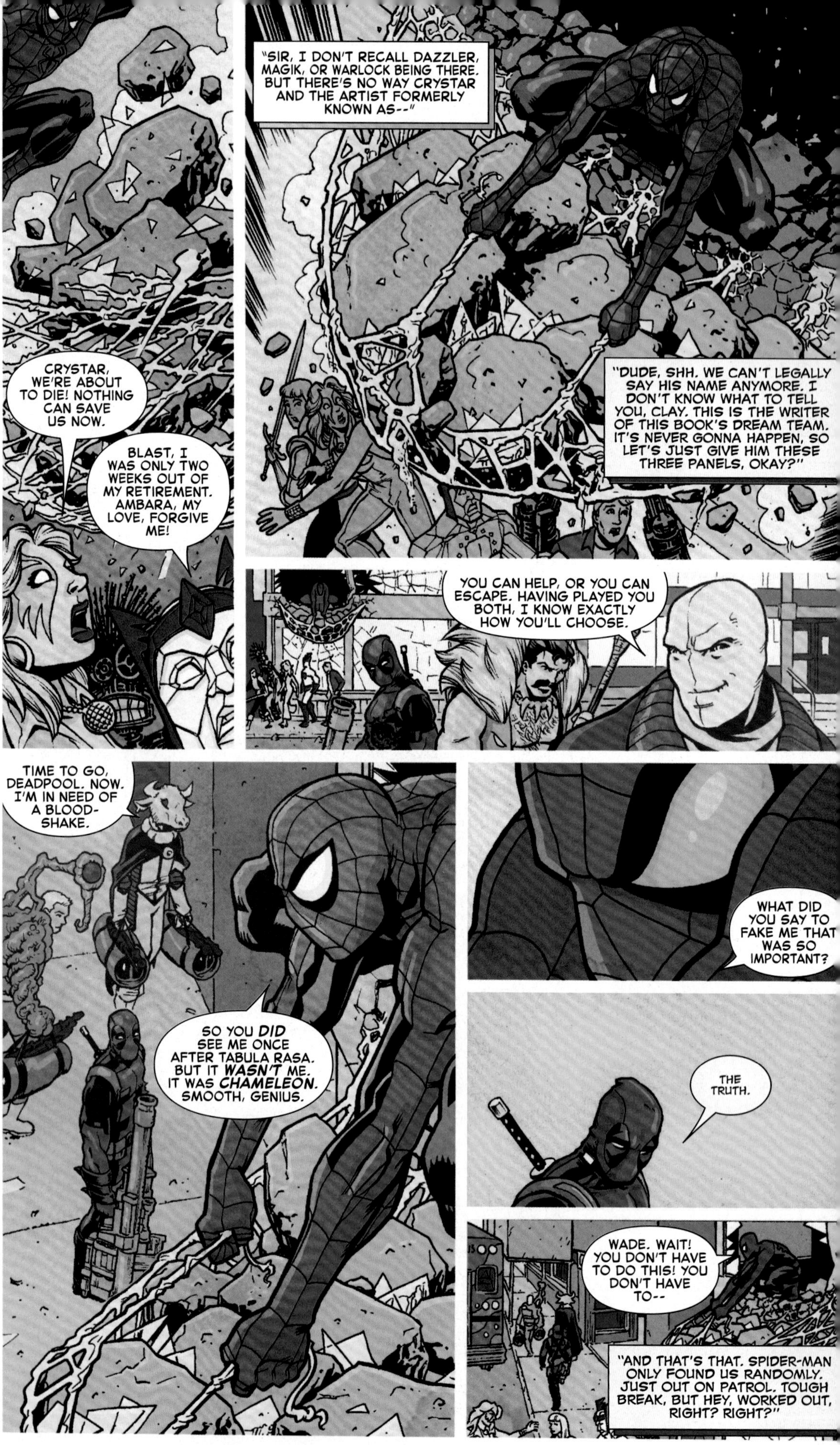
"SIR, I DON'T RECALL DAZZLER, MAGIK, OR WARLOCK BEING THERE. BUT THERE'S NO WAY CRYSTAR AND THE ARTIST FORMERLY KNOWN AS--"
CRYSTAR, WE'RE ABOUT TO DIE! NOTHING CAN SAVE US NOW.
BLAST, I WAS ONLY TWO WEEKS OUT OF MY RETIREMENT. AMBARA, MY LOVE, FORGIVE ME!
"DUDE, SHH. WE CAN'T LEGALLY SAY HIS NAME ANYMORE. I DON'T KNOW WHAT TO TELL YOU, CLAY. THIS IS THE WRITER OF THIS BOOK'S DREAM TEAM. IT'S NEVER GONNA HAPPEN, SO LET'S JUST GIVE HIM THESE THREE PANELS, OKAY?"
YOU CAN HELP, OR YOU CAN ESCAPE. HAVING PLAYED YOU BOTH, I KNOW EXACTLY HOW YOU'LL CHOOSE.
TIME TO GO, DEADPOOL. NOW. I'M IN NEED OF A BLOOD-SHAKE.
SO YOU DID SEE ME ONCE AFTER TABULA RASA. BUT IT WASN'T ME. IT WAS CHAMELEON. SMOOTH, GENIUS.
WHAT DID YOU SAY TO FAKE ME THAT WAS SO IMPORTANT?
THE TRUTH.
WADE. WAIT! YOU DON'T HAVE TO DO THIS! YOU DON'T HAVE TO--
"AND THAT'S THAT. SPIDER-MAN ONLY FOUND US RANDOMLY. JUST OUT ON PATROL. TOUGH BREAK, BUT HEY, WORKED OUT, RIGHT? RIGHT?"

WHAT?

YOU CAN READ MINDS... IS HE LYING, BRANCH?

NO. HE IS *CLOSED* TO ME IN THIS MOMENT. BUT I SENSE... *SOMETHING.* SOMETHING... *OFF.*

WHAT YOU SENSE IS *WORRY.* AND NOT ABOUT SPIDER-MAN.

CHAMELEON GOT THE DROP ON US. LIKE HE *KNEW* WE WERE COMING. HOW IS THAT POSSIBLE?

SPIDER-MAN WAS RIGHT FOR ONCE. YOU'RE NOT EXACTLY SUBTLE.

PERHAPS CHAMELEON'S USING STOLEN S.H.I.E.L.D. GEAR THAT WE DON'T KNOW ABOUT. SOMETHING THAT GIVES HIM AN EDGE. YOU ALL DID SAY HIS SUIT WAS ENHANCED.

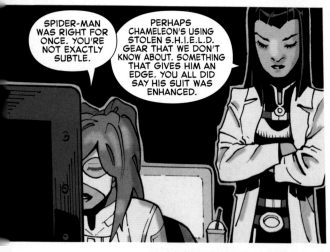

BUT CHAMELEON *ISN'T* THE ISSUE HERE, DEADPOOL--

YES. HE IS.

LAST TIME WE RAN INTO SPIDER-MAN, IT *WASN'T* SPIDER-MAN. IT WAS *CHAMELEON.*

HE'S *THAT* GOOD. HELL, HE COULD BE ONE OF YOU GUYS--HE COULD BE *ME,* FOR ALL I KNOW.

HOW DO YOU KNOW IT WASN'T SPIDER-MAN IN AREA 14?

HE DIDN'T REMEMBER WHAT WE TALKED ABOUT, SCREWBALL.

REALLY. WHAT *DID* YOU TALK ABOUT?

I DON'T CARE THAT I LET EVERYONE DOWN...

...EXCEPT YOU. I'M...

...I'M SORRY, WEBS.

IT WAS...IT WAS...

...NOTHING IMPORTANT. APPARENTLY.

YOU ALMOST GOT CAUGHT. WHICH MEANS WE ALMOST GOT CAUGHT.

I HATE TO ADMIT IT, BUT MANPHIBIAN IS RIGHT. FOR ONCE.

I HAVE NO INTENTION OF GOING BACK TO JAIL, DEADPOOL.

NONE OF US ARE GOING TO JAIL.

BECAUSE WE WORK FOR DEADPOOL.

THE WORLD'S GREATEST ASSASSIN.

NEXT TIME SPIDER-MAN GETS IN OUR WAY--

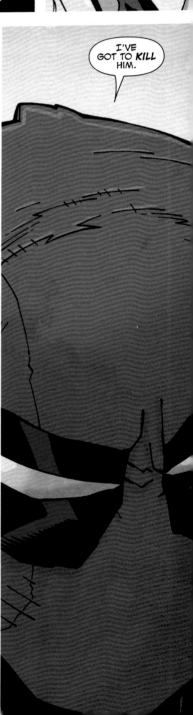

I'VE GOT TO KILL HIM.

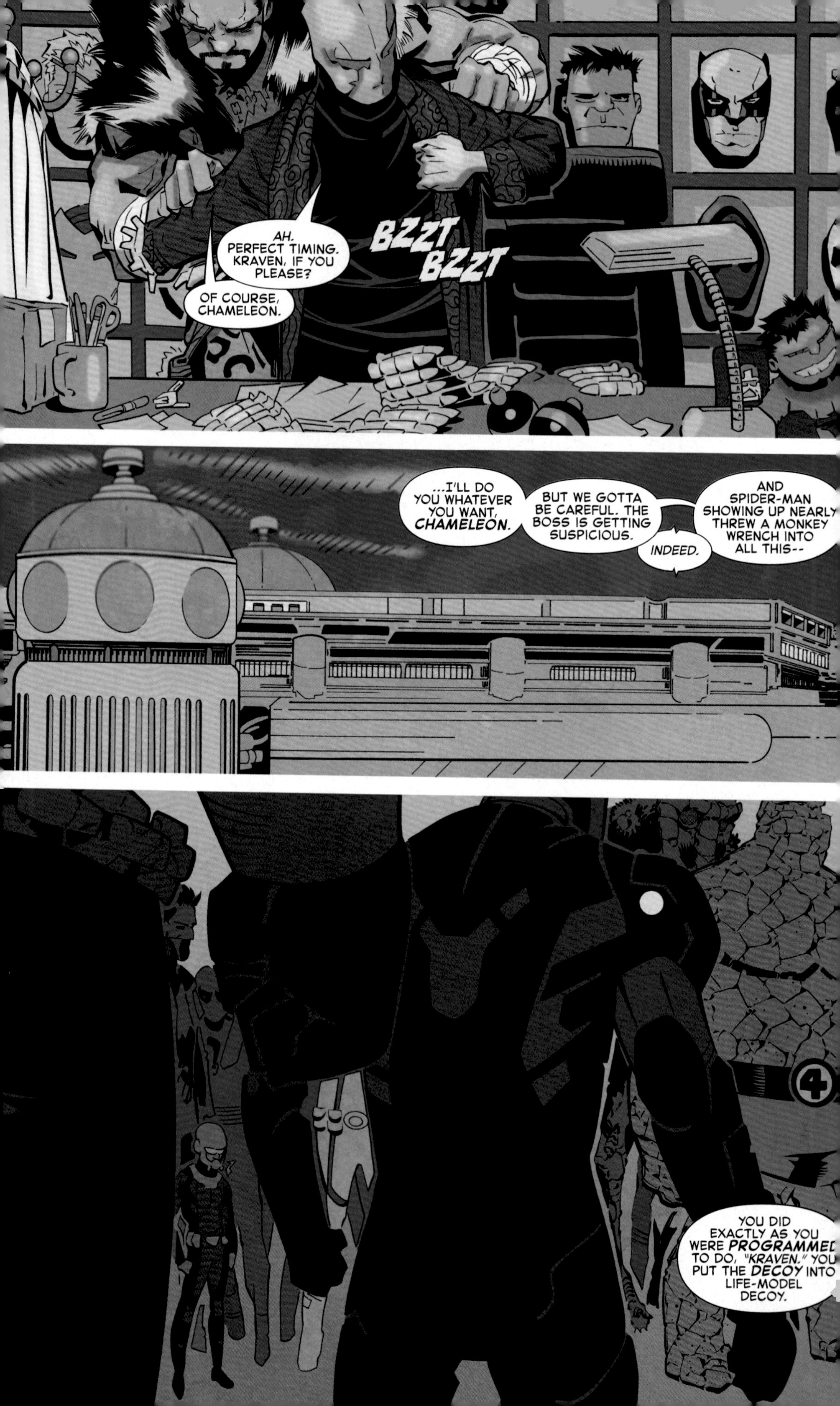
AH. PERFECT TIMING. KRAVEN, IF YOU PLEASE?
OF COURSE, CHAMELEON.
BZZT BZZT
...I'LL DO YOU WHATEVER YOU WANT, CHAMELEON.
BUT WE GOTTA BE CAREFUL. THE BOSS IS GETTING SUSPICIOUS.
AND SPIDER-MAN SHOWING UP NEARLY THREW A MONKEY WRENCH INTO ALL THIS--
INDEED.
YOU DID EXACTLY AS YOU WERE PROGRAMMED TO DO, "KRAVEN." YOU PUT THE DECOY INTO LIFE-MODEL DECOY.

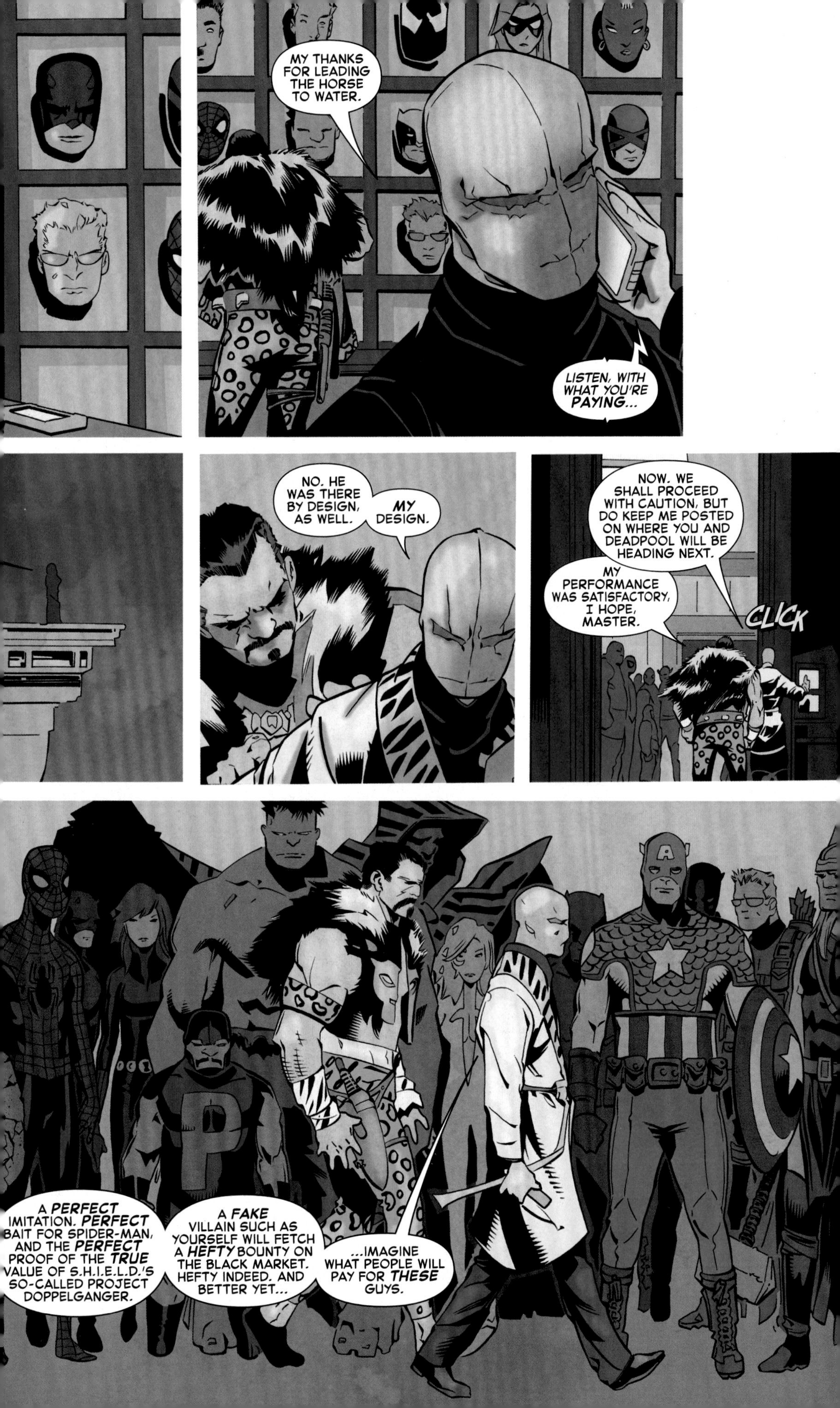
MY THANKS FOR LEADING THE HORSE TO WATER.
LISTEN, WITH WHAT YOU'RE PAYING...
NO. HE WAS THERE BY DESIGN, AS WELL.
MY DESIGN.
NOW. WE SHALL PROCEED WITH CAUTION, BUT DO KEEP ME POSTED ON WHERE YOU AND DEADPOOL WILL BE HEADING NEXT.
MY PERFORMANCE WAS SATISFACTORY, I HOPE, MASTER.
CLICK
A PERFECT IMITATION. PERFECT BAIT FOR SPIDER-MAN, AND THE PERFECT PROOF OF THE TRUE VALUE OF S.H.I.E.L.D.'S SO-CALLED PROJECT DOPPELGANGER.
A FAKE VILLAIN SUCH AS YOURSELF WILL FETCH A HEFTY BOUNTY ON THE BLACK MARKET. HEFTY INDEED. AND BETTER YET...
...IMAGINE WHAT PEOPLE WILL PAY FOR THESE GUYS.

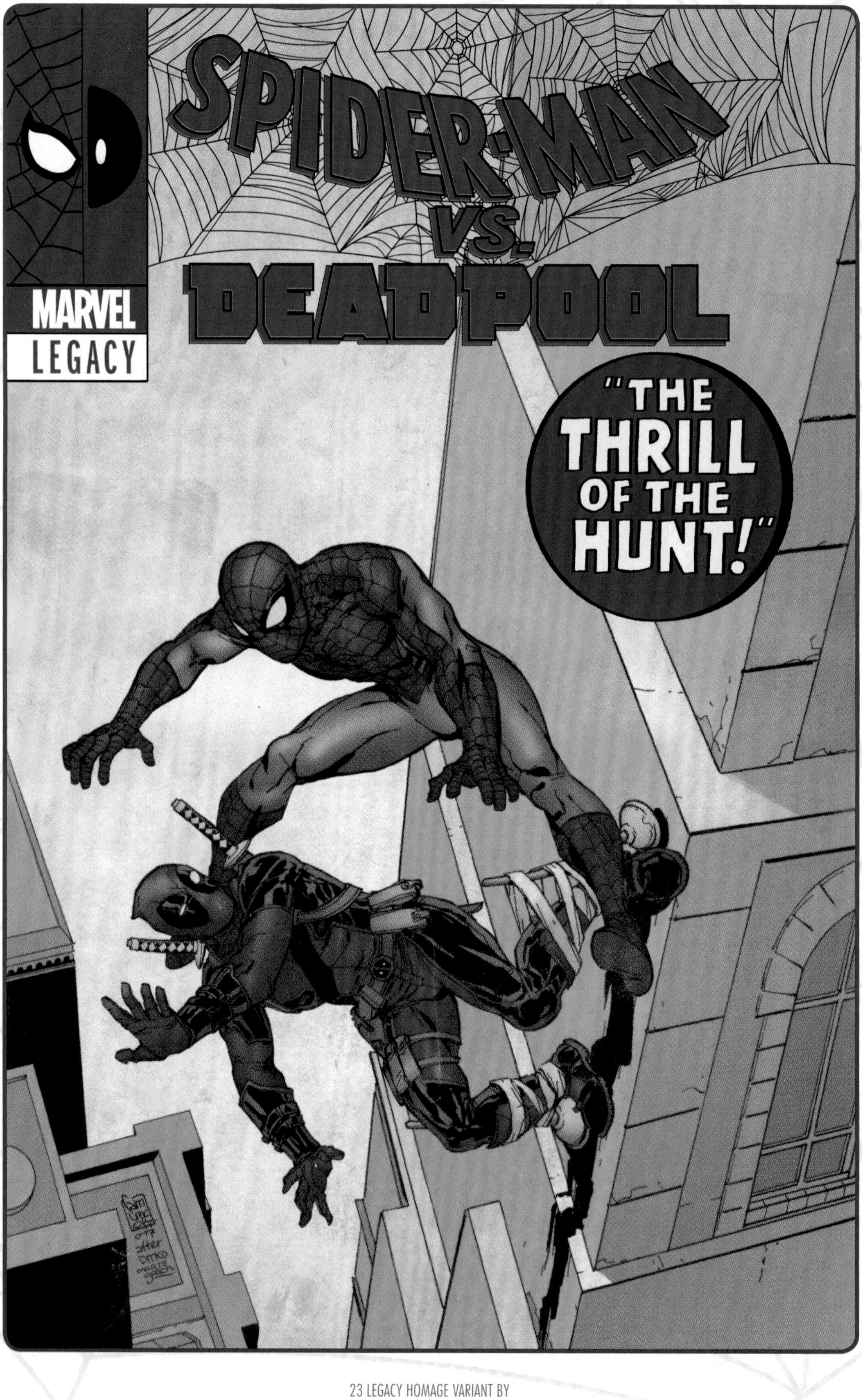
MARVEL
LEGACY
SPIDER-MAN
VS.
DEADPOOL
"THE THRILL OF THE HUNT!"

23 LEGACY HOMAGE VARIANT BY
GIUSEPPE CAMUNCOLI & MARTE GRACIA

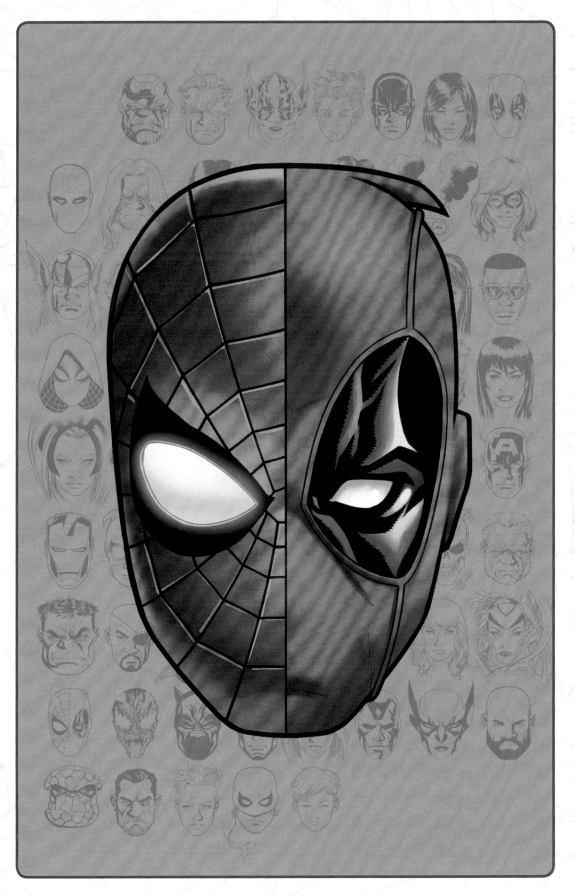

23 HEADSHOT VARIANT BY
MIKE McKONE & **RACHELLE ROSENBERG**

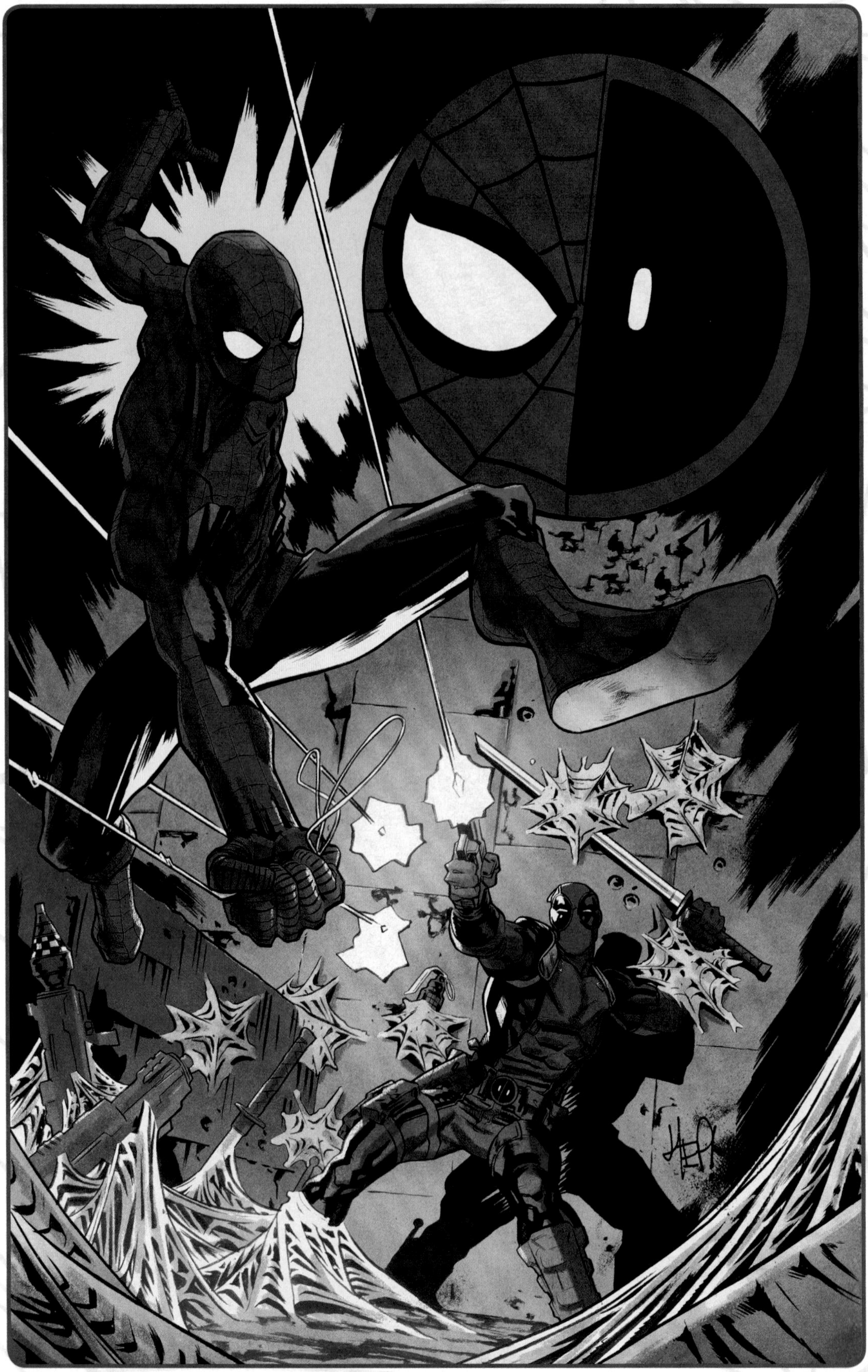

23 VARIANT BY
SCOTT HEPBURN & IAN HERRING

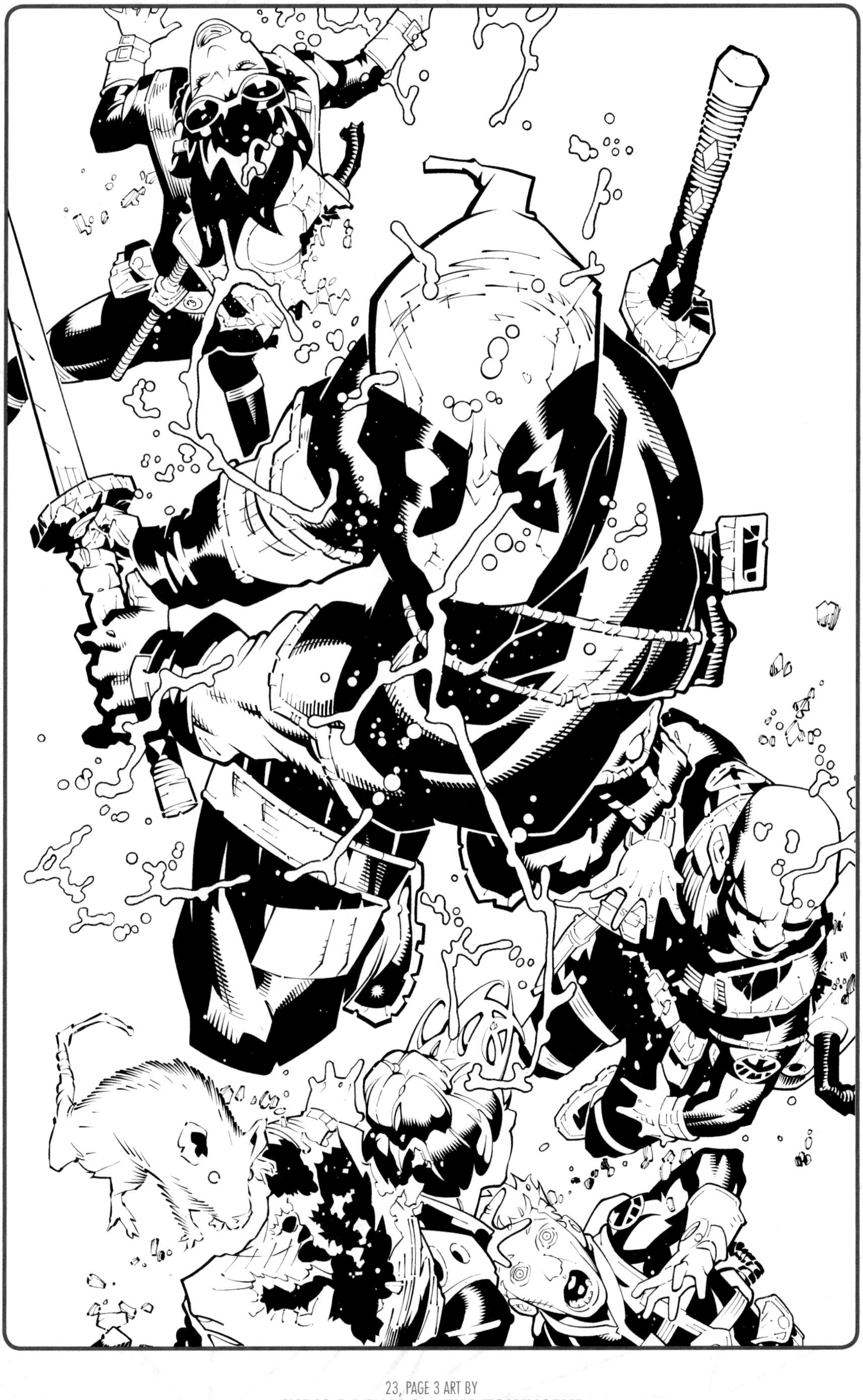

23, PAGE 3 ART BY
CHRIS BACHALO & TIM TOWNSEND

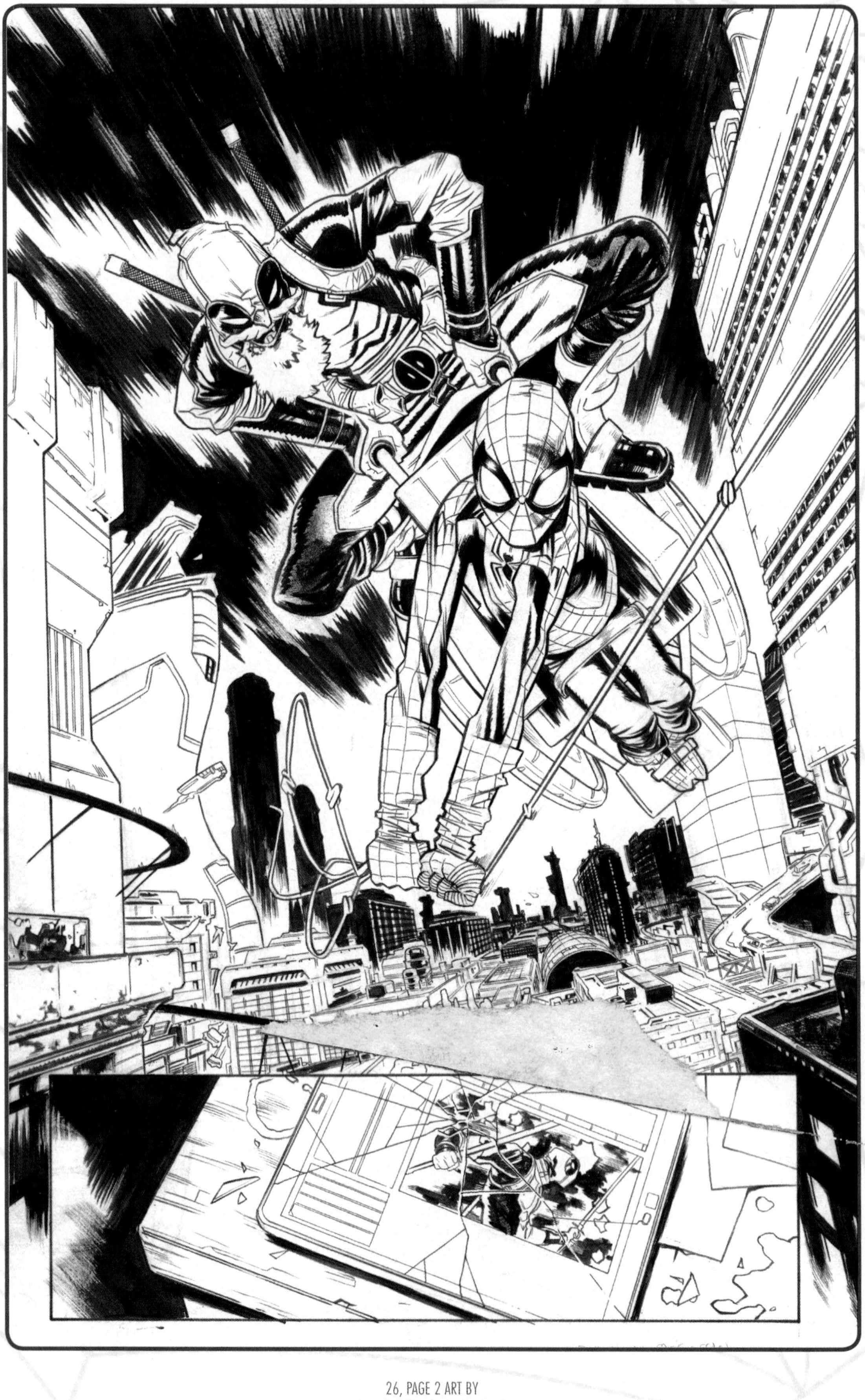

26, PAGE 2 ART BY
SCOTT HEPBURN

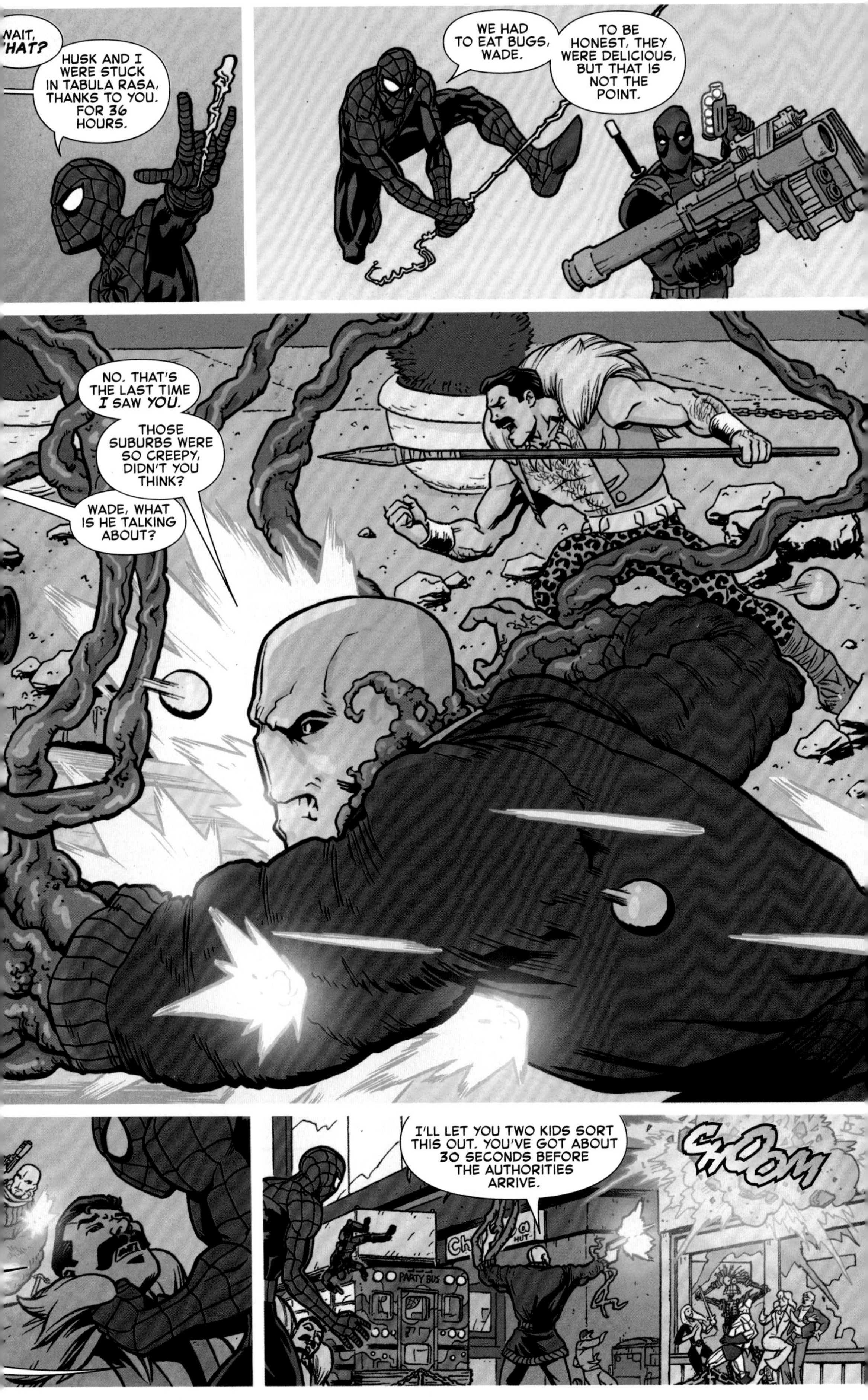

AIT, HAT?
HUSK AND I WERE STUCK IN TABULA RASA, THANKS TO YOU. FOR 36 HOURS.
WE HAD TO EAT BUGS, WADE.
TO BE HONEST, THEY WERE DELICIOUS, BUT THAT IS NOT THE POINT.
NO. THAT'S THE LAST TIME I SAW YOU.
THOSE SUBURBS WERE SO CREEPY, DIDN'T YOU THINK?
WADE, WHAT IS HE TALKING ABOUT?
I'LL LET YOU TWO KIDS SORT THIS OUT. YOU'VE GOT ABOUT 30 SECONDS BEFORE THE AUTHORITIES ARRIVE.
SKOOM
PARTY BUS